CREATIVE TEACHING *in* PRIMARY SCIENCE

Education at SAGE

SAGE is a leading international publisher of journals, books, and electronic media for academic, educational, and professional markets.

Our education publishing includes:

- accessible and comprehensive texts for aspiring education professionals and practitioners looking to further their careers through continuing professional development

- inspirational advice and guidance for the classroom

- authoritative state of the art reference from the leading authors in the field.

Find out more at: **www.sagepub.co.uk/education**

CREATIVE TEACHING in PRIMARY SCIENCE

Roger Cutting *and* Orla Kelly

Los Angeles | London | New Delhi
Singapore | Washington DC

Los Angeles | London | New Delhi
Singapore | Washington DC

SAGE Publications Ltd
1 Oliver's Yard
55 City Road
London EC1Y 1SP

SAGE Publications Inc.
2455 Teller Road
Thousand Oaks, California 91320

SAGE Publications India Pvt Ltd
B 1/I 1 Mohan Cooperative Industrial Area
Mathura Road
New Delhi 110 044

SAGE Publications Asia-Pacific Pte Ltd
3 Church Street
#10-04 Samsung Hub
Singapore 049483

Editor: James Clark
Assistant editor: Rachael Plant
Production editor: Imogen Roome
Copyeditor: Bryan Campbell
Proofreader: Rosemary Morlin
Indexer: Adam Pozner
Marketing manager: Dilhara Attygalle
Cover design: Naomi Robinson
Typeset by: C&M Digitals (P) Ltd, Chennai, India
Printed in India at Replika Press Pvt Ltd

© Roger Cutting and Orla Kelly 2015

First published 2015

Library of Congress Control Number: 2014935449

British Library Cataloguing in Publication data

A catalogue record for this book is available from
the British Library

ISBN 978–1–4462–5542–1
ISBN 978–1–4462–5543–8 (pbk)

CONTENTS

List of Figures vii
List of Tables viii
About the authors ix
Acknowledgements xi
Introduction xii

PART I **1**

1 Introducing creative science 3

2 Misconceptions and enabling conceptual change in science 14

3 Pedagogical approaches and the teaching of science 28

4 The importance of teacher knowledge in science 42

5 Planning and assessing creative approaches in science 54

6 Working scientifically 66

7 Getting creative with technology in science 77

PART II **87**

8 Art and design and creative science 89

9 Creative science through drama and storytelling 99

10 Sustainability and primary science   112

11 Teaching science outside the classroom   126

12 The science of health and wellbeing   138

13 Teaching controversial issues in science   149

14 A science of equality   160

Index   172

LIST OF FIGURES

2.1 Frequency of the words 'creative, creativity or creatively' across the
2014 National Curriculum for England (adapted from Department for
Education, 2013)   16

3.1 The stages of scientific enquiry (from Ward et al., 2008, p. 60)   32

3.2 The Five Dimensions of Practice (Bartholomew et al., 2004, p. 664)
which impact on the success of teaching about the nature of science   32

3.3 Case Example links to the 2014 National Curriculum for England
(Department for Education, 2013)   37

4.1 Overview of content areas in the 2014 National Curriculum
for England   47

4.2 Progression in grouping materials based on their properties from
Year 1 to Year 5 (adapted from Department for Education, 2013a)   49

4.3 Overview of progression in working scientifically   50

8.1 Scientific enquiry process – deductive and inductive reasoning
with observation as a key role in both processes   93

9.1 Mapping of the *Finding Nemo* drama activities against the 2014
Primary Science Curriculum for England   109

LIST OF TABLES

5.1   Example rubric for assessing working scientifically   60

5.2   Selected level descriptors for four of the science assessment
focusses (Department for Children, Schools and Families (2009))   61

8.1   Activity box   94

9.1   Activity box   103

10.1 The Great Acceleration   114

ABOUT THE AUTHORS

ROGER CUTTING

Dr Roger Cutting is an Associate Professor in Education at the Institute of Education at Plymouth University in England. Roger has a background in science research, but also has wide and complimentary experience of teaching science at many levels across the primary, secondary and tertiary sectors. Now at Plymouth University he contributes to a range of courses with particular emphasis on science education and sustainability, and has recently been awarded a number of teaching fellowships and nominations for teaching excellence. He is Programme Leader for the Masters in Learning for Sustainability and is an active member of the Learning Outside Formal Education (LOFE) research group. He is also a Research Fellow for the Centre for Sustainable Futures.

ORLA KELLY

Dr Orla Kelly is a Lecturer in Social, Environmental and Scientific Education in the Church of Ireland College of Education in Dublin, with responsibility for science, history and geography education on the primary BEd. Prior to this appointment in 2013, she was the subject leader for science at Plymouth University. She was appointed as a Lecturer in Science Education in 2006 and the beginnings of a productive and enjoyable research partnership with Roger Cutting began when they were awarded a Plymouth University Teaching Fellowship. It was also at Plymouth University that she had the opportunity to share her passion for drama, teaching it to students on both the primary BEd and PGCE programmes. As a qualified speech and drama teacher and a chemistry graduate, Orla has long been aware of the perceived tension between the creative arts and science. Her PhD research was centred around problem-based learning as an innovative approach to teaching practical chemistry. Her passion and interest in innovative teaching approaches continues and guides her research and practice. She is a member of the advisory panel for *Chemistry Education Research and Practice* and is a regular reviewer. She has a number of peer-reviewed publications and has presented widely at a variety of international conferences.

ACKNOWLEDGEMENTS

It is always something of a cliché to say that many people have been involved in the production of a book, but here it is genuinely the case.

We would therefore like to thank in particular James Clark, Rachael Plant, Imogen Roome and the team at SAGE for all their support and understanding. Gemma Howard at Plymouth University for her help on outdoor education. Oliver Quinlan at Nesta for invaluable help, guidance and ideas with the chapter on digital technologies. Thank you to all our colleagues at Plymouth University (past and present) for their support and encouragement, not just for this book, but for also understanding the chaos that at times we may have caused.

Finally, we'd like to thank our students (again, past and present) for allowing us to 'experiment' with ideas and approaches that hopefully you've taken with you into the teaching profession.

SAGE would like to thank the following reviewers whose comments have helped shape the original proposal:

Adenike Akinbode, *University of Hertfordshire*
Edwyn Anderton, *Sheffield Hallam University*
Claire Garven, *University of the West of England*
Jane Gibson, *University of St Mark & St John (Plymouth)*
Nicola Kitchen, *University of Cumbria*

INTRODUCTION

WHY WE CHANGED OUR APPROACH TO TEACHING SCIENCE

A few years ago we presented a paper at a teaching and learning conference at Plymouth University called 'Hating the Smell of Science'. The title was based on an overheard conversation between two, presumably non-science students who happened to be passing by the laboratories, when one said to the other 'Urrgh, I hate the smell of science'. Funnily enough we knew what they meant.

For a couple of years we had shared the teaching of science modules on an initial teacher education degree for those wishing to become primary school teachers. We had taught them pretty well and the students seemed to enjoy them, but when we talked about, or reviewed our teaching it always seemed to be with a certain sense of dissatisfaction. For us science had always been exciting because it was about the unknown. It was about trying to find things out, whether the answer to a question, or the solution to a problem, and that science was essentially creative. It was that sense of excitement and wonder that had brought us into science in the first place, but somewhere along the line, we had lost our way in terms of communicating that sense of excitement. For our students with non-science backgrounds in particular, it was becoming anything but. They were creative in all sorts of wonderful ways and through all sorts of interesting media, but we were effectively asking them to leave all that creativity at the door when they entered the science classes.

As a result we decided to quite radically change our approach to teaching science. We introduced problem-based learning, the use of film making as a means of assessment, we got students rapping about science, we put science into all sorts of issues and contexts, not so much socio-scientific concerns, but more immediate social and emotional issues, such as compassion and love. We used drama, story-telling, role play and art to help explain key concepts, not only in terms of processes, but also to help explore the nature and practice of science. We even had delegates at a number of international conferences singing!

Along the way some approaches and ideas were really successful and others were nothing less than spectacular disasters! You can read about the latter in Cutting and Kelly (2015). However, when we reviewed our teaching, we wanted to be creative and innovative in both contexts and approaches, but the trick was to do so and yet meticulously avoid compromising the authentic nature of science though inadvertently promoting any kind of pseudo-science.

This book represents something of a review of our time teaching together over the last few years. Part I considers aspects related to pedagogy for creative teaching and learning in science, including, among other things, misconceptions, scientific enquiry, the use of technology and even thinking creatively about assessment. Part II then considers what we call creative approaches and creative contexts. Creative approaches looks specifically at integrated approaches that can be employed to help children better understand science by the use of drama, art and the outdoor classroom in a wide range of imaginative ways. Creative contexts concern specific topic areas that may be addressed in science classes. Here we consider ideas for the inclusion of science relating to issues such as sustainability, well-being, social equality and the use of controversial issues to stimulate children's understanding of science and its wider applications. Each chapter asks you to reflect on various aspects through 'Time for reflection' sections, allowing you to consider your attitude to, and experiences of, science both as a student and teacher. It will also enable you to reflect on the nature of science and creativity among other things. Additionally, each chapter will provide opportunities to put some of the ideas raised into action through 'Activity' sections. These and the 'Time for reflection' sections will contribute to your professional development in both pedagogy and science.

WHY YOU MAY NEED TO CHANGE

In 2013 the UK Government published the new National Curriculum for England. In the accompanying documents, the following key points are made:

> It is the Government's intention that the National Curriculum be slimmed down so that it properly reflects the body of essential knowledge which all children should learn and does not absorb the overwhelming majority of teaching time in schools. Individual schools should have greater freedom to construct their own programmes of study in subjects outside the National Curriculum and develop approaches to learning and study which complement it. Remit for Review of the National Curriculum in England (2012)

Less content and more time does appear to present teachers with a really intriguing prospect to develop something new. Of course, the temptation may be to use this extra time to merely concentrate on the 'essential knowledge' rather than branching out and trying something different. For the first time in perhaps decades of curriculum constraint, teachers have the opportunity now to be really creative in both design and approach to teaching science. This book will provide you, not with resources, but hopefully with creative ideas for approaches and contexts that will help you develop not only your own science curriculum, but also your own teaching approaches to science.

When we changed our approach to teaching science, we would often worry out loud about what we were doing, whether the students were learning, how could we assess this? During one such angst-ridden discussion, a colleague said to us 'In my experience the only things that are ever really worth doing in teaching always involve adrenalin!' We have a chance now to accept the invitation to develop and construct our own programmes of study and although such challenges may appear daunting and intimidating and involve adrenalin, the opportunity to be really innovative and creative in teaching is why many of us came into the profession. We hope that this book will help you develop such imaginative and creative programmes and that you find the process, as we have done, genuinely rewarding.

REFERENCE

Cutting, R. and Kelly, O. (2015) 'We weren't taught this way'. Overcoming problems with the transition to new forms of pedagogy in Science and Sustainability in Science Teacher Training, in *Educating Science Teachers for Sustainability* ASTE Science Education Series. New York: Springer, Inc.

PART 1

CHAPTER 1

INTRODUCING CREATIVE SCIENCE

Chapter aims

By the end of this chapter, you should be able to:

- Define some aspects of creativity and what they might look like in the primary classroom

- Recognize a number of ways to promote creativity in the primary classroom

---

OPPORTUNITY IN A TIME OF CHANGE

2013 saw the publication of the new National Curriculum for England including the individual programmes of study for science in Key Stages 1 to 3. The main characteristic of the new National Curriculum is its return to the original intention of it providing an outline framework:

> The new national curriculum will set out only the essential knowledge that all children should acquire, and give schools and teachers more freedom to decide how to teach this most effectively and to design a wider school curriculum that best meets the needs of their pupils. (Department for Education (2013a))

Schools will now be expected to design their own additional curriculum and are allowed more flexibility in approaches to its delivery. Science remains a core subject at the primary levels of Key Stage 1 and 2 (although the Key Stages are now divided into years) and the content of the science programme of study has not been 'slimmed down' as have the non-core subjects.

The time line for the introduction is very short and the curriculum itself has had its share of criticism, however, its introduction does undoubtedly present schools and teachers with something of an opportunity. Indeed, that is in part its intention. We should not miss this chance. Innovative approaches and creative ideas will be key to developing a challenging, engaging and enjoyable learning experience for children and hopefully this book will provide some ideas and suggest some possibilities to you.

In 2014 an article appeared in the highly prestigious, peer-reviewed international science journal *Nature* on science education that called for social awareness to be recognized as a core scientific skill, for without this, science disengages itself from the world (Cech, 2014). If we are to genuinely engage children in science perhaps we too need to look beyond the traditional approaches to science teaching. To promote the idea that science does not stand alone, nor is it separate from people, but rather that it compliments and therefore enhances our understanding of all sorts of subjects and contemporary issues would be a good starting point.

WHY WE WROTE THIS BOOK

When we first sat down and discussed writing this book we had to think very carefully about who we were writing for. As you are reading this there's a very good chance that you are either training to be a teacher (if so, good luck with it!) or, you may already be a qualified teacher with an interest in teaching science. If so, you've potentially picked up the right book. We say *potentially* for if you are either a trainee or an experienced teacher and you are looking for a book to provide you with well-designed, practical ideas, with A4 monochrome worksheets to photocopy which specifically address precise aspects of the National Curriculum, well, thanks for your interest, but we'd suggest you put this one back on the shelf and look for something else.

However, if you are interested in taking a journey that will go deeper into not only methods and creative ideas for teaching, but also into the nature of science and what it may, surprisingly perhaps, offer to teaching in primary settings, well then, this might be the book for you. Again, we say *might*, as we want this book to help you to think about science in creative and innovative ways. In some chapters we will explore different sorts of pedagogical approaches that perhaps are not readily associated with science teaching. We like to think of these as 'creative approaches' as they rely on aspects of the creative arts. We also want to look at some of the contributions that teaching science topics can make not only to the broader curriculum, but also perhaps, to the wider school community, particularly in relation to its potential for promoting social education. We feel that science topics can have much to offer here to the personal and social development of children and can provide an effective way of reinforcing and enhancing these aspects of the curriculum. We like to call this 'science in creative contexts'.

DEFINING AND ENABLING CREATIVITY

Before embarking on this journey into creative science, it is necessary to explore what creativity is and what conditions allow it to flourish in the primary class-room. There are three main conceptions of creativity:

1. Sectoral – classifies creativity as belonging to a particular sector, for example, the Arts (and not science).

2. Elite – identifies creativity as only evident in very rare people such as the great inventors, painters, architects, etc.

3. Democratic – recognizes the ability for creativity in all sectors and in all people.

In this book we propose a democratic conception of creativity. Democratic crea-tivity was coined in the NACCCE Report (1999) to mean the creativity of the ordinary person, recognizing that all pupils can be creative. In this, creativity is defined by four main factors; using imagination, pursuing with purpose, being original and judging value. To be creative there needs to be a focus on both out-comes and process. Outcomes need to be original and appropriate. The latter is where judging value is important as are pursuing activities or tasks with a pur-pose. Originality interpreted as development of globally transformative products, processes, understanding or knowledge is not likely in the primary classroom. However, originality recognized as a child establishing new connections to old ideas or finding novel solutions to problems that are new to them is much more likely in primary classrooms. This fits with the model of 'little c' creativity reported by Schmidt (2010), which is concerned with construction of novel solutions to problems of limited relevance. 'Big C' creativity on the other hand is about the development of transformative performances or products and sits more in the 'elite' conception of creativity.

Creative Scotland (2013) defines creativity as the capacity to generate ideas that have value to the individual, to look at familiar things with a fresh eye, to examine problems with an open mind, make connections, learn from mistakes and use the imagination to explore new possibilities. Ultimately creativity is the ability to make the world anew, to shape the future and enrich the here and now. Education Scotland (2013) recognize that definitions of creativity have similar characteristics, these include; analysis and identification of problems and issues, the exploration of ideas and the processes by which these ideas are realized, implemented, evaluated and refined.

Creative processes and products therefore need both generative and analytical (or evaluative) thinking. Creative thinking is seen as the ability to move between the two. To be fixed in either generative thinking or evaluative thinking only will stifle creativity. Generative thinking, the process of generating and exploring new ideas, is certainly a key element of the creative process but without a reflective lens, the new ideas may not be appropriate or of value. Conversely, analytical thinking, the process of examining an idea and identifying strengths and weaknesses, will suppress any imaginative thought as each will be met with a critical judgment before they have a chance to develop. Therefore to harness and promote creativity, an environment that promotes generative and analytical thinking is essential and children should be encouraged to move between the two as they progress with their ideas.

The process of creativity requires particular learning conditions. Davies et al. (2013) carried out a systematic review of literature on creative environments for learning in schools. Their review identified several key characteristics of the environments and conditions that are most effective in promoting creative skills in children and young people. These included the physical environment, availability of resources/materials, use of the outdoor environment, pedagogical environment, use of environments beyond the school, play-based learning, effective and flexible use of time and relationships between teachers and learners including allowing children to work at their own pace without pressure (pp. 84–8). Howard-Jones (2008) stresses the importance of a relaxed and uncritical environment and working within an area of personal interest as crucial for generative thinking. Generative thinking is influenced also by intrinsic motivation. Fascination and curiosity are intrinsic motivators, therefore an environment that promotes questioning and interest will also support generative thinking. Curiosity is a key scientific attitude as is a willingness to change ideas in light of evidence. Therefore, science is, by its very nature, twinned with creative thinking. Furthermore, Murphy (2005) suggests that learning science enhances the development of creative thinking skills, such as fluency, flexibility, originality of ideas and imagination.

It is interesting that Torrance (1965), an eminent creativity researcher, put forward nearly 50 years ago the following definition of creativity,

> As the process of becoming sensitive to problems, deficiencies, gaps in knowledge, missing elements, disharmonies, and so on; identifying the difficulty; searching for solutions, making guesses, or formulating hypotheses about the deficiencies; testing and retesting these hypotheses and possibly modifying and retesting them; and finally communicating the results. (pp. 663–4)

This definition, a scientific definition of creativity, met resistance, with objections that he had no right to use the term 'creative' outside such fields as art, music, and writing. He argued that his definition seemed to fit the creativity of both artists and writers as well as it did that of the creative scientist (Torrance, 1965, p. 665). Fortunately, things have moved on from then and the notion that science and creativity may not be mutually exclusive is certainly plausible but this shall be discussed in more detail Chapter 2.

In his highly regarded Technology, Education and Design (TED) talk (Robinson, 2006), Sir Ken Robinson made a robust case for creativity in formal education stating that it should have equal status with literacy. He argued that all children have tremendous talent and have an extraordinary capacity for innovation. However, he declared unequivocally that children are 'being educated out of creativity'. To be creative, he asserted, you have to be prepared to be wrong, and that the current model of formal education leaves children frightened of being wrong. Unfortunately, this is particularly pertinent in science where there is often a perceived 'right' answer and this notion drives down creativity and divergent thinking. Scotland have rooted creativity firmly in their Curriculum for Excellence and it is seen as fundamental to the definition of what it means to be a 'successful learner' in the Scottish education system (Education Scotland, 2013). Unfortunately, the National Curriculum for England (Department for Education, 2013b) does not seem to be embracing creativity as much.

 Activity 1.1

Education Scotland (2013) recognizes three key factors in enabling children and young people to develop creative skills.

1   To help children to take greater responsibility for planning and managing their own learning.
2   The need to establish open-ended approaches to learning, where learners and teachers work together to explore a theme.
3   The potential to use external partnerships to broaden and enhance the learning experience.

As you read through this book, keep these three pillars for successful creativity at the forefront of your thinking.

WHY CREATIVITY IS IMPORTANT

Science is exciting and engaging in many of the ways in which it is already explained and taught. Some teachers, or trainee graduates, particularly with science backgrounds will already hold a clear and functional view of what science is and what is important in terms of teaching it. You may have very clear ideas of what constitutes a scientific approach and quite strongly held views on what is really important for children to understand about 'science methods'. However, such interpretations can framework and even confine your approach to teaching. The issue here of course is not everyone, even within the scientific community may share your view. We may be very different in terms of the subject we studied (such as physics, chemistry, biology) and the different skills and approaches that this imparts. Indeed, it is not uncommon for those with science degrees, training to be science specialists on initial teacher education courses, to express concerns about teaching areas of science that they 'know nothing about'!

If you don't have a science background; don't worry; you are actually in quite; a good position. You are coming to this with no preconceptions and therefore no confines as to what constitutes a scientific approach. If you have a creative arts background, or come from the humanities you may actually have an advantage in thinking innovatively and creatively about science and science teaching. It's the scientists that need to worry! Hopefully this book will be helpful to all.

In this book we suggest that science teaching can be approached in different ways. We can utilize all sorts of creative and imaginative methods and apply these to topics not normally associated with primary science curricula. Of course the obvious question is why should we bother to change? Well, the answer to this is twofold. First, we want to reassure those who are new to science that they have a whole range of valuable skills that can really promote and encourage children to see science as a creative and relevant subject and second, to address a wider issue; that something is going wrong in science education for across many of the 'high-income countries' (including the UK) a distinctive downward trend in the numbers studying science has been recognized (Fensham, 2004). Yet, for those of us who work around children, it is plainly obvious that they are natural scientists in that they have an almost universal curiosity about the world around them. Young children are always asking the question 'why?' Yet, somewhere along the line they appear to lose this curiosity and fascination.

Of course paradoxically in the last 20 years the advances in science and technology have bordered on the revolutionary, particularly in areas such as biomedicine and electronic communications. The technological tools that we have developed now allow us to explore not only adjacent planets but to view horizons that span from the edge of the known universe to sub-atomic space. Never before in our history have we understood so much about ourselves, or the physical world around us and never before have we had the means of communicating this understanding (as well as intriguing questions concerning that which we still do not understand) to such a wide and literate audience. The advances that we have made and the pace of such developments have been little less than spectacular.

It is also undoubtedly true that the planet is facing a seemingly worsening environmental decline and that there needs to be a profound change in the way we live that is based on sustainability. Science also has a profound role in providing the knowledge and skills that young people will need to face the problems that the future will certainly pose.

Given this, how can it be that young people, it would appear, are being put off science as early as 7–8 years old? The only possible answer is somewhat worrying. Children do not tend to 'do' science at home and only rarely in 'out of school' settings. They come across it predominantly at school and therefore something is quite clearly going wrong at this point. Put plainly, children appear to be put off science at school.

This book looks to suggest some ways in which we might not only halt this decline, but also propose methods to engage the natural enthusiasm and interest that children innately possess in the world around them. We suggest that one way in which this may be achieved is by removing the artificial barriers that lead to the compartmentalization of science in primary teaching. We suggest a more holistic approach to science teaching; one that both blurs the distinction between approaches in arts and science and also sees science as an integral part of social, emotional and personal development. In a way we would like children not to be able to necessarily distinguish science from any other area of the curriculum. Going even further, sometimes barriers are not just theoretical, but made from bricks and mortar and in the same way we would wish to see artificial divides removed, we'd extend that wish to the classroom walls. Teaching in the environment, for the environment may be a well-worn phrase now, but it is still a valuable sentiment.

This book's primary objective then is to break science teaching out of any artificial confines. First, it will look at various aspects of pedagogy for creative teaching and learning in primary science, looking among others at the role of misconceptions, working scientifically and, assessment and ways we can use an enquiry approach to teaching. Second, it will look at some creative contexts in the sense of the role of science in areas not traditionally associated with Science, Technology, Engineering and Mathematics (STEM) subjects. It will consider the contribution science can make to social development such as making friends and feeling safe and it will consider how it can be of use in other areas such as the promotion of well-being and sustainability. Other areas include the use of contexts usually confined to the creative arts, including art and drama.

We would like to move science away from being a distinct subject to having a more integral role across the wider curriculum. A potential problem with this lies in the way that science is sometimes perceived. How would you describe science? Logical? Precise? Analytical? Or creative, imaginative and inspiring? Most people would probably draw up a list close to the sentiments at least to the first set of words. We would like to think that the primary outcome of this book would be, having read it, for you to more strongly associate science with the second set. However, before we move on to consider some of these different ideas and approaches, it may be worth reflecting on our own views and experiences.

WHAT DO YOU THINK?

We'd like you to think about your own experiences of teachers and of teaching and reflect upon specific aspects of your own learning. We don't spend long at school (more or less depending where you are in the world) but the majority of us have still attended some form of formal learning and therefore have experiences to reflect on.

When you think back to your time at school there are certain things that will come to mind. If school was a generally positive experience, you will easily remember the ridiculous (and ridiculously funny) things that may have happened. Generally, lessons or/and even subjects that you were taught (perhaps seemingly endlessly at the time) are less well recalled. We have found with our students that it is not uncommon for them to remember almost verbatim certain things teachers said outside the classroom, but hardly anything that was said in it!

Before reading on, look at Time for reflection 1.1.

 Time for reflection 1.1

Spend a little time and try to think of the most profound learning experience that you have had? Try to identify one or two events from which you learnt the most.

Having thought of it, was it when you were at school or outside school? How old were you?

If the learning experience that you identified above was not at school, what learning experience do you remember most from your school days?

Again, was it in a classroom, or outside? Was it a special event?

How does reflecting on your own learning experiences influence your teaching?

Every year we ask students to write down their most profound learning experience and every year, it involves something that happened when they were travelling, or working somewhere, or on a placement. Rarely, if ever, do they mention school. When asked to identify key learning events at school, equally rarely does the most profound learning experience ever involve some sort of science. No one identifies 'sinking and floating' as deep, or making circuits (even with buzzers) as transformational. However, if you do have a science background, something must have hooked you, something made you want to carry on with it. If we are to promote and develop science and teach it in a way that inspires children to continue studying it as they progress, then it is important that we reflect on what it was that moved us. After all, what enthused us is likely to excite others; we perhaps need to harvest that enthusiasm and remind ourselves how it feels to really see something for the first time. It is, of course, not only seeing 'things', it is also the excitement of 'doing' science that can inspire. From role playing a marine habitat, to thinking about why it makes scientific sense to be nice to people, science can be without doubt genuinely exciting, inspiring and actually pretty useful.

CHALLENGES

Calls for new approaches to teaching science are undoubtedly not new (see Time for reflection 1.2), the famous Nuffield Science Teaching Project was developed in the 1960s and the Schools Council Integrated Science Project in the early 1970s.

 Time for reflection 1.2

'In the early 1960s most primary teachers had little scientific knowledge. Little was known about how children develop conceptual understanding of science. Few teachers had received any training in the use of scientific processes, they did not know what was meant by a variable, and could not design experiments, evaluate evidence or draw valid conclusions. They did not know how to ask or recognize appropriate questions for the children.

The first principle was that children should have the widest possible range of practical experiences rather than just learning facts at second hand. It was thought vital that children should handle materials as well as hear, smell and taste them where practicable. The overall aim was to produce children who are keenly observant, questioning, able to devise means of getting answers to their questions, rigorous in their work and able to communicate their findings and ideas.' Nuffield Junior Science (1966).

How far have things moved on? If you are starting teaching, to what extent does the first paragraph apply to you? How far do you agree with nearly 50-year-old comments on principles and aims?

We have over 50 years of pedagogic and curriculum development as a backdrop to the decline in numbers studying science. Given the amount of time, money and enthusiasm put into these projects to re-contextualize science and to change the approach to science teaching, one wonders about the real impact of any suggested change on teaching approaches. Perhaps the difference here is that we only want to utilize the skills and develop the confidence of teachers in primary settings, not to see science as something daunting and separate from everything else that goes on. In fact to see ways of teaching science that don't necessarily depend on designing and carrying out experiments, that maybe are creative and artistic in the way that data are presented, that can lead to discussions about 'bigger' ideas and concepts, not being afraid to engage in potentially controversial areas. In reality of course, all the characteristics of good science!

What we are **not** suggesting here is a 'new science' but rather different ways of teaching and seeing the old one. Whenever there is an attempt to change the way we approach teaching science, we have to be very wary of slipping into what could be called pseudo-science. Pseudo-science is perhaps best described as something that purports to be scientific, looks scientific, even sounds scientific (in terms of the language it uses) but on close inspection it is not. It is a bit like a science 'tribute band' – it looks a bit similar from a distance, but doesn't stand any degree of closer inspection. It normally lacks supporting evidence, employs non-scientific methods and cannot be reliably tested or verified. In this sense it is different from something that has come to be called 'Bad Science'. Bad Science is just that, poorly designed, erroneous results; it is generally just poor practice. Any endeavour, however noble and well intentioned can be carried out badly, it sometimes happens and can be understood. Pseudo-science cannot. In this book we have tried to be careful in avoiding any accusations of pseudo-science and so should you.

We've all come across ideas such as science in the kitchen or activities that involve onomatopoeic words like 'boom, bang, crash!' These are fine, but we consistently look at the subject and outcome, rather than the processes. This is curious, as science is a process, yet we rarely try to sell it as such. One very obvious activity that gives all sorts of wrong messages, is the 'kitchen volcano', when putting vinegar on a pile of baking soda is meant to give you a model volcanic eruption. Actually, the reaction tends to be short-lived, neither tells us much about volcano's nor the chemical reaction taking place. Yet still this activity is promoted. Simply putting the baking soda on a digital scale and looking at what happens to its mass as you add a known mass of vinegar might lead to some intriguing questions about reactions. Also, as the loss will be quite small the experiment would be need to be replicated a number of times, so again, a better introduction to real science.

This of course, is the objective of this book and it's not easy. How do we make science really engaging for children, but at the same time avoid the pitfalls of reducing the robustness of the subject?

Furthermore, while science remains a statutory subject in the national curriculum it is increasingly under pressure from other subjects. One way forward is to better integrate science across the curriculum. Of course this is easier said than done and often such integrative approaches do neither the primary subject area, nor the integrative science area much good.

Children should be involved in an exploration, both in the sense of hands-on and mind-on. In other words, being engaged in problem solving, designing experiments, drawing conclusions. Wherever possible you should go with them on the adventure. Don't feel that you need to know the answers; be a fellow explorer. It really doesn't matter, if you all come up with something that's not quite right; that's half the fun and that's the nature of science.

FURTHER READING

Craft, A., Cremin, T., Hay, P. and Clack, J. (2014) Creative primary schools: developing and maintaining pedagogy for creativity. *Ethnography and Education*, 9(1), 16–34.
This paper, an in-depth study of two primary schools recognized nationally for their creative approaches, offers pertinent insights into their creative teaching and learning practices. Three characteristics emerged co-construction, high value placed on children's ownership of their learning and high expectations in skilful creative engagement.

REFERENCES

Cech, E.A. (2014) Education: Embed social awareness in science curricula. *Nature* 505, 477–8
Creative Scotland (2013) What is creativity? A source of inspiration and summary of actions from Scotland's Creative Learning Partners. [Online] Available at: from http://www.creativescotland.com/__data/assets/pdf_file/0019/21394/Scotlands-Creative-Learning-Plan-2013-v-d4.pdf (accessed 31.01.2014)
Davies, D., Jindal-Snape, D., Collier, C., Digby, R., Hay, P. and Howe. A. (2013) Creative Environments for Learning in Schools. *Thinking Skills and Creativity*, 8, pp. 80–91. http://dx.doi.org/10.1016/j.tsc.2012.07.004

Department for Education (2013a) Science programmes of study: Key stages 1 and 2 National Curriculum in England. DFE-00182–2013

Department for Education (2013b) The national curriculum in England framework document. DFE-00177–2013

Education Scotland (2013) Creativity across learning 3–18 [Online] Available at: http://www. educationscotland.gov.uk/Images/Creativity3to18_tcm4–814361.pdf (accessed 31.01.2014).

Fensham, P. (2004) *Engagement with Science: An International Issue that Goes beyond Knowledge.* Paper presented at the Science and Maths Education for a New Century Conference, Dublin City University, Ireland. Retrieved 19/05/2013, from http://www.dcu.ie/ smec/plenary/Fensham,%20Peter.pdf

Howard-Jones, P. (2008) Fostering creative thinking: co-constructed insights from neuroscience and education. Bristol: Higher Education Academy Education Subject Centre ESCalate. [Online] Available at: http://escalate.ac.uk/downloads/4389.pdf (accessed 16.07.2013)

Murphy, C. (2005) Primary science in the UK: a scoping study. The Wellcome Trust [Online] Available at: http://www.wellcome.ac.uk/stellent/groups/corporatesite/@msh_peda/docu ments/web_document/wtx026636.pdf

National Advisory Committee on Creative and Cultural Education (1999) *All Our Futures: Creativity, Culture and Education.* [Online] Available at: http://sirkenrobinson.com/pdf/ allourfutures.pdf (accessed 19.05.2013)

Nuffield Junior Science (1966). Retrieved 19/05/2013, from http://www.nuffieldfoundation.org/ nuffield-junior-science-1966

Robinson, K. (2006) Sir Ken Robinson: how schools kill creativity. TED Talk. [Online] Available at: http://www.ted.com/talks/ken_robinson_says_schools_kill_creativity.html

Schmidt, A.L. (2010) The battle for creativity: frontiers in science and science education. *BioEssays*, 32,1016–9 DOI 10.1002/bies.201000092

Torrance, E.P. (1965) Scientific views of creativity and factors affecting its growth. Daedalus, *Creativity and Learning*, 94(3), 663–81

CHAPTER 2

MISCONCEPTIONS AND ENABLING CONCEPTUAL CHANGE IN SCIENCE

Chapter aims

By the end of this chapter, you should be able to:

- Challenge the conception that science is not a creative subject
- Examine your own conception of the nature of science
- Explain the theories which underpin conceptual change in children
- Develop creative strategies for challenging children's naïve conceptions

---

INTRODUCTION

Anecdotal evidence from years of working with initial teacher education students is that there is a well-held belief that science is about learning facts, with clear right and wrong answers and is in stark contrast to 'creative' subjects such as art and music, where other attributes such as individuality, interpretation and aesthetics are valued. This is a belief that science education teaching teams challenge as their teacher trainees progress through their modules on initial teacher education programmes. By the time they leave, we hope that we have provided them with enough evidence, the right opportunities to discuss and develop their ideas and a positive classroom environment to change this concept of science. In a way, this is the biggest challenge we face as science educators.

We all know about Leonardo da Vinci, who is known the world round as both an artist and inventor. More recently, Brian Cox is known for his integral role in 'sexing' up physics and astronomy as well as being the keyboard player for 1990s band D:Ream. Here we have two examples of well-known accomplished scientists having a definite creative side too. And these two are not alone! Brunelleschi was the architect who made the beautiful and magnificent cupola of Florence cathedral and he was also recognized for using geometric principles in creating perspective. American computer scientist Jaron Lanier is best known for popularizing the term virtual reality as a pioneer in the field. He is also an accomplished classical composer, film director and author. And Root-Bernstein (1987) has identified over 400 such examples. Additionally, it is reported by Root-Bernstein et al. (2008, p. 54) that Nobel laureates in the sciences are at least a factor of 7 more likely to be a visual artist, sculptor, or printmaker; at least a factor of 7.5 more likely to be a craftsperson engaged in woodwork, mechanics, electronics, glassblowing; at least a factor of 12 more likely to write poetry, short stories, plays, essays, novels, or popular books; and at least a factor of 22 more likely to be an amateur actor, dancer, magician, or other performer than the average scientist. Einstein furthermore sums up the interplay of science and art by saying,

> After a certain high level of technical skill is achieved, science and art tend to coalesce in esthetics, plasticity, and form. The greatest scientists are always artists as well. (cited in Kaplan 2001, p. 37)

Therefore, the notion that the sciences and the more creative arts subjects are polar opposites of each other needs to be challenged. This is a misconception which we hope to address throughout this book. It is not helped by a legacy of national documents, reviews and initiatives which further embed the connection between the Arts and creativity such as the Creative Partnerships Programme (CCE, 2002) managed by Arts Council England, the Excellence and Enjoyment framework (DfES, 2003, p. 4) which states 'primary education is about children … being creative in writing, art, music' and the Independent Review of the Primary Curriculum (Rose, 2009) which reported that 'Both at home and abroad there is little dispute that a primary curriculum must develop young people's … artistic and creative development'. 'Understanding the Arts' was one of the areas of learning in the proposed curriculum under the previous government, which was seen as a progression from creative development in the early years (Rose, 2009). Similarly, the Cambridge Primary Review (Alexander, 2010) suggested 'Arts and Creativity' as one of eight domains of knowledge, skill, enquiry and disposition (p. 267). Juliet Desailly discusses this and the historical journey of 'creativity' in the primary curriculum in more depth in her book 'Creativity in the Primary Classroom' (2012) and it is clear that there is an underlying assumption that creativity fits best with the Arts. On a final note, Figure 2.1 below shows the frequency of the words 'creative, creativity or creatively' across the 2014 National Curriculum for England (Department for Education, 2013). It is clear that art and design has a strong creative focus along with music, whereas the core subjects of English, mathematics and science have a limited creative demand. Additionally, the instances in science were limited to

Subject	English	Mathematics	Science	Art and Design	Computing	Design and Technology	Music
Frequency of 'creative' words	1	1	3	6	2	6	3
In 'purpose', 'aims' or 'subject content'	0	0	3	6	2	6	3

Figure 2.1 Frequency of the words 'creative, creativity or creatively' across the 2014 National Curriculum for England (adapted from Department for Education, 2013)

the *creative use* of everyday materials, different magnets and new materials and this was in the non-statutory guidance. Interestingly, design and technology and computing have a clear expectation for creativity. As you have hopefully seen from Chapter 1, being creative is not just about generating creative products but also being creative in the process with a purpose and value attached to it.

Nonetheless, in this chapter we will consider children's own conceptions and how creativity can be used to challenge these often naïve conceptions and enable conceptual change towards accepted scientific concepts. Initially however, we need to challenge the concept that science is a fact-based subject concerned with the acquisition of bodies of knowledge. Instead, science should be seen as a subject which is ultimately concerned with the very processes which lead to the development of such knowledge. Respecting evidence, asking questions, evaluating and arguing science is what science is really all about and certainly should be at the heart of all primary science lessons.

 Activity 2.1

Consider the following statements in relation to your own understanding of science and learning in science (or when you last studied science) – to what extent do you agree or disagree?

- Knowledge in science consists of many disconnected topics.
- As scientists learn more, most science ideas we use today are likely to be proven wrong.
- It is possible for scientists to carefully perform the same experiment and get two very different results that are both correct.
- When studying science, I relate the important information to what I already know rather than just memorizing it the way it is presented.
- I find that reading the text in detail is a good way for me to learn science.
- Why scientific phenomena happen the way they do does not usually make sense to me; I just memorize what happens.

(adapted from the CLASS survey http://www.colorado.edu/sei/surveys/Faculty/CLASS-PHYS-faculty.html)

Time for reflection 2.1

Do you see science as a fact-driven subject or as a subject which by its very nature demands flexibility and creativity?

What experiences have led to this attitude?

How will this attitude impact on your teaching of science?

What evidence from the classroom, your own experiences of learning science or from your personal life can you think of to support the notion that science is a creative subject?

CHALLENGING THE NATURE OF SCIENCE – HOW WE KNOW WHAT WE KNOW

Let's start with science in the curriculum. In the 2014 National Curriculum for England (Department for Education, 2013, p. 144), it states 'all pupils should be taught essential aspects of the knowledge, methods, processes and uses of science'. This is supported by the aims of the curriculum which are to ensure that all pupils:

- develop scientific knowledge and conceptual understanding through the specific disciplines of biology, chemistry and physics

- develop understanding of the nature, processes and methods of science through different types of science enquiries that help them to answer scientific questions about the world around them

- are equipped with the scientific knowledge required to understand the uses and implications of science, today and for the future.

Additionally, it describes 'working scientifically' (p. 145) as specifying the understanding of the nature, processes and methods of science. It stresses it should always be taught through and clearly related to the teaching of substantive science content in the programme of study across both Key Stage 1 and upper and lower Key Stage 2. In this way, the 2014 curriculum is building on the 1999 National Curriculum (DfEE/QCA, 1999) which states teaching should ensure that 'scientific enquiry' is taught through contexts taken from the sections on 'life processes and living things', 'materials and their properties' and 'physical processes'. This is best practice in science education. Furthermore, as much as possible children should be involved in all stages of the science process, in teaching and learning environments which encourage questioning and curiosity about the world around us. This requires active involvement of the children in their own learning, with opportunities for discussion and effective co-operative group learning. This discussion should allow for review and evaluation, with children recognizing improvements and showing openness to others' ideas. Osborne argues that debate and discussion with others are most likely to enable new meanings and that comprehending why ideas are wrong matters as much as understanding why other ideas might be right. (Osborne, 2010, p. 464) Enabling children to come up with their own ideas to scientific questions and giving them ownership of how they want to go about their investigations as well as choice in how they communicate their results are vital to the success of such an approach. This also encourages the development of key scientific attitudes, such as creativity, flexibility, objectivity, open-mindedness and respect for evidence.

CONCEPTUAL CHANGE

We all have 'gaps' in our knowledge, a popular TV programme had a whole episode around the gaps in knowledge and ability of the key characters: Lily couldn't throw, Ted mispronounced 'chameleon' and Robin believed the North Pole was not actually a real place. Yes, it's fictional, but no doubt most of us can remember a moment (or probably moments) when gaps in our knowledge were revealed. This is normal and probably a result of miscommunication at some point. The important thing to remember is that our ideas are very real to us and come from previous experiences; in the playground, school, youth club, in the pub, parents, siblings, friends and the classroom. This is not necessarily problematic so long as teachers start from children's ideas and move them forward. To do this we need to have an appreciation for the theoretical underpinning of conceptual change.

THEORETICAL FRAMEWORK

The teaching of science in schools, particularly in primary, has seen a shift in recent times, where teachers and researchers are recognizing the value of children constructing their own knowledge and understanding, rather than merely receiving knowledge transmitted from their teacher. One leading theorist in the field, David Ausubel, has made a clear distinction between rote learning and meaningful learning. Meaningful learning derives from the combination of ideas linked to any given concept and is further influenced by emotional associations, the experiences during which concepts were acquired and the context of the learning. To enable meaningful learning, new material needs to be incorporated into existing cognitive structures. From Ausubel's perspective, this is the meaning of learning. He recognizes two ways this can be done: correlative subsumption, where it is an extension or elaboration of what is already known and derivative subsumption, where new material can be linked to other concepts or ideas to create new interpretations or understanding. In this latter approach completely new concepts can emerge, and previous concepts can be changed or expanded to include more of the previously existing information. Interestingly, Ausubel was a proponent of didactic, expository approaches, which is in sharp contrast to the current thinking on classroom methods. Conversely, Jerome Bruner, who had similar theories on how we learn, was a strong proponent of a discovery and problem-solving approach to teaching and learning. These and other approaches will be discussed in more depth in the next chapter. Bruner's sees learning as an active process, including selection and transformation of information, decision making, generating hypotheses, and making meaning from information and experiences. Bruner held similar views to Jean Piaget and was influenced by the work of Lev Vygotsky, both his peers. Piaget recognized 'schema' as the basic building block of intelligent behaviour. These can be seen as 'units' of knowledge, each relating to one aspect of the world, including objects, actions and abstract theoretical concepts. Piaget emphasized the importance of schemas in cognitive development, and described how they were developed or acquired. He suggested a process of accommodation and assimilation, whereby accommodation is using an existing schema to deal with a new object or situation and assimilation happening when the existing schema does not work, and needs to be changed to deal with a new object or situation. In this way, Piaget is often called the 'father of constructivism'. However, his view was somewhat limited in terms of the potential influence of external factors on learning and cognition. Lev Vygotsky, a peer of Piaget, put a lot more value on the role social interaction plays in the development of cognition. In essence, an individual can achieve a certain amount of understanding, but with others through social interaction can achieve more. This gap between what people can achieve on their own and what they can potentially achieve with the help of others is called the 'Zone of Proximal Development'.

Constructivism, as you will see throughout this book, is a key approach to effective science teaching and learning. A fundamental learning outcome of constructivist approaches to science education is the achievement of conceptual change in learners and there is a wealth of researchers who dedicate themselves to this. Children come to science lessons, just as we do to situations in everyday life, with conceptions that may differ from accepted scientific ones that we expect them to acquire. Using elicitation strategies, teachers need to explore their children's existing conceptions and use these to build new understandings (Morton, 2012). Posner et al. (1982) suggest that learners are more likely to accept new conceptions if they are dissatisfied with the old ones, and find the new ones make sense, offer solutions to other problems and fit in with other knowledge, and if they potentially open up new areas of enquiry. In this way, children need to be very much part of the process of constructing their scientific knowledge and understanding. Murphy suggests that many criticisms have been levelled against the constructivist approach to science teaching in the primary school, recognizing that there is little advice for teachers regarding specific strategies to develop these ideas so that they become more 'scientific' (Murphy, 2003, p. 3). Hopefully this chapter will go some way to rectify this.

Conceptual change needs to consider epistemological, ontological and social/affective factors (Treagust and Duit, 2008; Venville and Treagust, 1998). Epistemology considers the origin, nature, and limits of human knowledge. Of significance to this chapter is whether some human knowledge is innate or whether instead all significant knowledge is acquired through experience. Ontology is concerned with the nature of being and with various categories of being. It considers 'What exists? And how can it be grouped as related to other things that exist? When individuals' experiences change, the relationships between things can change and the categories can change. Social factors include the learning environment and the class organization. Affective factors take account of the emotional factors which influence learning. These can be negative or positive.

Morton (2012) argues that as well as these factors the role dialogue plays in conceptual change needs to be considered. This links strongly with the constructivist perspective where there is a strong social dimension. Mercer (2000, 2008 cited in Morton 2012) strongly advocates for recognition of the role both participants have in the joint construction of new knowledge, or 'thinking together'.

The importance of spoken language in science is emphasized in the 2014 curriculum (Department for Education, 2013, p. 145), noting that 'the quality and variety of language that pupils hear and speak are key factors in developing their scientific vocabulary and articulating scientific concepts clearly and precisely. They must be assisted in making their thinking clear, both to themselves and others, and teachers should ensure that pupils build secure foundations by using discussion to probe and remedy their misconceptions.' This is a welcome addition and recognizes best practice in science education where the role of discussion, as mentioned earlier, is paramount in developing knowledge and understanding and enabling conceptual change. If discussion and working scientifically are the foundation of primary science classrooms, this will directly impact on children's progression in scientific knowledge, concepts and processes and will develop their understanding of the nature of science.

Allen (2010, pp. 12–13) offers some general qualities of a constructivist teaching approach when considering misconceptions. These are summarized here:

- assimilation

- accommodation

- experiential learning

- cognitive conflict

- social and collaborative learning

- student autonomy and independent learning

- open-ended questions

- higher-level thinking

- peer dialogue

- responsibility with the learner

İpek and Çalık (2008, p. 145) suggest a 4-step constructivist teaching model to enable conceptual change. In the first phase, eliciting students' pre-existing ideas, the teacher tries to enhance students' motivation for the topic and to become aware of their pre-existing knowledge and alternative conceptions to allow identification of appropriate activities. In the second phase, focusing on the target concept, the teacher attempts to enrich the learning environment for the students through engagement in activities and experiences about the target concept. The teacher also encourages the students to think about related concepts by asking questions. However, they refrain from giving any clue. In the third phase, challenging students' ideas, students compare their prior knowledge with their newly structured one. The teacher makes reasonable explanations to confirm or refute their gained experiences. In the last phase, applying newly constructed ideas to similar situations, the students apply their newly structured knowledge to new situations to reinforce their understanding. This latter point is very important as it has long been recognized that learners have an inability to transfer knowledge, giving rise to the notion of situated learning (Novak, 2002).

Reasoning skills that science education might seek to develop include the following abilities (Osborne, 2010, p. 465):

- to identify patterns in data, such as covariation (how two variables change together), and to make inferences;

- to coordinate theory with evidence and to discriminate between evidence that supports (inclusive) or does not support (exclusive) or that is simply indeterminate;

- to construct evidence-based, explanatory hypotheses or models of scientific phenomena and persuasive arguments that justify their validity; and

- to resolve uncertainty, which requires a body of knowledge about concepts of evidence such as the role of statistical techniques, the measurement of error, and the appropriate use of experimental designs, such as randomized double-blind trials (see Chapter 6 – Key methods).

CHILDREN'S NAÏVE CONCEPTIONS

There are many different ways to describe children's ideas in science: misconceptions, alternative conceptions, common sense, non-scientific ideas, intuitive conceptions, naïve conceptions. In reality these mean the same thing, ideas which are not yet developed into accepted science ones. Researchers are interested in the theories which underpin the barriers to, and strategies for, conceptual change in science; as teachers we are interested in knowing what children's ideas are so we can use them as starting points to develop, or where necessary change, their ideas, thus allowing children to make progress. Either way, both communities are very interested in children's ideas. We of course, need to exercise caution as sometimes children can have the 'correct' scientific idea in their head but may lack the language to communicate it. Chi and Roscoe (2002) also recognize the difference between naïve knowledge that can be readily revised or removed through instruction and naïve knowledge which seems highly resistant to change, referring to the latter as misconceptions (p. 3).

Shtulman and Valcarcel (2012) investigated what happened to children's ideas when exposed to new ones. They found that children verified scientific concepts much more slowly and less accurately across 10 domains of scientific knowledge, when these concepts did not match with their intuitive ideas, suggesting that naïve theories survive the acquisition of a mutually incompatible scientific theory, coexisting with that theory for many years to follow. This means that we can tell a child that the water in a puddle has not disappeared, but instead changed state into a gas and evaporated into the atmosphere but unless we actually give them evidence and the opportunity to discuss and construct such meaning for themselves, their intuitive idea that the water has simply disappeared will stick. Chi and Roscoe (2002) also recognized this, stating that such misconceptions can persist even when they are confronted by ingenious forms of instruction.

Research encourages secondary pre-service teachers to incorporate misconceptions into their teaching as learning platforms to build on, instead of obstacles to learning (Larkin, 2012) and we would advocate this in primary science teaching too. Earlier strategies used to explore children's conceptions included minimal use of written language, using visual images and often the presentation of alternative concepts or questions relating to one central idea or word. The use of concept cartoons is one such approach that has been, and still is, used effectively to explore children's conceptions (Keogh and Naylor, 1999). Concept mapping (Liu, 2004) and computer simulations (Trundle and Bell, 2010) have also been used to explore concepts and promote conceptual change. Foster (2012) suggests the discussion of socio-cultural issues can be used as a means to explore concepts and enable conceptual change about evolution. His paper suggests that 'teachers can be confident that evolution has nothing to fear from a free and frank discussion in which claims can be rebutted with evidence to drive out pre-scientific superstitions. It also models the scientific process more authentically and develops students' ability to think critically' (Foster, 2012). Research carried out by Monteiro et al. (2012) on children's conceptions of 'minerals' suggests that teachers need to promote the understanding of the evolution of the mineral concept through time, highlighting that 'Definitions naturally change as a consequence of the growth of scientific knowledge and may, over time, become inappropriate due to new findings' (p. 2721). This reflects the spiral curriculum advocated by Bruner, where basic ideas should be repeatedly revisited, building upon them until the student has grasped the full formal apparatus that goes with them. Finally, it is important to recognize the seminal work of Shayer and Adey (1981) on cognitive acceleration through science education (CASE) which draws heavily from a constructivist pedagogy and has cognitive conflict as a key factor in developing cognition. This means presenting children with something which is puzzling, unexpected perhaps, which makes them stop to think. It is not simply a matter of presenting difficult material, but rather of leading to certain expectations which are then not met, so we have to 'think again' (www.letsthink.org.uk).

CREATIVE APPROACHES TO CONCEPTUAL CHANGE

These are all useful approaches and strategies but we want to encourage creative approaches, which will lead to conceptual change and the development of creative thinkers. It has been already described how psychologists and social scientists recognize two forms of creativity: big-C creativity (BC); and little-c creativity (LC). Big-C creativity describes development of transformative performances or products, whereas little-c is concerned with the construction of novel solutions to problems of limited relevance. Within this framework, little-c creativity may be combinatorial, where new connections are established between old ideas or exploratory, operating within a limited domain, or limiting set of rules (Schmidt, 2010, p. 1016).

In this vein, little-c creativity can be developed and utilized in the primary science classroom to establish new connections between old ideas and when exploring ideas within a limited domain, for example exploring melting. Teachers need to see these naïve conceptions not as barriers to get over but productive starting points. One suggestion is to consider the resources we use when teaching. Textbooks can and do contain misconceptions and if we think a bit outside the box, we will be able to find resources that may unintentionally support children's naïve ideas. Why not explore and discuss this with children?

 Activity 2.2 – Resources

Look at the photograph below. It is an orrery, a mechanical model of the solar system. Many schools will have one of these and possibly on display. List the scientific ideas that you could draw from this resource. Which of these might lead to alternative conceptions about our solar system?

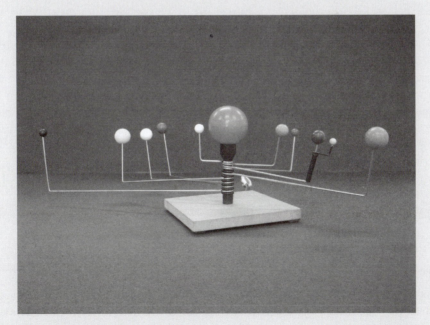

Photo © Richard Fowler, 2014

(Continued)

(Continued)

Now look at this picture of the solar system. Again, list the scientific ideas that you could draw from this picture. How might this lead to alternative conceptions about the solar system?

©iStock.com/pialhovik

As well as considering the classroom resources we use, another creative approach could be consideration of the textbooks and written resources that we use (or maybe shouldn't use). Traditionally, science teaching relied heavily on textbooks and worksheets and Van de Broek (2010) highlights the factors which can hinder the learning of science from texts, recognizing a number of reader and text characteristics. Text characteristics include the organization of the text, verbal complexity and typographical prompts. The reader's availability of working memory capacity and relevant background knowledge coupled with skills factors such as reasoning and reading impact on their ability to comprehend text. Taking into account a reader's personal motivation for the subject and task, it is clear how learning from texts may be hindered. This situation is not helped by the fact that school textbooks themselves often contain inaccurate knowledge (King, 2010) Additionally, among the most commonly noted features of academic language are conciseness, achieved by avoiding redundancy; using a high density of information-bearing words, ensuring precision of expression; and relying on grammatical processes to compress complex ideas into few words (Snow, 2010, p. 450). Therefore, a creative approach to challenging misconceptions is not to use work sheets and textbooks in the traditional way. Instead, consider getting children to pick out words from worksheets or books that they think are scientific words and discuss their meaning in pairs or groups. Think of all the words which have more than one meaning and which we use in the primary science classroom for example bark, energy, force, mass, plant, shoot, the list goes on. Will the children pick these out or will they ignore them? We can probably all think about children who have spent the majority of a lesson with a totally different understanding of a particular word. Without exploring the meaning of such words, a perfectly planned, resourced and executed lesson will fail! Carefully selected images and visuals can be an excellent starting point for exploring children's ideas so long as discussion and then concrete experiences follow to challenge and move their ideas and conceptual understanding on.

CONCLUSION

The key message in this chapter is about enabling conceptual change in children to move their naïve conceptions to accepted scientific ones. Several strategies and suggestions were put forward to challenge children's misconceptions. Starting from children's ideas is crucial and strategies to elicit children's ideas are discussed in Chapter 5. The key theories underlying conceptual change were highlighted, in particular constructivism.

The chapter started with a consideration for the dichotomy between the Arts and science when considering creativity. A case was made for this to be challenged. This highlighted the importance of teacher's considering their attitude and understanding of the nature of science.

FURTHER READING

Allen, M. (2010) *Misconceptions in Primary Science.* Maidenhead: Open University Press, McGraw-Hill Education

This book offers clear support and practical advice for dealing with the common misconceptions encountered in the primary science classroom.

Hadjiachilleos, S., Valanides, N. and Angeli, C. (2013) The impact of cognitive and affective aspects of cognitive conflict on learners' conceptual change about floating and sinking. *Research in Science & Technological Education,* 31(2), pp. 133–52.

This research paper describes a small-scale study into the contribution of cognitive and affective aspects on students' conceptual change in floating and sinking.

Marin, N., Benarroch, A. and Jimenez Gomez, E. (2000) What is the relationship between social constructivism and Piagetian constructivism? An analysis of the characteristics of the ideas within both theories. *International Journal of Science Education,* 22:3, pp. 225–38.

In this research paper, the authors consider the characteristics of social constructivism and 'Piagetian' constructivism and attempt to find connections and bridges between them for the benefit of science teaching.

REFERENCES

Allen, M. (2010) *Misconceptions in Primary Science*. Maidenhead: Open University Press, McGraw-Hill Education

Alexander, R. (ed.) (2010) *Children, their World, their Education. Final Report and Recommendations of the Cambridge Primary Review*. Oxon: Routledge

CCE (2002) Creative partnerships. [Online] Available at: http://www.creativitycultureeducation.org/creative-partnerships

Chi, M.T.H. and Roscoe, R.D. (2002) The processes and challenges of conceptual change, in M. Limón and L. Mason (eds) *Reconsidering Conceptual Change. Issues in Theory and Practice*. Dordrecht: Kluwer, pp. 3–28

Department for Education (2013) The National Curriculum in England. [Online] Available at: https://www.gov.uk/government/uploads/system/uploads/attachment_data/file/260481/PRIMARY_national_curriculum_11-9-13_2.pdf

DfEE/QCA (1999) *The National Curriculum. Handbook for Primary Teachers in England*. Department for Education and Employment/ Qualifications and Curriculum Authority. [Online] Available at: http://www.educationengland.org.uk/documents/pdfs/1999-nc-primary-handbook.pdf

DfES (2003) *Excellence and Enjoyment – A Strategy for Primary Schools* DfES/0377/2003 [Online] Available at: http://webarchive.nationalarchives.gov.uk/20040722013944/dfes.gov.uk/primary document/

Desailly, J. (2012) *Creativity in the Primary Classroom*. London: Sage

Foster, C. (2012) Creationism as a misconception: socio-cognitive conflict in the teaching of evolution. *International Journal of Science Education*, 34(14), pp. 2171–80

İpek, H. and Çalık, M. (2008) Combining different conceptual change methods within four-step constructivist teaching model: a sample teaching of series and parallel circuits. *International Journal of Environmental & Science Education*, 3(3), pp. 143–53

Kaplan, R. (ed.) (2001) *Science Says: A Collection of Quotations on the History, Meaning, and Practice of Science*. New York: The Stonesong Press

Keogh, B. and Naylor, S., (1999) Concept cartoons, teaching and learning in science: an evaluation. *International Journal of Science Education*, 21(4), pp. 431–46

King, C.J.H. (2010) An analysis of misconceptions in science textbooks: earth science in England and Wales. *International Journal of Science Education*, 32(5), pp. 565–601

Larkin, D. (2012) Misconceptions about 'misconceptions': preservice secondary science teachers' views on the value and role of student ideas. *Science Education*, 96(5), pp. 927–59

Let's think (2012) cognitive conflict. [Online] Available at: http://www.letsthink.org.uk/ca_approach/cognitive_conflict.html

Liu, X. (2004) Using concept mapping for assessing and promoting relational conceptual change in science. *Science Education*, 88(3), pp. 373–96

Monteiro, A., Nóbrega, C., Abrantes, I. and Gomes, C. (2012) Diagnosing Portuguese students' misconceptions about the mineral concept. *International Journal of Science Education*, 34(17), pp. 2705–26

Morton, T. (2012) Classroom talk, conceptual change and teacher reflection in bilingual science teaching. *Teaching and Teacher Education*, 28, pp. 101–10

Murphy, C. (2003) Literature review in primary science and ICT. [Online] Available at: http://archive.futurelab.org.uk/resources/documents/lit_reviews/Primary_Science_Review.pdf

Novak, J.D. (2002) Meaningful learning: the essential factor for conceptual change in limited or inappropriate propositional hierarchies leading to empowerment of learners. *Science Education,* 86(4), pp. 548–71.

Osborne, J. (2010) Arguing to learn in science: the role of collaborative, critical discourse. *Science*, 328 (5977), pp. 463–6

Posner, G.J., Strike, K.A., Hewson, P.W. and Gertzog, W.A. (1982) Accommodation of a scientific conception: toward a theory of conceptual change. *Science Education*, 66(2), pp. 211–27

Root-Bernstein, R.S. (1987) Tools of thought: designing an integrated curriculum for lifelong learners. *Roeper Review*, 10(1), pp. 17–21

Root-Bernstein R.S., Allen, L., Beach, L., Bhadula, R., Fast, J., Hosey, C., Kremkow, B., Lapp, J., Lonc, K., Pawelec, K., Podufaly, A., Russ, C., Tennant, L., Vrtis, E. and Weinlander, S. (2008) Arts foster success: comparison of Nobel Prizewinners, Royal Society, National Academy, and Sigma Xi members. *Journal of Psychology of Science and Technology*, 1(2), pp. 51–63

Rose, J. (2009) *Independent Review of the Primary Curriculum: Final report*. DCSF Publications 00499–2009DOM-EN [Online] Available at: http://www.educationengland.org.uk/documents/pdfs/2009-IRPC-final-report.pdf

Schmidt, A.L. (2010) The battle for creativity: frontiers in science and science education. *Insights and Perspectives, Bioessays*, 32, pp. 1016–19

Shayer, M. and Adey, P.S. (1981). *Towards a Science of Science Teaching*. London: Heinemann Educational Books

Shtulman, A. and Valcarcel, J. (2012) Scientific knowledge suppresses but does not supplant earlier intuitions. *Cognition*, 124(2), pp. 209–15

Snow, C.E. (2010) Academic language and the challenge of reading for learning about science. *Science*, 328(5977) pp. 450–2.

Treagust, D. and Duit, R. (2008) Conceptual change: a discussion of theoretical, methodological and practical challenges for science education. *Cultural Studies of Science Education*, 3(2), pp. 297–328

Trundle, K.C. and Bell R.L. (2010) The use of a computer simulation to promote conceptual change: a quasi-experimental study. *Computers & Education*, 54(4), pp. 1078–88

Van de Broek, P. (2010) Using texts in science education: cognitive processes and knowledge representation. *Science*, 328(5977), pp. 453–6

Venville, G.J. and Treagust, D.F. (1998) Exploring conceptual change in genetics using a multidimensional interpretive framework. *Journal of Research in Science Teaching*, 35(9), pp. 1031–55

CHAPTER 3

PEDAGOGICAL APPROACHES AND THE TEACHING OF SCIENCE

Chapter aims

By the end of this chapter, you should be able to:

- Examine dimensions of teaching that enable effective learning about the nature of science

- Explore a range of approaches to scientific enquiry in the primary classroom

- Develop strategies for enquiry-based science education

INTRODUCTION

Teachers are continually striving to raise standards as well as provide children with a holistic education that develops the whole child and promotes their well-being. The real pressures that teachers are under means that some may argue that there is little space outside of the traditional Arts subjects for creativity. Fortunately, Ofsted's report (2010) *Learning: Creative Approaches that Raise Standards* states that 'In schools with good teaching, there is not a conflict between the National Curriculum, national standards in core subjects and creative approaches to learning' (p. 5).

In relation to science and the other STEM (science, technology, engineering and mathematics) subjects, the report noted the commitments of these schools to promoting investigation, invention and evaluation. They also reported the use of practitioners, both in and out of the classroom, to extend pupils' opportunities for creative learning (Ofsted, 2010, p. 5). Opportunities for creative science outside the classroom are explored in-depth in Chapter 11. Other contributing factors were the use of approaches traditionally used in creative subjects being incorporated into science and mathematics (p. 5). Sadly, in Ofsted's most recent report on schools successful in science (Ofsted, 2013), there is no reference to creativity and the previous one (Ofsted, 2011) contains only one reference to being creative and that refers to being creative with a budget!

Therefore, this book (and this chapter in particular) aims to empower teachers to embrace creative approaches and know that this will not be to the detriment of meeting internal or external performance targets. Instead, with the right planning and confidence in their understanding of the core concepts underpinning science, teachers can deliver creative lessons with engaged children, who are taking ownership of their own learning and developing as active, informed citizens.

WHAT ARE CREATIVE APPROACHES TO SCIENCE?

There is no simple answer to this. Creativity can mean, as has been discussed in Chapter 1, different things to different people and at different times depending on the context. This chapter will make a case for some key ingredients to successful teaching and learning in science. By combining elements of these with creative contexts, as explored in Chapters 8–14 (Part II of this book), effective and creative learning in the primary science classroom can happen.

National curricula and accompanying guidance are excellent sources for ideas and exemplars on how to approach teaching particular subject areas. The 2014 National Curriculum for England (Department for Education, 2013) identifies a number of approaches to teaching and learning including direct teaching, drama and discussion across the range of subject areas. In science, it suggests using a variety of approaches. Scotland's Curriculum for Excellence (Education Scotland, 2013) offers guidance on a number of key approaches including first-hand experience outdoors, active learning and co-operative and collaborative learning across all subjects. Northern Ireland's curriculum (CCEA, 2007) states that teachers should make use of a wide range of teaching methods, balancing whole class, group and individual activities, to engage children in effective learning. Wales' curriculum (ACCAC, 2003) offers an exemplar on using the outdoors as an approach to effective science teaching. The Irish National Curriculum Teacher Guidelines (NCCA/DES, 1997) offers clear direction for how to approach teaching the different strand areas of science and identifies relevant and appropriate methods.

Underlying all this is a common understanding and valuing of the importance of a variety of teaching and learning approaches, particularly in the context of increasing pupil diversity in our classrooms. No one approach is best and certainly when considering the range of learners and their needs a varied approach to teaching and learning is seen as best practice.

NATURE OF SCIENCE

The most recent Ofsted reports on schools successful in science (2013, 2011, 2008) clearly recognize that scientific enquiry is at the heart of effective science teaching and learning. Most recently, it was observed that science teaching was most effective when teachers' set out to sustain pupils' natural curiosity, so that they were eager to learn the subject content as well as develop the necessary investigative skills (Ofsted, 2013). Instances where science lessons were more practical and focussed on the development of the skills of scientific enquiry (Ofsted, 2010) and where emphasis was placed on children designing and carrying out investigations for themselves (Ofsted, 2008) were also noted. However, each report also recognizes the need for further engagement with scientific enquiry. Education Scotland (2012) also report that while there is some evidence of high quality scientific enquiry, there is scope for children to be engaged further in such fruitful investigative work as this is not a consistent enough feature of learning in the sciences across primary school. This is particularly interesting given that Scotland has a longer history of teacher assessment in science, and studies (Murphy, 2005) have indicated that teaching investigative science was considerably constrained by preparation for national tests. This suggests that other factors play a part in teachers' desire and ability to teach through scientific enquiry.

Underpinning effective scientific enquiry is the need for a common understanding of and appreciation for the nature of science. This is reflected explicitly in the 2014 National Curriculum for England (Department for Education, 2013) through 'Working scientifically' which specifies the understanding of the nature, processes and methods of science. A similar focus is implicit and explicit in other national curricula. These combine the key elements of working and thinking scientifically and promote understanding of the nature of science.

The nature of science, in particular scientific methods, will be explored in more depth in Chapter 6 but for now a brief consideration is required. Osbourne et al. (2003) in their research identified nine elements that should underpin ideas about science and the nature of science:

1. Scientific methods and critical testing

2. Science and certainty

3. Diversity of scientific thinking

4. Hypothesis and prediction

5. Historical development of scientific knowledge

6. Creativity

7. Science and questioning

8. Analysis and interpretation of data

9. Cooperation and collaboration in the development of scientific knowledge.

See Osbourne et al. (2003) for an explanation of each of these elements.

While there is a common understanding that engaging in scientific enquiry will help develop ideas about the nature of science, Schwarz et al. (2004) state that research does not generally support the idea that engaging in scientific enquiry alone will enhance conceptions of the nature of science. Further research was carried out by Bartholomew et al. (2004) and they reported five dimensions of practice which impact on teachers' success with teaching about the nature of science. It was most successful where teachers were confident that they had a sufficient understanding of the nature of science, saw their role as facilitators of learning, promoted open and dialogic discourse in the classroom, valued knowledge and reasoning outcomes and learning activities were authentic and owned by the students. These dimensions, as shall be discussed in more depth in this chapter, strengthen a creative approach to science teaching and learning, and foster understanding of the nature of science.

ENQUIRY-BASED SCIENCE EDUCATION

Investigations and enquiry lie at the heart of science. Though science is a practical subject by its very nature, research evidence clearly shows that a lot of practical work makes little difference to students' understanding of scientific ideas. Many studies have found no significant difference in understanding between students taught a range of topics with and without hands-on practical work. Some of the studies suggest the reasons may lie in the way practical work is used (Millar, 2010, p. 133). Traditionally, students of science experienced a didactic approach to this, whereby the teacher had control over the various aspects of the investigation including the question to be investigated, how it would be investigated, the expected outcome and how results would be recorded and communicated. This is defined as a transmissive, deductive approach to learning. In this the teacher has a clear knowledge outcome which the students are expected to meet through a singular pre-determined route. This was certainly the case when we studied science in secondary school and for part of our university degree courses. It wasn't until we had the opportunity to undertake research projects that we really felt we were actually *doing* science.

There is value to a transmissive approach however and in the primary classroom it would be best described as an illustrative approach or closed investigation whereby the question is defined by the teacher and the variables identified, the teacher tells the children what to do and there is one expected answer. In an illustrative approach the aim is to enable the children to experience a particular phenomenon or concept. It is about clarifying or exemplifying a particular scientific idea. It is particularly useful when a shared understanding among the children is desired. This may be appropriate as an enquiry in itself, such as a closed investigation, or before children start investigating their own questions and ideas or equally as effective after to consolidate understanding. It may also be used to teach children how to use particular equipment or tools. Figure 3.1 shows the stages in scientific enquiry and an illustrative approach or closed investigation would typically see the teacher control steps 1–5.

1. Selection of the global question*
2. Identification of the independent variables
3. Thinking of how to measure/observe the outcome (dependent variable)
4. Question generation
5. Selecting the equipment and deciding how to use it
6. Deciding what might happen (making a prediction) if needed*
7. Data collection methods – type and amount of data to be collected*
8. Making observations and measurements
9. Recording and evaluating the data (reliability)
10. Interpreting the data
11. Drawing conclusions
12. Evaluating the process*

* Using secondary sources of information can occur at a number of points. It will differ according to the investigation as well as age of learners, but is an important part of the process.

Figure 3.1   The stages of scientific enquiry (from Ward et al., 2008, p. 60)

 # Time for reflection 3.1

Remember the five dimensions of practice developed by Bartholomew et al. (2004, p. 664), where teachers had success in teaching about the nature of science. Review the scale below in Figure 3.2 and reflect on each dimension. Consider which end of the scale for each dimension of practice an illustrative approach or closed investigation supports.

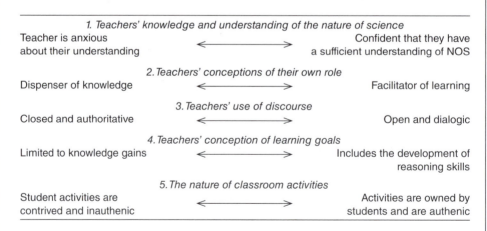

Figure 3.2   The five dimensions of practice (Bartholomew et al., 2004, p. 664) which impact on the success of teaching about the nature of science

Reflect on your experience of teaching science or from your experiences of being taught science either in university, college, secondary or primary school. Which dimensions and to what degree were they evident in your experiences of science?

Finally, consider how each of these dimensions might encourage creativity.

A contrasting approach, which is defined by its inductive approach to developing scientific ideas, is inquiry-based science education (IBSE). Wolk (2008) writes that enquiry-based teaching 'transforms the aims of school from short term memorization of facts into disciplined questioning and investigating' (p. 117), which as we know are core elements of working scientifically. Enquiry-based learning gets students asking questions and investigating possible answers, using a variety of skills to collect reliable and accurate data, analyse secondary sources, draw conclusions, reason and debate (Wellcome Trust, 2012). IBSE sees a shift in the teacher's role to one of facilitator and centres the learning around the child. IBSE has proved its efficiency at both primary and secondary levels in increasing children's and students' interest and attainment levels while at the same time stimulating teacher motivations (Rocard et al., 2007). Furthermore, Rocard et al. (2007, p. 2) report 'IBSE is effective with all kinds of students from the weakest to the most able and is fully compatible with the ambition of excellence. Moreover IBSE is beneficial to promoting girls' interest and participation in science activities.'

The evidence is such that the European Commission has shown its support for IBSE through its FP7 funding (2007–2013). This has resulted in a significant number of large-scale Europe-wide projects investigating, developing and disseminating relevant research, practice and professional development around IBSE. These include ESTABLISH, FIBONACCI, PRIMAS, PROFILES, PATHWAY, INQUIRE and Pri-Sci-Net (Europa, 2007). However, Peacock (2012) raises the question to what extent, if any, IBSE has affected the curriculum, teaching methods and professional development in England. His answer suggests little. Instead he recognizes the positive directions of Wales, Northern Ireland and Scotland towards more creative approaches to science. Particularly in the case of the Northern Ireland curriculum, he notes the positive impact of teacher independence and freedom in terms of assessment methods on creative approaches to science, including IBSE. However, despite a more open curriculum, Education Scotland (2012) note that at times, practical work in all sectors is still too prescriptive and teacher-led thereby not allowing the development of learners' creativity and enquiry skills.

There are many different degrees to IBSE and a range of interpretations and practice. On one end you have guided enquiry and on the other you have fully open ended, child-led investigations or free exploration, where the children identify the question, decide how to go about doing it and offer their solution to the problem based on their question and evidence gathered.

PROCESS-ORIENTED GUIDED ENQUIRY LEARNING

Process-oriented guided inquiry learning (POGIL) is, as the term suggests, a guided approach to enquiry. It originated in college chemistry departments in America (pogil.org) in 1994 and has gained widespread popularity since across a range of disciplines. It is defined as a learning cycle of exploration, concept invention and application to guide the students to construct new knowledge. POGIL activities focus on core concepts and encourage a deep understanding of the curriculum content while developing higher-order thinking and process skills. The resources used supply students with data or information followed by leading questions designed to guide them toward formulation of their own valid conclusions and conceptual understanding. Thus making it guided enquiry.

Martin (2011) discusses a number of constructivist approaches to primary science including POGIL and states that POGIL is reported as the most effective for elementary (primary) children.

PROBLEM-BASED LEARNING

Problem-based learning (PBL) is another such 'enquiry-based' teaching methodology and has its origins in the medical field. It is attributed to Howard S. Barrows and Robyn M. Tamblyn at McMaster University, Ontario, Canada. Like other methodologies it has evolved and taken different forms. However, the underlying principle is consistent, that PBL is any learning environment in which the problem drives the learning. And in this vein, it has been around a lot longer than you or me. From the Stone Age people have developed skills and knowledge in the face of problems. However, in its purest state as a teaching methodology, PBL is small group, self-directed, self-assessed learning (Woods, n.d.). PBL requires students to identify and develop new knowledge, understanding and skills before they can solve the problem. Additionally, they should come to that realization, the gap in their knowledge, themselves rather than being made aware of it by the teacher. Furthermore, the students having identified these knowledge gaps, then go about finding and making sense of these new ideas and apply them to the problem. In this way the teacher takes on the role of facilitator throughout the process. This is where the primary school teacher has a much easier job adapting to such an approach compared to the university teacher (the authors included!), who is used to being in the position of 'fount of all knowledge'. Here the role of the teacher is to ask questions (not answer them) and support discussion by challenging assumptions. Facilitators should use different question types when facilitating, including informational, application and problem-solving ones (Walsh, 2005), which promote both lower and higher order thinking.

A problem-based investigation naturally demands problem-solving and the National Advisory Committee on Creative and Cultural Education (NACCCE) has long since recognized the importance of developing this skill in younger children. 'Problem-solving is now a key skill in education. Developing young peoples' abilities to solve problems is fundamental to preparing them for an independent life and a somewhat uncertain future. Creative education can contribute directly to problem-solving abilities in all disciplines and fields of work' (NACCCE, 1999, p. 37). This NACCCE report also stated that more opportunities should be given to young people to sense and define problems for themselves, as well as identifying solutions to given problems.

PBL supports both a constructivist and social constructivist approach to learning, as students work together to solve the problem. Through PBL students are starting from their learning. Their own ideas, experiences and knowledge are examined in the context of the problem and misconceptions are challenged and new learning connected to existing ideas. It is important that problems or scenarios are relevant, this is particularly the case with children. They need to be able to relate to the problem or scenario; this encourages them and will allow them to make progress with the problem.

Problems can be set up as 'real' experiences. There is a wonderful example of this in Ashbridge and Joesphidou (2012). It is a cross-curricular scheme of work for infants. While on a walk in the school grounds, the children come across a bear, with a parachute on, stuck in a tree. This leads to lots of questioning and a range of learning opportunities across the curriculum, including science, as the children find out where the bear has come from, who he is and how he will get home. Such an approach is to be recommended when working with younger children. With older children, written scenarios with pictures and/or objects would also work well.

 Case example

Scenario: The children are out in the playground when one of them discovers a small tooth (this is set up by the teacher). The children don't know where it came from. They are at the age when they are losing their baby teeth and are beginning to grow their adult teeth so it is relevant to them. There are also a few schools pets and they might offer that it could have belonged to one of them. There is some scope for some whole class discussion at this stage so initial excitement and motivation can be shared. Then it would be important to divide the children into small groups (no more than five) to work on the problem. Next follows a 7-step approach to this problem, as suggested by Walsh (2005).

Step 1: Identify the problem

As facilitator, you, the teacher, should encourage questioning around the problem among the group. Who does the tooth belong to? How did it get here? Why did the tooth come out? You should encourage talk and discussion among the children, rather than teacher-directed talk.

Step 2: Explore pre-existing knowledge

The children should discuss and share their existing knowledge. What do they know about teeth? Why do humans have different kinds of teeth? What do different teeth look like? What animals do they know that have teeth? What are they like? At this stage, you should allow children to share their experiences and ideas about the problem and encourage some critical thinking around the ideas being expressed.

(Continued)

(Continued)

Step 3: Generate hypotheses and possible ways to investigate these

Next, children should be encouraged to discuss possible solutions to the problem and how they are going to approach solving it. You need to ensure all ideas are being heard and considered and that the group have a clear plan of action.

Step 4: Identify learning issues

These are questions that can't be answered by the existing knowledge within the group. These might be: Has anyone lost a tooth recently and not found it? What are the shapes of different human teeth? Why do we have different kinds of teeth? Why do we look after our teeth by brushing regularly? What pets are in the school? What type of teeth do they have? What diets do the different pets have and what kind of teeth would they need for this? Why might an animal's tooth fall out? How do animals look after their teeth?

Step 5: Self study

As this stage, children should be encouraged to do some primary and/or secondary research to help solve the problem. Primary research could involve doing an observational drawing of the tooth and doing a comparison to a child's tooth, identifying similarities and differences or this could again be done by consulting secondary sources. Primary research could also involve collecting data around the diets of the school pets or this could be done through secondary research using the internet or information books. Perhaps the local vet would be able to help. It is important that you set a clear time frame for this stage so that children know how much time they have and how best to use this time to tackle the identified learning issues. During this stage, you should confer with individuals and groups to ensure they are focussed on their work and addressing issues that will help solve the original problem.

Step 6: Re-evaluation and application of new knowledge to the problem

During this stage, the children should share all the new knowledge and understanding they have gained from their self-study. As well as encouraging sharing, you should also encourage children to ask each other questions, explain concepts to each other and identify and understand the key concepts that will help to solve the problem. The children apply the knowledge gained to the original problem and offer a solution.

Step 7: Assessment and reflection on learning

In this final stage, the children should reflect on the skills and processes they used and how well they worked together as a group. They should evaluate their learning and identify ways to improve next time.

Good PBL problems don't have one clear solution. Instead, given the children's experiences, prior learning and information, or resources available, the children may come up with any number of different solutions. There is no right answer! The tooth could be a rabbit's tooth if it hasn't had enough hard things to chew on; the tooth could be a cat's tooth, particularly if the cat is over 10-years-old. Poor diet can also lead to gum disease and a cat losing teeth due to the build-up of plaque from canned or dry food. Older hamsters are prone to teeth that may break easily. Some vets also think that a hamster's teeth may break more easily if the diet is low in calcium. It could be a part of a tooth from a fight between animals. The possibilities are many. If you are thinking, 'my school doesn't have any pets' then be creative. What way could you rework the problem so that the children are still developing their scientific enquiry skills and engaging with similar content?

As an extension to this, you could get your local vet to come in and talk about dental care for pets. As highlighted earlier, Ofsted's 2010 report praised the use of practitioners, both in and out of the classroom, to extend pupils' opportunities for creative learning. They also are probably the person to ask to get hold of some animal teeth!

The case example links to the following objectives of the 2014 National Curriculum for England (Department for Education, 2013), under the content area 'Animals, including humans'. As can be seen, this problem can be used from Year 1 to Year 4.

Year	Statutory requirements
1	Identify and name a variety of common animals that are carnivores, herbivores and omnivores
	Describe and compare the structure of a variety of common animals (including pets)
3	Identify that animals, including humans, need the right types and amount of nutrition and that they cannot make their own food. They get nutrition from what they eat
4	Describe the simple functions of the basic parts of the digestive system in humans
	Identify the different types of teeth in humans and their simple functions

Figure 3.3 Case example links to the 2014 National Curriculum for England (Department for Education, 2013)

Activity 3.1

Consider which of the working scientifically objectives for Year 1 and 2 and/or Year 3 and 4 could be developed by the case example.
    Year 1 and 2 – Working scientifically (Department for Education, 2013, p. 147)

- asking simple questions and recognizing that they can be answered in different ways
- observing closely, using simple equipment

(Continued)

(Continued)

- performing simple tests
- identifying and classifying
- using their observations and ideas to suggest answers to questions
- gathering and recording data to help in answering questions.

Year 3 and 4 (Department for Education, 2013, p. 155)

- asking relevant questions and using different types of scientific enquiries to answer them
- setting up simple practical enquiries, comparative and fair tests
- making systematic and careful observations and, where appropriate, taking accurate measurements using standard units, using a range of equipment including thermometers and data loggers
- gathering, recording, classifying and presenting data in a variety of ways to help in answering questions
- recording findings using simple scientific language, drawings, labelled diagrams, keys, bar charts, and tables
- reporting on findings from enquiries including oral and written explanations, displays or presentations of results and conclusions
- using results to draw simple conclusions, make predictions for new values, suggest improvements and raise further questions
- identifying differences, similarities or changes related to simple scientific ideas and processes
- using straightforward scientific evidence to answer questions or to support their findings.

Now let's think back to the five dimensions of practice identified by Bartholomew et al. (2004, p. 664). Would a teacher adopting this kind of problem-based approach to science have to have a sufficient knowledge and understanding of the nature of science? What would they see as their role, dispenser of knowledge or facilitator of learning? Would the teacher's use of discourse be closed and authoritative or open and dialogic? Would the teacher see the learning benefits of both knowledge gains and skills? Who would have ownership of such an activity? How confident would you feel to adopt such an approach to your science teaching and learning?

Now compose a checklist of the attributes needed to adopt this approach.

CONCLUSION

According to the Council for Curriculum, Examinations and Assessment in Northern Ireland (CCEA, 2007) children should be able to use creative approaches to be imaginative and inventive, to explore possibilities and take risks in their learning. Some of the ways they suggest that children do this is by experimenting with questions and ideas in a playful way; seeking out questions to explore and problems to solve; challenging the routine method, accepting that there is not always a 'right' answer; learning from and building on own and others' experiences; using all the senses to stimulate and contribute to ideas; making ideas real by experimenting with different designs, actions and outcomes; and valuing other people's ideas to stimulate their own thinking. By adopting an enquiry-based approach to teaching and learning in science there is more opportunity and scope for children to be creative in all of the above ways.

At the heart of good practice in science education is investigation. Hopefully a case has been made for adopting an open, child-led enquiry-based approach but Rocard et al. (2007) note that 'IBSE and traditional deductive approaches are not mutually exclusive and they should be combined in any science classroom to accommodate different mind sets and age-group preferences' (p. 2). Indeed, whether it is teacher- or child-led, open or closed, primary or secondary data collection, the key elements that are required are discussion and questioning, both teacher and children's questions, starting from children's ideas and experiences and opportunity for evaluation and reflection. These are the consistent elements of teaching and learning in schools which are successful in primary science in England and they are simply good practice.

FURTHER READING

Dunlop, L., Compton, K., Clarke, L. and McKelvey-Martin, V. (2013) Child-led enquiry in primary science, *Education 3–13: International Journal of Primary, Elementary and Early Years Education*. Available at: http://dx.doi.org/10.1080/03004279.2013.822013

In this research paper, the authors describe and evaluate the application of a child-led approach to scientific enquiry to children aged 8–11. It offers useful insights into the experience of both the teachers and children engaged with scientific enquiry.

Wellcome Trust (2011) Perspectives on education: enquiry-based learning. [Online] Available at: http://www.wellcome.ac.uk/stellent/groups/corporatesite/@msh_peda/documents/web_document/wtvm055190.pdf

This article presents four perspectives on enquiry-based teaching; a secondary teacher's perspective, a policy perspective, an international perspective and a research perspective. It addresses the need for informed debate to consider what enquiry-based learning means in practice and what role it has in inspiring science education.

Primary Science Teaching Trust (2013) Focused assessment of science enquiry. [Online] Available at: http://www.pstt.org.uk/resources/curriculum-materials/focused-assessment-of-science-enquiry-.aspx

Assessment is a key driver of learning and this website provides guidance on how to assess during enquiry work. See also Chapter 5 for more on how to assess skills and content knowledge.

REFERENCES

ACCAC (Qualifications, Curriculum and Assessment Authority for Wales) (2003) Developing the Curriculum Cymreig. Cardiff: ACCAC Publications. Available at: http://wales.gov.uk/docs/dcells/publications/090902curriculumcymreigen.pdf

Ashbridge, J. and Joesphidou, J. (2012).Who am I? How can we learn to value ourselves and others through thematic work supporting the development of children's knowledge and understanding of the world in the Foundation Stage?, in Rowley, C. and Cooper, H. (eds), *Cross Curricular Approaches to Teaching and Learning.* London: Sage, pp. 17–33

Bartholomew, H., Osborne, J. and Ratcliffe, M. (2004) Teaching students 'ideas-about-science': five dimensions of effective practice. *Science Education,* 88(5), pp. 654–82

CCEA (2007) The Northern Ireland Curriculum Primary. Council for the Curriculum, Examinations and Assessment [Online] Available at: http://www.nicurriculum.org.uk/docs/key_stages_1_and_2/northern_ireland_curriculum_primary.pdf

Department for Education (2013) The National Curriculum in England. [Online] Available at: https://www.gov.uk/government/uploads/system/uploads/attachment_data/file/260481/PRIMARY_national_curriculum_11–9–13_2.pdf

Education Scotland (2012) The sciences 3–18. Available at: http://www.educationscotland.gov.uk/Images/Science3to18v4_tcm4–731895.pdf September 2012

Education Scotland (2013) http://www.educationscotland.gov.uk/learningteachingandassessment/

Europa (2007) http://ec.europa.eu/research/science-society/document_library/pdf_06/fp7-science-education-contracts-2007–2010_en.pdf

Martin, D.J. (2011) *Elementary Science Methods: A Constructivist Approach.* 6th ed. Stamford, CT: CENGAGE Learning Custom Publishing

Millar, R. (2010) Practical Work, in Osborne, J. and Dillin, J. (eds) *Good Practice in Science Teaching. What Research Has to Say.* 2nd ed. Maidenhead: Open University Press

Murphy, C. (2005) Primary science in the UK: a scoping study. Wellcome Trust. [Online] Available at: http://www.wellcome.ac.uk/stellent/groups/corporatesite/@msh_peda/documents/web_document/wtx026636.pdf

NACCCE (1999) All our futures: creativity, culture and education. National Advisory Committee on Creative and Cultural Education. [Online] Available at: http://sirkenrobinson.com/pdf/allourfutures.pdf

NCCA/DES National Council for Curriculum and Assessment/Department of Education and Science (1997) *Science: Social, Environmental and Scientific Education Teacher Guidelines.* Dublin: The Stationery Office

Ofsted (2008) Success in science. [Online] Available at: http://www.ofsted.gov.uk/resources/success-science June 2008

Ofsted (2010) Learning: creative approaches that raise standards. [Online] Available at: http://www.ofsted.gov.uk/node/2405 January 2010

Ofsted (2011) Successful science. [Online] Available at: http://www.ofsted.gov.uk/resources/successful-science January 2011

Ofsted (2013) Maintaining curiosity: a survey into science education in schools. [Online] Available at: http://www.ofsted.gov.uk/resources/maintaining-curiosity-survey-science-education-schools

Osborne, J.F., Ratcliffe, M., Collins, S., Millar, R. and Duschl, R. (2003) What 'ideas-about-science'should be taught in school science? A Delphi Study of the 'Expert' Community. *Journal of Research in Science Teaching,* 40(7), pp. 692–720

Peacock, A. (2012) Learning from elsewhere: an international perspective in the development of primary science, in Dunne, M. and Peacock, A. (eds) *Primary Science: A Guide to Teaching Practice.* London: Sage

Rocard, M., Csermely, P., Jorde, D., Lenzen, D., Walberg-Henriksson, H., and Hemmo, V. (2007) *Science Education Now: A Renewed Pedagogy for the Future of Europe.* Luxembourg: Office for Official Publications of the European Communities

Schwartz, R.S., Lederman, N.G. and Crawford, B.A. (2004) Developing views of nature of science in an authentic context: an explicit approach to bridging the gap between nature of science and scientific inquiry. *Science Education*, 88(4), pp. 610–45

Walsh, A. (2005) The tutor in problem based learning: a novice's guide. Hamilton: programme for faculty development. [Online] Available at: http://www.fhs.mcmaster.ca/facdev/documents/tutorPBL.pdf

Ward, H., Roden, J., Hewlett, C. and Foreman, J. (2008) *Teaching Science in the Primary Classroom. A Practical Guide.* 2nd ed. London: Sage

Wellcome Trust (2012) Inquiry-based learning – what is its role in an inspiring science education? [Online] Available at: http://www.wellcome.ac.uk/News/2012/News/WTVM054002.htm

Wolk, S. (2008) School as Inquiry. *Phi Delta Kappan* October 2008. [Online] Available at: http://www.pdkmembers.org/members_online/publications/Archive/pdf/k0810wol.pdf

Woods, D. (n.d.) Problem-based learning. [Online] Available at: http://chemeng.mcmaster.ca/problem-based-learning (accessed 16.01.14)

CHAPTER 4

THE IMPORTANCE OF TEACHER KNOWLEDGE IN SCIENCE

Chapter aims

By the end of this chapter, you should be able to:

- Recognize the various aspects of teacher knowledge required for effective teaching in science

- Explore your own knowledge and understanding of the core concepts underpinning the National Curriculum for England

- Develop a working knowledge of the key indicators of progression in working scientifically across the curriculum

---

INTRODUCTION

Typically when we ask our initial teacher education students 'what is science?' we get a large number who recognize science as a study of the three main subject areas – biology, chemistry and physics and an encouraging number who identify science as a study of the world around us and sometimes the processes by which we do this. At the other end of scale we get that science is about learning facts from textbooks! This is perhaps not surprising since many people can identify with this view of science from some stage in their life. Our experiences were a little different as we were naturally inquisitive and interested in science and enjoyed the various aspects but we certainly remember science lessons which were of the textbook kind. Unfortunately, it often appears that students who once had positive experiences of science, particularly in primary, have been left with negative feelings and memories from their formal education in science at secondary level and beyond.

Science is both a body of knowledge and a process and as you progress in science, the knowledge and understanding of particular disciplines and the core concepts that underpin them become increasingly important. This coupled with the demands of assessment procedures, over-loaded curricula and practical and resource issues can be to the detriment of scientific, student-led enquiry, leading to the over reliance on textbooks. Luckily, in primary science we are not constrained by such factors, particularly given the slimmed down 2014 National Curriculum for England (Department for Education, 2013a) and would strongly advocate for the enquiry side of science taking the central position, embedding the thinking, attitudes, values and ways of working scientifically. It is therefore right and appropriate that working scientifically (formerly scientific enquiry) is central to the National Curriculum in England. A similar focus on the processes of science is seen in the national curricula in Scotland, Wales, Northern Ireland and Ireland. So when thinking about what you need to know to teach primary science effectively, it is important to recognize and value the key role that the processes of science play.

Time for reflection 4.1

Think about the following statements. To what extent do you agree or disagree with them?

- I'm no good at science
- I enjoy practical science
- I never liked chemistry (or biology or physics as the case may be)
- I know how to carry out a scientific investigation
- I get nervous when I think about teaching science
- I look forward to teaching practical science.

Ask most science enthusiasts and educators and they will probably tell you they have a preferred discipline within science and maybe one which they struggled with or still struggle with, or maybe even that they don't like. However, despite this they should acknowledge the key role engaging in scientific enquiry will have played in developing their understanding and enjoyment of that area of science. Additionally, for educators they will certainly value the process of planning for and teaching the subject had on their enjoyment and conceptual understanding, particularly if there was a shared hands-on, investigative approach with their students. So if you enjoy practical work and are developing your understanding of working scientifically and what it is to carry out a scientific investigation, you are well on your way to developing your subject knowledge and enjoyment of science. Alternatively, if you get nervous when thinking about teaching science or feel you are no good at science, hopefully this book will give you confidence to take an enquiry approach to your science teaching. This will enable you and your children to immerse yourselves in the processes of science and through this develop knowledge and understanding. Chapter 3 had described a range of approaches for effective science teaching and learning through enquiry.

However, subject matter knowledge does play a part and this shall be explored in more detail now.

SUBJECT MATTER KNOWLEDGE

Gilbert (2010) recognizes three necessary characteristics of a science teacher; subject matter knowledge, pedagogic knowledge and pedagogic content knowledge. Within subject matter knowledge, Gilbert (2010, p. 279) further recognizes three components; substantive, syntactic and beliefs. The substantive components are the concepts that make up the core of the curriculum such as forces, materials, plants, and so on. The syntactic component is the knowledge concerned with the processes of science. The beliefs component is to do with the beliefs held about the nature of particular sciences and of science itself. Teachers' perceptions of a discipline have been shown to significantly influence their teaching of the subject (Parker, 2004). According to Gilbert (2010), each of these, substantive, syntactic and beliefs, play a crucial role in developing the necessary characteristics for effective science teaching. This supports the notion that knowledge and understanding of scientific enquiry and working scientifically are important aspects of science subject knowledge.

In a review of the first ten years of compulsory primary science in England and Wales, Harlen (1998) identified concerns around teachers' subject knowledge and the balance between process skills and science content among other factors. It is interesting that the latter continues to be an issue with each of the last Ofsted reports on science (Ofsted, 2013, 2011, 2008) identifying scientific enquiry and child-led investigations as areas for development. Conversely, according to the latest report (Ofsted, 2013, p. 12) 'Despite concerns raised by various government agencies and professional associations about the lack of science subject specialists in primary schools, the evidence from this survey indicates that this (teachers' subject knowledge) was not a serious barrier to pupils' achievement in terms of teachers' knowledge and understanding. Additionally, in an earlier report (Ofsted, 2011), teachers' subject knowledge was found to be at least satisfactory and in the large majority of the schools, the teachers' knowledge and understanding of the National Curriculum science requirements were good or outstanding. The supports available to, and used by, teachers who were aware of the limitations of their knowledge and their conscientious planning were also acknowledged (Ofsted, 2013). Here we begin to appreciate the importance of teachers' pedagogic knowledge. Parker and Heywood (2000) also suggest that knowing the subject does not necessarily translate into effective teaching of that subject. Findings from a research study on secondary science teacher trainees

(Kind, 2009) offer further insights. The study reported somewhat counter-intuitively that the trainees were found to teach more successful lessons outside their specialism, particularly in the early stages. This was enabled by using a richer range of subject matter knowledge sources, including crucially, advice from experienced colleagues and practising unfamiliar experiments and seeking advice from technicians. Additionally, in the Ofsted report on primary teachers' subject knowledge (Ofsted, 2009, p. 7) it was reported that where lessons were judged to be good were sometimes so because teachers' strong general teaching skills more than made up for any weaknesses in their knowledge of the subject they were teaching. Furthermore, studies have shown that integrating science can compensate for primary teachers' lack of confidence in science teaching (Gresnigt et al., 2014).

However, Pollard (2008) states that though an association between sound subject knowledge and effective teaching may be unproven, recognizing in particular the myriad of factors that play a part in effective teaching and learning, he expresses the crucial role substantive knowledge plays in teachers being able to explain and scaffold children's knowledge and understanding. He argues that there does, in fact, seem to be something of a consensus that teachers with sound subject knowledge can do this more effectively, citing several research studies in science education. Furthermore, Ofsted (2013, 2009) reported that teachers' lack of subject knowledge meant some teachers did not spot and tackle errors or misconceptions in pupils' work. Occasional inaccuracies in terms of technical explanation were also noted. However, it was noted that these did not necessarily impede learning. The role of substantive or content knowledge is complex but it is clear that applying good pedagogy and valuing the role of the processes or syntactic knowledge of science can contribute significantly to effective teaching and learning in science.

PEDAGOGIC CONTENT KNOWLEDGE

A theme underpinning this book had been the recognition of the importance of teaching that supports conceptual understanding and children constructing their own ideas rather than rote memorizing in science. As teacher educators it is impossible to 'teach' all the required substantive and syntactic knowledge as well develop our students' skills and expertise in teaching science in the primary classroom. It is in supporting student teachers in acquiring content knowledge in science that the tension between subject knowledge and conceptual understanding manifests itself most acutely. Parker and Heywood (2000, p. 89) suggest that it concerns not simply knowing something (for example that the seasons are caused by the tilt of the earth's axis), but having a coherent, causal explanation which makes sense to the teacher such that they feel skilled in teaching the concept to children.

Shulman introduced the idea of pedagogical content knowledge (PCK) as 'a special amalgam of content and pedagogy that is uniquely the province of teachers, their own special form of professional understanding' (Shulman, 1987, p. 8). It is the ways of representing and formulating the subject that make it comprehensible to others. Shulman (1987) described it as 'taking what he or she (the teacher) understands and making it ready for effective instruction' (p. 14). Asoko (2002) recognizes the need for teachers to be confident enough in their own knowledge of science to identify those ideas which they considered appropriate for their class, the level at which these would be discussed and ways to exploit opportunities to introduce and apply them (p. 161). These are all aspects of PCK.

PCK was valued in the 2008 Teacher Standard Q14, 'Those recommended for the award of QTS should have a secure knowledge and understanding of their subjects/curriculum areas and related pedagogy to enable them to teach effectively across the age and ability range for which they are trained' (TDA, 2008, p. 7). This reflected an appreciation for the role subject specific pedagogy played. In the latest Teachers' Standards for England (Department for Education, 2013b) there is again an emphasis on secure knowledge including being able to address misunderstandings. In relation to the earlier discussion, Pollard (2008) suggested that substantive subject knowledge is needed for this.

The purpose of the discussion here is to relieve fears of the often assumed central role of substantive subject knowledge to teach science effectively. Syntactic knowledge of the processes of science, and pedagogic content knowledge have equally important roles in effective teaching and learning in primary science. Additionally, it is important to recognize the role that knowledge of the curriculum requirements has. We will now look at the substantive and syntactic content of the National Curriculum for England.

OVERVIEW OF THE 2014 NATIONAL CURRICULUM FOR ENGLAND

According to the Department for Education (2013a) a high-quality science education provides the foundations for understanding the world through the specific disciplines of biology, chemistry and physics. Figure 4.1 shows the content covered for each school year from Year 1 to Year 6. It is clear that apart from working scientifically, the content area 'Animals, including humans' is the only one that is covered across all six years, additionally, 'living things and their habitats' and 'plants' are strongly represented. In fact, a simple tally of the different content areas shows that over half of the content areas relate to biology (15 of 28), with areas related to physics being slightly more represented than chemistry, eight of 28 and five of 28 respectively. While we welcome the focus on plants, animals and habitats, in particular the inclusion of evolution, it is a concern that children's understanding of chemical and physical processes are not being given as much attention in these crucial early stages.

Interestingly, Chiu et al. (2007) suggested that it might be wise for science curriculum frameworks, textbooks, and science teachers to emphasize a minimum number of core concepts and to deal with them in greater depth (p. 387) and a slimmed down curriculum was a stated aim of the revised curriculum (Department for Education, 2012). Also, the US is making moves in this direction (McGraw Hill

Discipline area	Content area	Key Stage 1		Lower Key Stage 2		Upper Key Stage 2	
Class		1st	2nd	3rd	4th	5th	6th
Working scientifically		✓	✓	✓	✓	✓	✓
Biology	Animals (including humans)	✓	✓	✓	✓	✓	✓
	Living things and their habitats		✓		✓	✓	✓
	Plants	✓	✓	✓			
	Seasonal changes	✓					
	Evolution and inheritance						✓
Chemistry	(Use of*) everyday materials	✓	✓*				
	Rocks			✓			
	States of matter				✓		
	Properties and changes of materials					✓	
Physics	Forces (and magnets*)			✓*		✓	
	Light			✓			✓
	Sound				✓		
	Electricity				✓		✓
	Earth and space					✓	

Figure 4.1   Overview of content areas in the 2014 National Curriculum for England

(2014), see the recommended further reading for more on this). The idea of a slimmed-down curriculum focussing on core concepts is something that has clear merit when thinking of the creative classroom. Rather than considering a long list of specific facts and criteria, the focus should shift to some general principles and underlying concepts.

 Activity 4.1

Thinking about one of the disciplines of science: biology, chemistry or physics, consider how you would describe it to someone who has never heard of it before.

Biology is …   Chemistry is …   Physics is …

Now having done this, create a concept map for your chosen discipline. A concept map is a diagram that depicts suggested relationships between concepts, allowing you to organize and structure your knowledge and understanding. It is

(Continued)

(Continued)

more demanding than a spider diagram as concept maps show the connection between ideas. As an example, let's consider light within physics, rather than just linking 'light→ shadows'. It is necessary to state your understanding of how these are related for example 'shadows→ **are formed when an object blocks**→ light, a second connection could then be made to show further understanding 'light→ **travels in**→ straight lines'. Use the questions below to develop your ideas for your concept map:

- Which three words come to mind first when you think of this subject?
- What subject-specific language would you use to describe this subject?
- What physical resources would you use to exemplify this subject in the classroom?
- What examples of it can you see around you?
- What connections does it have to other areas of science?

It would be useful to repeat this for the other areas of science too.

It is important to step back from the details of the curriculum and try to recognize the core concepts which underpin each discipline and the core processes which drive the development of science. However, there is not space in this book to offer a comprehensive and worthwhile discussion of all the core concepts and indeed development of such understanding takes time. Moreover, the National Research Council in the US (2007) noted that one of the best ways for students to learn the core concepts of science is to learn successively more sophisticated ways of thinking about these ideas over multiple years, as evident through progression. However, to exemplify what this might look like in practice, progression in materials is described here.

 ## Case example 4.1

Chemistry is all about atoms and molecules. It is fascinating that various combinations of these make up everything, both in the living and non-living world, the natural and the man-made. Single atoms, the smallest particle of matter that retains the properties of a given element, make up precious metals like gold (Au) and platinum (Pt), liquids like mercury (Hg) and gases like helium (He) and krypton (Kr). Simple molecules are made up of two or more atoms joined together. Everyday examples of simple molecules are carbon dioxide, CO_2; hydrogen, H_2; water, H_2O; salt (sodium chloride) NaCl. The idea that unimaginable combinations of the 98 naturally occurring elements give rise to all matter is impressive and this identifies one of the fundamental concepts: that all matter is made up of the elements. Furthermore, matter is anything that occupies space and has mass; this includes all that we can see and, most of the time, what we can't see. Chemistry is all about the study of the composition, structure, properties and changes of matter. In primary science, children encounter chemistry, the study of matter, through materials.

Progression in materials

On close inspection of the statutory content for materials in the 2014 National Curriculum for England (Department for Education, 2013a), it is clear that there are two key areas to consider. The first one is investigating materials based on their properties, with implicit links to the following skills of working scientifically, observation, identification and classification. Progression is evident from Year 1 to 5. See Figure 4.2 for more details. It is important that subject-specific language is encouraged as the children progress in their observations and descriptions. They should also be encouraged to group materials in a variety of different ways. Initially children will classify and sort into groups based on obvious properties, for example colour and size. To progress in this you could get children to rank them from smallest to largest, or darkest to lightest. They should then be encouraged to classify based on other properties such as texture or use. The teacher's choice of materials for sorting is important here as well as the classroom environment. A wide range of familiar materials should be provided. Additionally, time should be allowed for free exploration of the materials, with the teacher encouraging use of all the children's senses as appropriate, for example the sound the objects make. Additionally, magnifying glasses and teacher questions should further promote observations. As children progress, they should also be encouraged to classify based on similarities as well as differences. Finally, children observing and classifying based on chemical properties, such as magnetism, or conductivity (a material's ability to allow electric current to pass through it) show an appreciation for the internal make-up of the material and thus begins their understanding that all things are made up of atoms and molecules which give rise to different properties and characteristics of materials.

Year	Materials should be grouped based on:
1	Simple physical properties
2	Suitability or use
3	Appearance and simple physical properties (rocks)
4	Whether they are solid, liquid or gas
5	A range of physical and chemical properties

Figure 4.2 Progression in grouping materials based on their properties from Year 1 to Year 5 (adapted from Department for Education, 2013a)

PROGRESSION IN WORKING SCIENTIFICALLY

It is expected that the content areas of science are taught through the processes of working scientifically (Department for Education, 2013a). One of the key characteristics of teacher knowledge in science is knowing how to progress and develop children's ability to work scientifically through the primary phase. Figure 4.3 gives an overview of the various elements of progression in the key areas of working scientifically. These generally reflect the requirements of the 2014 National Curriculum for England (Department for Education, 2013a) but level of independence and explanations have been added to provide a fuller picture of progression when children are working scientifically.

	1st and 2nd class	3rd and 4th class	5th and 6th class
Questioning	Asking simple questions	Asking relevant questions	
Observation	Observing closely	Systematic and careful observation	
Level of independence	Carrying out simple tests with support from the teacher as appropriate	Setting up simple enquiries with some support from the teacher	Planning their own enquiries in response to their own questions/observations
Investigation	Performing simple tests	Setting up practical enquiries, considering comparative and fair tests	Planning different types of scientific enquiries recognizing and controlling variables where appropriate
Measurement	Using simple (including non-standard) equipment	Accurate measurement with standard units	Increasing accuracy and precision by repeating measurements
Recording	Using class bar chart or simple tables, for example with ✓✗ or ☺☺☹ or numbers	In a variety of ways, using simple scientific language, drawings, labelled diagrams, keys, bar charts and tables	Using scientific diagrams and labels, classification keys, tables, scatter graphs, bar and line graphs
Analysing	Identifying and classifying	Classifying and identifying differences, similarities or change	Identifying causal relationships
Using observations, ideas, and results	To help answer questions	To answer questions, draw simple conclusions, make predictions for new values, suggest improvements and raise further questions	To support or refute ideas, make predictions to set up further comparative and fair tests
Reporting	What they found out in simple ways, e.g. talk partners	Through oral and written explanations, displays or presentations	Through oral and written explanations, displays or presentations with evaluation
Explanations	Linked to evidence from enquiry or investigation	Linked to evidence from enquiry or investigation with some attempt to link to scientific ideas	Linked to evidence from enquiry or investigation and justified by scientific ideas

Figure 4.3 Overview of progression in working scientifically

CONCLUSION

In this chapter we have explored the importance of teacher knowledge for effective teaching and learning in science, emphasizing the importance of substantive or content knowledge in allowing teachers to offer explanations, scaffold learning, as well as recognize and challenge misconceptions or naïve ideas. However, other areas of teacher knowledge are equally valuable, in particular the role of syntactic knowledge, that of working scientifically, as well as teachers' beliefs about science. Moreover, evidence shows that teachers teach good science lessons by drawing on their general teaching skills or pedagogic knowledge. A case is made for a specific kind of pedagogic knowledge in science, that of pedagogical content knowledge, which brings together pedagogic and content knowledge to enable effective learning experiences in science. Teachers should therefore strive to develop their own conceptual understanding of science, as well as develop their general teaching skills.

The value of a slimmed down curriculum is noted and we encourage you as teachers to step back from the curriculum and recognize the key elements of progression in the various curriculum areas. Case example 4.1 provided, as an example, an overview of progression in materials and their properties in primary school. This showed how experiences in primary school link to developing core concepts, which children will further develop in secondary school and beyond. The central role of scientific enquiry and working scientifically is again highlighted in this chapter alongside concepts of progression across the primary age phase.

FURTHER READING

Kind, V. (2009) Pedagogical content knowledge in science education: perspectives and potential for progress, *Studies in Science Education*, 45(2), pp. 169–204
In this paper, the author puts forward an argument for pedagogical content knowledge (PCK) having a higher profile in teacher education. It offers useful perspectives for both the trainee and the experienced teacher.

ASE (2014) Subject knowledge [Online] Available at: http://www.ase.org.uk/resources/scitutors/subject-knowledge/
This is an excellent overview of the different areas of learning within primary science, though they are currently grouped as per the 1999 National Curriculum, the ideas presented are relevant and highly useful.

Dunne, M. and Howard, D. (2012) Tricky topics and how to teach them, in Dunne, M. and Peacock, A. (eds) *Primary Science: A Guide to Teaching Practice*, London: Sage, pp. 125–36
This chapter offers some practical advice on using analogies, metaphors, similes and models to support children's conceptual development in science and some of the issues with them. Consideration is also given for how children develop their own ideas.

McGraw-Hill Education (2014) New generation science standards – White papers. [Online] Available at: https://www.mheonline.com/ngss/view/9

The New Generation Science Standards (NGSS) framework has been collabora- tively developed in the US and acts as the foundation for science education standards, with consideration for practices, cross cutting concepts and discipli- nary core ideas. This offers a perspective on reducing the content and considering the big ideas and underlying concepts and processes in science. In the white papers there are a number of useful discussions. Particularly relevant to this chap- ter are the ones entitled 'Twelve Core Ideas' and 'Learning Progressions: What Are They, and Why Are They Important?'

REFERENCES

Asoko, H. (2002) Developing conceptual understanding in primary science. *Cambridge Journal of Education*, 32(2), 153–64

Chiu, M-H., Guo, C-J. and Treagust, D.F. (2007) Assessing students' conceptual understanding in science: an introduction about a national project in Taiwan. *International Journal of Science Education*, 29(4), 379–90

Department for Education (2012) Remit for review of the National Curriculum in England. [Online] Available at: http://webarchive.nationalarchives.gov.uk/20130904095427/https:// www.education.gov.uk/schools/teachingandlearning/curriculum/nationalcurriculum2014/ nationalcurriculum/b0073043/remit-for-review-of-the-national-curriculum-in-england

Department for Education (2013a) The National Curriculum in England. [Online] Available at: https://www.gov.uk/government/uploads/system/uploads/attachment_data/file/260481/ PRIMARY_national_curriculum_11–9–13_2.pdf

Department for Education (2013b) The Teachers' Standards. Statutory guidance for school lead- ers, school staff and governing bodies. [Online] Available at: https://www.gov.uk/government/ uploads/system/uploads/attachment_data/file/208682/Teachers__Standards_2013.pdf

Gilbert, J.K. (2010) Supporting the development of effective science teachers, in Osborne, J. and Dillon, J. (eds) *Good Practice in Science Teaching. What Research Has to Say.* 2nd ed. Maidenhead: Open University Press, pp. 274–300

Gresnigt, R., Taconis, R., van Keulen, H., Gravemeijer, K. and Baartman, L. (2014) Promoting science and technology in primary education: a review of integrated curricula. *Studies in Science Education*, 50(1), pp. 47–84

Harlen, W. (1998). The last ten years; the next ten years, in Sherrington, R. (1998) *ASE Guide to Primary Science Education.* Cheltenham: Stanley Thornes

Kind, V. (2009) A conflict in your head: an exploration of trainee science teachers' subject matter knowledge development and its impact on teacher self-confidence. *International Journal of Science Education*, 31(11), 1529–62

McGraw-Hill Education (2014) New generation science standards – White papers. [Online] Available at: https://www.mheonline.com/ngss/view/9

National Research Council (2007) *Ready, Set, SCIENCE!: Putting Research to Work in K-8 Science Classrooms.* Washington: The National Academies Press

Ofsted (2008) Success in science. [Online] Available at: http://www.ofsted.gov.uk/resources/ success-science June 2008

Ofsted (2009) Improving primary teachers' subject knowledge across the curriculum [Online] Available at: http://www.ofsted.gov.uk/resources/improving-primary-teachers-subject- knowledge-across-curriculum June 2009

Ofsted (2011) Successful science. [Online] Available at: http://www.ofsted.gov.uk/resources/ successful-science January 2011

Ofsted (2013) Maintaining curiosity: a survey into science education in schools. [Online] Available at: http://www.ofsted.gov.uk/resources/maintaining-curiosity-survey-science-education-schools

Parker, J. (2004) The synthesis of subject and pedagogy for effective learning and teaching in primary science education. *British Educational Research Journal*, 30(6), pp. 819–39

Parker, J. and Heywood, D. (2000) Exploring the relationship between subject knowledge and pedagogic content knowledge in primary teachers' learning about forces. *International Journal of Science Education*, 22(1), pp. 89–111

Pollard, A. (2008) *Reflective Teaching: Evidence-informed Professional Practice*. 3rd ed. London: Bloomsbury

Shulman, L. (1987) Knowledge and teaching: foundations of the new reform. *Harvard Educational Review*, 57(1), 1–22

Training and Development Agency for School (2008) Professional standards for qualified teacher status and requirements for initial teacher training (Revised 2008). [Online] Available at: http://webarchive.nationalarchives.gov.uk/20090606145859/http://tda.gov.uk/upload/resources/pdf/p/professional_standards_2008.pdf

CHAPTER 5

PLANNING AND ASSESSING CREATIVE APPROACHES IN SCIENCE

Chapter aims

By the end of this chapter, you should be able to:

- Recognize a number of key strategies for effective planning for creativity in science

- Discuss the issues and concerns surrounding assessment in science

- Develop ideas around effective assessment in science and assessing creativity

INTRODUCTION

A creative classroom doesn't just happen with a change in mind-set. A creative classroom requires reconsideration for a range of factors including the physical environment, the teacher's role and identity, the behaviour and learning expectations and the role of assessment. This all requires careful planning and there can be tension for teachers and children with moves towards a more creative classroom.

One of the first things that happens when children start in primary school is that they begin to learn routines. These range from the practical (what to do when you first come into the class in the morning, what to do when you need to use the toilet); to routines for learning (how to use group resources, what to do when you don't understand something or an instruction). These routines provide reassurance for the child and a safe place for learning. However, children like adults, will get used to these routines and expectations for behaviour and learning in the classroom and some may struggle with a sudden change in the learning environment. This is particularly the case for children with an autism spectrum disorder, where small and big changes in routines need to be carefully planned and managed. Equally for the teacher, who will have worked hard to build and establish routines and procedures in the classroom, there may be reluctance to alter the status quo. However, risk-taking is part and parcel of creativity so to ensure smooth transitions to a more creative classroom a number of factors need to be considered.

TEACHER IDENTITY

Planning for a creative learning environment requires focusing on your own identity as a teacher. Odena (2001) suggests that conceptions of creativity held by individual teachers have been found to influence their pedagogic approach and assessment of activities that are meant to develop creativity of their children. Cunliffe (2008, p. 315) highlights the conditions for fostering creativity, including elements of the teacher's ability and desire. He suggests that in order to foster creativity the teacher should:

- Have a cooperative, socially integrated style of teaching
- Enable children to learn to cope with frustration and failure, so that they have the courage to try the new and unusual
- Encourage children to learn independently
- Promote self-evaluation
- Encourage flexible thinking
- Offer children opportunities to work with a wide variety of materials under different conditions
- Take children's ideas and questions seriously.

Fostering creativity in children also requires teachers to think creatively themselves. Desailly (2012) describes the need for combinatorial, exploratory and transformative creativity, the very elements of creativity that we are encouraging in the children. The ability to combine ideas in unpredicted or alternative ways, thus providing the children with a broad and rich curriculum (2012, p. 84), requires relevant subject knowledge and the confidence to apply it. Exploratory creativity allows for exploration of ideas, even if they lead to 'failure', coming to the realization that something not working is in itself a useful outcome. This is something children (and teachers) will have to learn to deal with and come to expect when working creatively. Coupled with this, when considering creativity in science, teachers may have to challenge their existing ideas about the nature of science and how scientists come to develop knowledge and understanding. This has been considered in more detail in Chapter 3.

Time for reflection 5.1

It is nearing the autumn half-term break and the local amateur drama group have asked your class to sing as part of their matinee Christmas Pantomime. The children are very excited about the prospect of this. As the class teacher, you have a decision to make. Do you:

a) Say thank you but no thanks. It will take too much time away from the curriculum and planned activities.
b) Say thank you. We would love to and use the singing time to prepare.
c) Say thank you. We would love to and use the children's excitement and motivation to plan a whole scheme of work around the theatre, including linking with their earlier work on light and sound in science.

The creative teacher will answer (c) but this is not without potential problems.

Teachers will have responsibility for teaching certain curricular areas and this must be taken into consideration. Does this creative opportunity allow for extended learning on concepts already covered? Will it clash with concepts and ideas which are planned for the next year? Does it allow for further skills development? These are all things which need to be deliberated and discussed with the other teachers involved. There is a balance between recognizing the potential for enquiry and taking advantage of such opportunities as described above and teacher's responsibility for teaching certain curriculum areas during the school year (Desailly, 2012, p. 83).

ASSESSMENT

Assessment is a word that immediately conjures up a lot of ideas and emotions and quite often negative ones. Luckily assessment can take many different forms, particularly in the primary classroom. There are generally two accepted purposes of assessment, formative or assessment for learning which is used as part of everyday practice and summative or assessment of learning which is used to sum up learning on an individual, class, school, local and national level. An important point raised by Harlen (2012) is that what determines whether assessment is formative or summative is not what information is collected or how it is collected but how it is used (p. 9). Therefore, this chapter will not discuss strategies for formative or summative assessment, instead strategies will be discussed which could be used to inform or sum up learning. Wynder (2008) suggests that assessment can impact upon the development of creativity by motivating or impairing the implementation of creative activities. Furthermore, Davies (2000) suggests that use of assessment for summative purposes, combined with a rigid and prescriptive curriculum, is a huge obstacle against creative education. This is further supported by Ponchaud (cited in Murphy, 2005, p. 113) who states that the prescriptive nature of the National Curriculum and the imposed assessment tasks can work against teachers' creativity and their willingness to step outside the box. However, Craft et al. (2014, p. 26), in their study of two primary schools recognized nationally for their creative approaches, reported one headteacher as saying 'it's really important that people don't think that standards and creativity or having fun being outside are somehow mutually exclusive' and this is something which will be addressed in this chapter.

CURRENT STATE OF PRIMARY SCIENCE ASSESSMENT

The 2014 National Curriculum for England has brought about changes to the assessment regime in science with the reintroduction of Key Stage 2 tests in science, based on the new national curriculum, which will be sat by pupils for the first time in the summer of 2016 (Department for Education, 2013, p. 2). This reverses the earlier decision to abolish science testing at the end of Key Stage 2 in 2010 in England. The science tests were abolished in recognition that they failed to provide relevant and useful information about pupils' performance and had a constraining impact on teaching (Harlen, 2012, p. 7). Perhaps not surprisingly, one outcome from the abolition of end of Key Stage 2 testing in science is a general decline in attention to science. Ofsted in their most recent report on science in school (2013), report that half of the school leaders surveyed in the study cite the removal of end of Key Stage 2 testing as the main reason for less attention to science. Furthermore, the Bew report (2011, p. 64) stated that many respondents felt that the removal of statutory tests had significantly downgraded the place of science within the curriculum. However, others felt that this allowed more freedom 'Teachers are free to teach science as it was intended to be taught now, and do not have to teach to the test'. Either way, beyond the tests at Key Stage 2 (and GCSEs at Key Stage 4), it will be for schools to decide how they assess pupils' progress in science and across the curriculum (Department for Education, 2013, p. 2). Additionally, levels have been removed from the 2014 National Curriculum for England. Therefore, until additional guidance or a new assessment framework is put forward by the Department of Education, it is in the reliable hands of classroom teachers.

However, Harlen (2012) reports that some teachers continue to use past or published tests in science as there is no alternative framework for assessment designed to support learning and provide dependable information for reporting achievement at pupil, school and national levels. This is the crux of the issue. While the classroom provides a rich source of data for assessment, issues to do with validity and reliability and lack of attention to quality mean some teachers' stick with the tried and tested method of standardized testing in science.

This is a particular problem in the creative science classroom, whereby working scientifically can only be validly assessed when children are in situations where scientific work such as planning and carrying out investigations is taking place. Worryingly, Murphy (2005, p. 11) reported that fewer than 1 per cent of the teachers surveyed, from a sample size of 300, indicated that they assessed children's investigative skills. The application of knowledge is best assessed through discussion of events and phenomena that are new to the pupils (Harlen, 2012, p. 13), which does not necessarily align with standardized tests. These creative situations offer more authentic assessment opportunities and with the right planning and support can be both valid and reliable.

VALIDITY AND RELIABILITY

Assessment should be both reliable and valid and this can be difficult to achieve in teacher assessment. When we assess we want to know that on another day or if it was done by another teacher, the same outcome would be achieved, this gives a sense of reliability. However, we also want to know that we are assessing what we set out to measure, this is validity. This justifies the implications of assessment.

Harlen (2012, pp. 17–18) suggests using exemplars, group moderation, and using some form of test or special task as a check of teachers' judgments but not to be reported as a part of the result as ways to increase quality and reliability and teacher's confidence in assessment. One way of moderation found in practice includes professional collaboration, where teachers meet to review examples of pupils' work and in doing so clarify their understanding of the assessment criteria.

Teachers have long been effectively assessing their children and Harlen (2009, p. 253) highlights the benefits of teacher assessment:

- there is the potential for the full range of goals to be included as teachers collect evidence as part of their normal work with children; teachers' assessment can provide information about learning processes as well as outcomes;

- it relieves the pressure of tests and releases time and other resources for alternative use;

- when teachers gather evidence from pupils' on-going work, they can use information about students to help learning as well as for summative purposes;

- pupils can share in the process through self-assessment and focus on their 'learning goals' as distinct from 'performance goals'.

ELICITATION

Pre-assessment or elicitation of children's ideas is crucial to children's learning. Starting from children's ideas is critical in constructivist science teaching, allowing children to begin with what they know and to develop or adapt their own ideas in light of evidence and their experiences. The importance of this is highlighted and discussed in Chapter 2 and is of particular importance in creative teaching, where children have a lot more responsibility for their learning and independence.

There are a range of strategies that can be used to assess children's existing ideas. Common strategies include questioning, brainstorming and KWL grids, which allow children to recognize what they already know about a particular subject, K; what they want to know about it, W; and then what they have learnt after, L. In science, concept maps are a particularly effective strategy. These can be done as a class, as a group or individually. Depending on the age range of the children, concept maps may need scaffolding to maximize their use. Providing pictures for younger children where they have to describe the connections between them is more appropriate, whereas for slightly older children providing them with a word bank from which to make their own concept map is best. At upper Key Stage 2, children should be encouraged to come up with their own words and connections and to use scientific language and notation where possible. However, the focus here is for children to share their existing ideas and some children may struggle with having to organize their ideas using the structure of a concept map.

Another option in science is annotated drawings. Some children may find it easier to do a drawing to share their ideas about a concept or phenomenon, with either their own annotations or the teacher can annotate for them as they describe their drawing. This was a particularly effective method used for finding out children's ideas in the SPACE project (Nuffield Foundation, n.d.) carried out between 1989 and 1998. Using physical objects can also be valuable. Allowing children time to explore objects and share their ideas about it or describing how it works or how it is similar or different to another.

As the aim is to give children the opportunity to share their existing ideas, it is important to use a variety of strategies that allow the range of learners in the class to consider and share their existing ideas. Moreover, Ofsted (2013) reported that effective practice in science allowed for extended opportunities for children to explain, either orally or in writing, their understanding. This may be particularly relevant in classrooms with children with English as an additional language. For example, drawings may be best for them to share their ideas in science, where the scientific language provides an additional barrier to their verbal communication.

ASSESSING CREATIVE SCIENCE

Creative science has a strong focus on enquiry and investigation. Problem-based and enquiry approaches were put forward in Chapter 3 as appropriate teaching and learning methodologies for more creative science. Assessment that can happen while children are engaged in such enquiry and investigation, from the initial questioning and planning to the communication and evaluation, is what is needed. This will require you to observe and step back from the process, to listen to children's ideas and discussion, to watch them work with materials and objects, to hear them review and consider ideas, to see them communicate ideas in a variety of ways, to notice how they respond to other children's ideas and evidence. The importance of children's explanations cannot be understated, both as a tool for the children to make sense of their experiences and for the teacher as an assessment opportunity as well as reinforcing the central position of explanations to the development of scientific ideas. Newton (2010) suggests it is these very scientific explanations that evidence creative thought.

Abrahams et al. (2013) highlight another issue, that of assessing practical skills in science. They report that while practical skills in school science are clearly valued as being of importance, there is a lack of clarity as to what these skills actually are and how they might, most effectively, be validly assessed. In their international study, they found that there was too great a reliance on indirect assessment of practical skills, whereby a student's level of competence is inferred from the data they generate or reports of the practical work that they undertook. They suggest that this reduces the likelihood that practical work will be taught and learnt as well as it might be. This emphasizes the key role teacher observation should play in assessment when children are involved in practical enquiry and investigation.

Teacher observations can be recorded in a number of ways. For example, a simple rubric could be used, such as that shown in Table 5.1. A rubric is a type of matrix that provides scaled levels of achievement or understanding for a set of criteria. This could be used to monitor individuals in a particular group that you are working closely with and used over a number of scientific investigations. A similar rubric could be developed to assess their written work or how they communicated and evaluated their work. Other ways of recording observations are on post-its, noting particular phrases or skills which children demonstrate, or using video or audio clips which can be analysed later. Even better, these video and audio clips could be ones children have produced themselves as part of their science work. Reviewing the full range of children's work offers excellent opportunities for assessment of children's abilities, understanding and skills across science.

The approach described above is akin to the strategy put forward by an earlier government – Assessing Pupils' Progress (APP). APP was developed by QCA to help teachers in their assessments of student progress in the National Curriculum, summatively at the end of the key stage, and to inform teaching formatively throughout the key stage (Department for Education, 2011). In this, teachers were encouraged to periodically consider the full range of children's work; including written and oral contributions. There is little research evidence on the effectiveness of this strategy in primary science. However, an Ofsted report into the impact of APP (2011) across English, mathematics and science, described a secondary science department that used it to help define the precise learning outcomes for all practical activities. Subsequently, the teachers could talk precisely about the

Table 5.1 Example rubric for assessing working scientifically

	Initial stages	Developing	Well developed
Questioning	Can identify a question when prompted	Can identify one question in response to an observation	Can pose a range of questions in response to an observation
Scientific language	Can use everyday language only to describe their ideas	Can use some scientific keywords to describe their ideas	Can use appropriate keywords and language to explain their ideas
Investigation skills	Need some help planning and/or carrying-out an investigation to test their ideas	Can plan and carry-out an investigation to test their ideas	Can design and conduct a simple investigation to answer their question

purpose of practical work and saw how the intended learning linked with, and consolidated, other aspects of subject knowledge. While there were some issues with implementation and how it works in practice day to day in the classroom, the assessment grids do offer a useful framework to consider children's enquiry and practical work in science. As described earlier, this is where we are likely to encounter children's creativity in science. It is not possible to show all the levels and descriptors but a selection has been chosen and shown in Table 5.2.

However, other elements need to be considered with assessment. To what extent will the children be involved? The benefits of involving children in assessment through self- and peer-assessment have long been identified (Black and William, 1990), so teachers need to consider ways to allow for self- and peer-assessment.

Table 5.2 Selected level descriptors for four of the science assessment focusses (Department for Children, Schools and Families (2009))

	AF1 – Thinking scientifically	AF3 – Communicating and collaborating in science	AF4 – Using investigative approaches	AF5 – Working critically with evidence
Level 5	Explain processes or phenomena, suggest solutions to problems or answer questions by drawing on abstract ideas or models	Distinguish between opinion and scientific evidence in contexts related to science, and use evidence rather than opinion to support or challenge scientific arguments	Explain why particular pieces of equipment or information sources are appropriate for the questions or ideas under investigation	Interpret data in a variety of formats, recognizing obvious inconsistencies
Level 4	Use simple models to describe scientific ideas	Use appropriate scientific forms of language to communicate scientific ideas, processes or phenomena	Make sets of observations or measurements, identifying the ranges and intervals used	Identify scientific evidence they have used in drawing conclusions
Level 3	Respond to ideas given to them to answer to questions or suggest solutions to problems	Present simple scientific data in more than one way, including tables and bar charts	Select equipment or information sources from those provided to address a question or idea under investigation	Suggest improvements to their working methods
Level 2	Draw on their observations and ideas to offer answers to questions	Work together on an experiment or investigation and recognize contributions made by others	Make some suggestions about how to find things out or how to collect data to answer a question or idea they are investigating	Say whether what happened was what they expected, acknowledging any unexpected outcomes
Level 1	Ask questions stimulated by their exploration of their world	Share their own ideas and listen to the ideas of others	Use their senses and simple equipment to make observations	Say what has changed when observing objects, living things or events

How the assessment will be recorded and who it is for are also big considerations. The recognition of the importance of feedback in the assessment process is evident in all education spheres and allowing children time to respond to feedback.

Additionally, Black highlighted the importance of increased clarity of what was expected of children and, importantly, how it would be recognized when they had achieved 'it' (Nuffield, 2012, p. 3). In this way, Black recognizes the importance of sharing the learning intentions, with examples, with the children and sharing how intended learning would be demonstrated. This was referred to as the 'front loading' of assessment. Taking such an approach will ensure that the teacher is clear on the key learning foci for the lesson and will recognize the learning when it happens.

 Activity 5.1

Considering the key characteristics of creativity below, explore the connections between these and the APP assessment grid descriptors given in Table 5.2.
   Key characteristics of creativity:
   • Using imagination
   • Identification of problems and issues
   • Analysis of problems and issues
   • Exploration of ideas
   • Pursuing activities/tasks with a purpose
   • Establishing new connections to old ideas
   • Finding novel solutions to problems
   • Being original
   • Judging value
   • Exploration of processes by which these ideas are realized, implemented, evaluated and refined.

• Which elements of creativity could be assessed when observing and supporting children working scientifically?
• Which elements of working scientifically could be assessed when observing and supporting children working creatively?
• In both cases, think about what children might be saying, doing, writing or drawing.

Time for reflection 5.2

   Can you think about a time when you were involved in an activity in school, college or university and you displayed some of the creative characteristics described? What did it look like? What did it feel like? What do you think would have been the most effective way of assessing the creative elements and the subject-based knowledge and skills?

CONCLUSION

When considering assessment, teachers need to think carefully about their role in the process and how their own conceptions of assessment, creativity and science will impact on their planning and classroom practice. By considering the learning environment when planning, teachers can promote creativity as well as through modelling of creative thinking. Finding out children's ideas are crucial first steps in the teaching, learning and assessment process in science. For assessment, teachers should consider the rich opportunity investigative work provides for assessment of science knowledge, skills and attitudes as well as creativity. It is recognized that teacher-led assessment may have issues around validity and reliability. However, using a moderation process can go a long way towards minimizing such issues.

Good practice in teaching and learning will allow for more creative planning in the classroom. Planning for collaborative learning and for children to discuss and share ideas in a co-operative environment will encourage imagination and for children to be freer with their ideas. Making connections between subjects and doing integrated work will foster a wider view of science and encourage more 'out-of-the-box' thinking. Encouraging the exploration of science ideas through alternative media such as drama will again encourage creativity. Additionally, enabling children to work in more authentic contexts which are relevant to them will make learning more meaningful. The practical nature of science is a key motivator and done in the right way, can promote creative thinking and exploratory investigations. These are some of the teaching and learning issues that will be explored in other chapters in this book.

FURTHER READING

Harlen, W. (2012) *Developing Policy, Principles and Practice in Primary School Science Assessment*. London: Nuffield Foundation. [Online] Available at: http://www.nuffieldfoundation.org/sites/default/files/files/Developing_policy_principles_and_practice_in_primary_school_science_assessment_Nuffield_Foundation_v_FINAL.pdf

This is an excellent overview of best practice in primary science assessment. While it was written before the 2014 curriculum was finalized, including the assessment requirements, the guidance is pertinent as it focuses on teacher-led assessment.

Newton, D.P. (2010) Assessing the creativity of scientific explanations in elementary science: an insider-outsider view of intuitive assessment in the hypothesis space. *Research in Science and Technological Education*, 28(3), pp. 187–201

In this research paper, initial teacher education students assessed children's explanations of simple science events. The study revealed that that the assessment was more reliable when assessment switched to particular assessment criteria related to creativity, e.g. novelty. Overall, this is an interesting study and provides an excellent review of literature on creativity and assessment.

Wellcome Trust (2010) The effects of national testing in science at KS2 in England and Wales. Executive summary. [Online] Available at: http://www.wellcome.ac.uk/Aboutus/Publications/Reports/Education/WTX062723.htm

In this report the effects of national testing in science at KS2 in England and Wales are discussed. It highlights in particular, the continued reliance on standardized tests due to a range of factors including teacher confidence.

REFERENCES

Abrahams, I., Reiss, M.J. and Sharpe, R.M. (2013) The assessment of practical work in school science. *Studies in Science Education*, 49(2), pp. 209–51

Bew, P. (2011) Independent Review of Key Stage 2 testing, assessment and accountability. [Online] available at: https://www.gov.uk/government/uploads/system/uploads/attachment_data/file/176180/Review-KS2-Testing_final-report.pdf. pp. 64–5

Black, P. and William, D. (1990) *Inside the Black Box: Raising Standards Through Classroom Assessment*. London: GL Assessment Limited

Craft, A., Cremin, T., Hay, P. and Clack, J. (2014) Creative primary schools: developing and maintaining pedagogy for creativity. *Ethnography and Education*, 9(1), pp. 16–34

Cunliffe, L. (2008) Using assessment to nurture knowledge-rich creativity. *Innovations in Education and Teaching International*, 45(3), 309–17

Davies, T. (2000). Confidence! Its role in the creative teaching and learning of design and technology. *Journal of Technology Education*, 12(1), pp. 18–31

Department for Children, Schools and Families (2009) Assessing pupil's progress: science assessment criteria. [Online] Available at: http://webarchive.nationalarchives.gov.uk/20110809101133/http://wsassets.s3.amazonaws.com/ws/nso/pdf/7afb9e56503e0c974f694e40871f57bd.pdf

Department for Education (2011) Assessing pupils' progress. The national strategies. [Online] Available at: http://webarchive.nationalarchives.gov.uk/20110202093118/http:/nationalstrategies.standards.dcsf.gov.uk/primary/assessment/assessingpupilsprogressapp

Department for Education (2013) National curriculum and assessment from September 2014: information for school. [Online] Available at: https://www.gov.uk/government/uploads/system/uploads/attachment_data/file/275165/Curriculum_and_assessment_information_sheet.pdf

Desailly, J. (2012) *Creativity in the Primary Classroom*. London: Sage

Harlen, W. (2009) Improving assessment of learning and for learning. *Education 3–13: International Journal of Primary, Elementary and Early Years Education*, 37(3), pp. 247–57

Harlen, W. (2012) *Developing Policy, Principles and Practice in Primary School Science Assessment*. London: Nuffield Foundation. [Online] Available at: http://www.nuffieldfoundation.org/sites/default/files/files/Developing_policy_principles_and_practice_in_primary_school_science_assessment_Nuffield_Foundation_v_FINAL.pdf

Murphy, C. (2005) Primary science in the UK: a scoping study. The Wellcome Trust. [Online] Available at: http://www.wellcome.ac.uk/stellent/groups/corporatesite/@msh_peda/documents/web_document/wtx026636.pdf

Newton, D.P. (2010) Assessing the creativity of scientific explanations in elementary science: an insider-outsider view of intuitive assessment in the hypothesis space. *Research in Science and Technological Education*, 28(3), pp. 187–201

Nuffield Foundation (n.d.) Primary Science and SPACE. [Online] Available at: http://www.nuffieldfoundation.org/primary-science-and-space

Nuffield Foundation (2012) Primary school science assessment. Report from a seminar held at the Nuffield Foundation on 18 September 2012. [Online] Available at: http://www.nationalstemcentre.org.uk/dl/ed24c631038f9184cb80ebe25e4cca15a14478a9/26802-PrimSciAss-Stakeholder%20seminar%20report-v_%2003_10_12.pdf

Odena, O. (2001) Developing a framework for the study of teachers' views of creativity in music education. *Goldsmiths Journal of Education*, 4(1), pp. 59–67

Ofsted (2011) The impact of the 'Assessing pupils' progress' initiative. [Online] Available at: http://www.ofsted.gov.uk/resources/impact-of-assessing-pupils-progress-initiative

Ofsted (2013) Maintaining curiosity: a survey into science education in schools. [Online] Available at: http://www.ofsted.gov.uk/resources/maintaining-curiosity-survey-science-education-schools

Wynder, M. (2008) Motivating creativity through appropriate assessment: lessons for management accounting educators. *E-Journal of Business Education & Scholarship of Teaching*, 2(2), pp. 12–27

CHAPTER 6

WORKING SCIENTIFICALLY

Chapter aims

This chapter aims to:

- Help you understand the steps that a scientific investigation should go through
- Provide the framework onto which you can place creative approaches, designs, reporting and communication of the findings

In the new science programme of study in the 2014 National Curriculum for England (DfE 2013) the term 'scientific enquiry' has been replaced with 'working scientifically'. However, the skills that are described, with only the omission of 'fair testing' and a greater emphasis on classification, have remained broadly similar. Children, across the primary years are still encouraged to ask questions, make observations, test and record and to make suggestions based on results. However, the phrase 'working scientifically' does have much wider implications. The methods of observation, the type of testing, even the way we present our data can all involve some degree of creativity and invention.

In Chapter 1 you were asked how you would describe science. If you were asked to do the same again, but this time the phrase was 'science methods' do you think terms like 'enthusiasm', 'excitement' and 'delight' might have appeared on your list? On a chapter dealing with science methods it should not be unusual to talk about excitement and enthusiasm. These are after all key features of primary science.

It has almost become clichéd now in the literature, but fostering children's 'sense of wonder' and enthusiasm must be one of the key aims of not only science education, but education generally. While this is recognized as essential (who would disagree after all?) enthusiasm and excitement do at some point need to be appropriately focussed if we are to effectively utilize them. Joseph Cornell's (1989) 'Flow Learning' approach is a good starting point for science sessions. Here, early activities embrace and utilize the children's excitement and enthusiasm, but through staged activities begin to focus more their attention.

In science education it is important that we do not make the mistake of assuming that interest is somehow innately present in all science topics. The design of experiments and activities needs to take that into account. Sometimes simple observation and recording may fail to inspire or even maintain children's attention because they do not engage a child's imagination. If we are not very careful, we not only fail to channel and focus enthusiasm; we may very well extinguish it.

Key Stage 1 of the 2014 National Curriculum for England (DfE, 2013) provides both the guidance (content) and requirements (outcomes) for science and places the child at the centre of the process. Indeed in Year 1 they should:

> be encouraged to be curious and ask questions about what they notice. They should be helped to develop their understanding of scientific ideas by using different types of scientific enquiry to answer their own questions, including observing changes over a period of time, noticing patterns, grouping and classifying things, carrying out simple comparative tests, and finding things out using secondary. (DfE, 2013)

In an activity based on observation, children can make connections and have ideas that can be imaginative and creative. They will not always be right but should we at this early stage encourage children to 'chase' predetermined right answers? Being given the answer isn't even how science works, so why should we teach it that way? It really doesn't matter if their explanations are incorrect; exploring the question is the key scientific process here, not the result. After all, suggested answers can always be tested and that's good science.

Children should be involved in the exploration both in the sense of hands-on and mind-on, in other words being engaged in problem solving, designing experiments and drawing conclusions. If possible you can go with them on the adventure. Don't feel that you need to know the answers. Be a fellow explorer. It really doesn't matter, if you all come up with something that's not quite right. That is the nature of science.

 Time for reflection 6.1

But the reason I call myself by my childhood name is to remind myself that a scientist must also be absolutely like a child. If he sees a thing, he must say that he sees it, whether it was what he thought he was going to see or

(Continued)

> *(Continued)*
>
> not. See first, think later, then test. But always see first. Otherwise you will only see what you were expecting. (Douglas Adams, *So Long, and Thanks for All the Fish*)
>
> Think carefully about the sentiment of this Douglas Adams quote and reflect on how, beyond challenging its gender specificity, it may influence your approach to teaching science to young children.

THE MYTH OF SCIENTIFIC METHOD

From the outside looking in science often seems to be full of difficult terminology, technical equipment and befuddling analysis, numerical results (that may be significant, or not, whatever that means) and produces inexplicable graphical displays that no one, other than scientists, can seemingly understand.

Well, actually, some of that is true! However, in reality science, at a basic level, is a simple and particular way of looking for answers to questions that we may have about the world around us. As a method it doesn't always provide clear answers, perhaps because on occasion our questions are not very clear, but it is unarguably successful in progressing our understanding of the world around us.

Occasionally science is seen as a single entity and references about scientific method may imply that there is some universal format that needs to be followed for something to 'be science'. This, of course, is actually a common misconception as science is practised in all sorts of ways and in all sorts of places. Not all science involves experiments and of course it can be practised in all sorts of different environments. It does in fact have a range of different methodological approaches that can be both practical and theoretical and these in turn may be pragmatic, inventive and in some cases, even accidental! The National Curriculum identifies key features of scientific enquiry namely;

> observing over time; pattern seeking; identifying, classifying and grouping; comparative and fair testing (controlled investigations); and researching using secondary sources. (2014 National Curriculum for England (DfE, 2013))

It suggests that answers should be arrived at through collecting, analysing and presenting data. Often the results are presented in similar ways but the ways in which the results are arrived at can therefore be exceptionally varied. This is good news for those who wish to bring creativity to the practice of science because it does afford plenty of opportunities to do just that. In fact, another common misconception in science is that it discourages creativity, in that it is a linear process going through a number of well-defined and clearly prescribed steps. In fact the best science is often founded on creative thinking and creative approaches to problem solving. Far from stifling creativeness, science actually encourages it.

Having said that there are wide ranges of methods and that science does not have to be a linear process, for clarity this chapter will consider certain characteristics of science-based enquiry that are perhaps useful at the primary school level and that are also suggested in the 2014 National Curriculum for England (DfE, 2013) guidelines. However, any practice in science needs to creative and that often involves the development of new methods and approaches. It is at the heart of good science investigations and practice and it is a point that we make no apology about returning to several times.

 Time for reflection 6.2

When I think of innovation and I think of creativity, I don't necessarily think of thousands of scientists getting together to create a gigantic space program. I think of the individual scientists. The people who have this 'ah-ha' moment, this 'eureka' moment that allows them to see farther, to make that incredible breakthrough, to open up whole new worlds that were never seen before. (Dr Michio Kaku, Theoretical Physicist and Author http://curiosity.discovery.com/question/creativity-role-in-science)

Consider this quotation. To what extent are the children in your class involved in the creative process of science? Are they involved in designing experiments to answer questions? Do they have the opportunity to test their ideas? To what degree do you explore with them?

OBSERVATION

Trying to understand the world we observe around us is perhaps the basis for all human enquiry and not simply science, so as such it's a pretty good place to start. Simple observation is the basis of much of science and it shouldn't be underestimated as an investigative tool in itself. After all, Charles Darwin formulated the theory of natural selection on work that was essentially observational. It may seem like a long way from Darwin to the National Curriculum, yet scientific observation is a key feature in the first section of Key Stage 1. It is also a significant advantage to us as teachers that it is something that children do all the time.

Of course the problem with observation as a method is that there is far more to it than a cursory glance over things. Observing requires not only very careful looking, but also some degree of thoughtful or rather intellectual engagement.

In terms of observation there are a number of tricks of the trade. One of these is to promote what could be called 'attentive watching' meaning looking with some form of purpose, as opposed to simply observing something. Of course, imaginative engagements in observation (shapes of clouds, patterns on water surfaces) are an excellent way of initially engaging children. Once they have begun to observe however, their observations may need to be focussed and the simplest way of achieving this is through simple questions. Observing with a question to answer can be much more focussed than general observation.

With the latter we rarely notice detail.

Before going on, read Activity 2.1 as this a practical example of promoting active observation.

 ## Activity 6.1

Collect together a variety of about 30 everyday objects. Don't choose anything too large, as you need to be able to easily carry them all. Chose some objects that are brightly coloured (such as a red ball, a bright marker pen) and others that are simply wooden (a peg, a wooden spoon, a pencil).

In a wildlife, or wooded area, certainly beyond the sight of children (or even colleagues) pace out about 30 metres along a path, marking both the start point and the end point. Walk back along the path that you have marked out and randomly place each object somewhere along it. Don't place them too far from the path, as they need to be clearly visible (you'll need to find them all to collect at the end of the activity!). Also, try to place some of the objects above ground, on the branches of shrubs or trees. Once all the items have been secreted the activity is ready.

Line up the children and (your colleagues) and tell them that along the path there are a number of items that should not be there (you need to stress that they are everyday items). Ask them to walk quietly along the path and count the number that they see. At the end of the path, ask the children how many they counted. The number is normally pretty low (normally well below half) and your colleagues might not have spotted many more! Make a note of what has been seen, and ask them to walk back and count again, only this time looking really carefully, and also looking up into the branches. When they've completed the path for the second time, ask them how many this time? They will have improved an awful lot, but all the time we've done this activity with children and trainee teachers, they have never spotted them all. Of course it is the wooden objects that are the hardest to find. The brightly coloured objects are seen almost straight away. This last point of course can provide some interesting discussions with older groups about camouflage in nature and its use in avoiding predators. However, with all groups it introduces the idea of close and purposeful observation.

ASKING THE RIGHT QUESTIONS

From observations, science comes to ask questions, either about ourselves or about the wider environment. Of course asking questions is not unique to science, as sociologists, philosophers, theologians and all sorts of non-science methods of enquiry also ask questions and seek to understand more about the nature of the world around us. Given that, what makes science different? Well, the primary difference is that science has a peculiar approach to providing answers to questions that relies on producing evidence normally, but not always, through experimentation. We do ask questions of course but we often set out to find answers in science by using a peculiar method known as 'hypothesis testing'. A hypothesis tends to take the form of an initial guess at an outcome, or explanation, so just to make things even more complicated, they sometimes aren't even questions, but may take the form of a statement of a possible explanation. It is this explanation that we then set out to test.

A hypothesis therefore will lead to some form of testing and more often than not in science this is through experimentation. It is very important to understand the idea of a hypothesis, because it allows us to ask appropriate questions even before we start to design experiments.

The easiest way of thinking about a hypothesis is that by and large they can be answered by three responses, namely, 'yes', 'no' and 'perhaps' and results should not be dependent on personal preference or relate to phenomena that cannot be measured.

For example, the question 'How many leaves are there on that tree' is not really a hypothesis, as it will lead, if you could be bothered to count them, to a definitive number – say 12,345. Answers like this should promote the response, 'so what?'

A different question might be 'Are the leaves broader on the south facing side of the tree than the north facing side?' This is better, for this allows us to test that statement and to perhaps suggest why, or why there is not, a difference. It also fits with our simple test, in that the answer is likely to be 'yes', 'no' or 'perhaps'. If the result shows a difference and this result still promotes the response, 'so what?' we can now talk about why there is a difference and explore further some ideas for why this appears to be the case.

This is a really key idea in the methodology of science as investigation of one hypothesis will invariably lead on to others. Simple questions have definitive answers and are often full stops in investigations. A key issue here is to let the children develop their own hypotheses and then to help them test them. It is required at Key Stage 1, but more importantly it empowers the child to see that all explanations have validity at this stage. Their explanations at this stage can be as imaginative and as creative as they like as such engagement will facilitate their direct involvement in the next stage, namely that of experimental designs and hands-on experiments.

DESIGNING GOOD, SIMPLE TESTS AND EXPERIMENTS

Having spent some time thinking about the nature of questions, we are now in a position to start to think about designing experiments. Now without labouring the point and also stating the obvious, it is very important to design an experiment that actually goes at least some way to attempting to provide evidence to support, or not to support the hypothesis. You'd be surprised by how many people lose focus at this point; perhaps in part because, as you should be aware now, not all experiments provide direct and irrefutable evidence. They are normally a small part of a much longer process.

Generally, experimental design needs to consider all of the factors that are not in the experimenter's control that may influence the result. We call these factors 'variables'. So, if you were designing an experiment to measure the acceleration of two toy cars travelling down a slope that was to be set at different angles, what other variables may influence the toy cars' acceleration? These might include the type of tyres, the efficiency of any bearings on the axles, the relative masses of the two cars; in fact there are quite a few. Even perhaps the different shape of the cars might produce variable drag. This last one probably wouldn't be much of an influence, but is probably worth thinking about, just in case. Good experimental design identifies as many 'potential' variables as possible and then tries to eradicate them, or at least reduce their influence as much as possible. Thinking about other influencing variables can be quite creative in its own right. All sorts of suggestions may be forthcoming. Again, it can empower children to offer ideas and to get involved in a design process and help to develop their confidence where there are no 'right' and 'wrongs' only ideas.

A good deal of this reduction may be achieved by standardizing the equipment used, so for example, you might use the same type of toy car on both slopes. The idea in this experiment would be to make sure, as far as reasonably possible, that only the changing angle of slope of the surface influences both cars' descent.

When carrying out an experiment it is always worth remembering that any variable that the experimenter controls or changes (in the previous example it might be the different angles that the slope is set at) is known as the 'independent variable'. A good experiment normally only involves one independent variable. The variable that we are looking at to record any change to as we alter the independent variable is called the 'dependent variable'. It really is important for teachers to understand this, as it is a very simple way (despite the confusing language) to make experiments really robust. A good experiment is one where only the changes made to the independent variable (the one that is controlled/altered by the experimenter) could result in changes to the dependent variable.

LIVING WITH ERROR, LOOKING FOR PRECISION AND ACCURACY

Once you have understood the idea of variables, the next stage is quite straightforward. In some cases we cannot keep the dependant variable as the sole influence on the experiment. Other factors, however careful we may be, might influence the outcome. In fact sometimes we can only reduce the influence of other factors as no matter how hard we try it is sometimes simply not practically possible to do so. This provides us with so called 'sources of error' in our experimental design. We try as hard as we can to make the independent variable the sole influence on changes to the dependent variable, but sometimes those sources of error may still be there influencing the results. At this point of course, we just have to live with it and accept that there may be some error in our results, but that is not a problem, because we have a way around this. An important characteristic of experimental science is 'replication'. This word has a number of different meanings in science, but in this instance it simply means doing the experiment several times over. This produces a number, or a set, of results. If there is variation between the results for the same experiment it will be due to sources error. Children should not be concerned about this, as it will inevitably happen. They need to know that sometimes it is just part of doing an experiment.

Perhaps the simplest way of dealing with these variations is to look initially at the results and see if there are any glaringly obvious errors that can be easily sorted out.

If not, then we can begin to think about ways of living with experimental error. One of the most usual ways is to repeat the experiment a few times. This provides a number of results, or what is referred to as a 'set' of data. From the data set derived from repeating the experiment, you should be able to calculate a simple mean. Of course this brings us on to data presentation and simple analyses. However, before we move on to the next stage, it may be valuable to clarify a couple of terms that are often used erroneously in relation to experiments, namely 'accuracy' and 'precision'.

To explain these terms let's start with a question. If you were a footballer and had several shots at goal during a match, would you prefer your shots to be accurate or would you prefer them to be precise?

You would most probably go for accurate, because accuracy is a measure of how close you come to an aimed at value, in this case the goal. An accurate range of shots would be on target to go into the goalmouth, but may be spread around rather than clustered in one area of the goal. You'd certainly give the goalkeeper something to do.

A precise range of shots would indeed be closely clustered together. In fact, a precise range of shots would hit exactly the same spot each time. The problem of course, is that the location of that same spot the shots hit may be the corner flag! Hitting the corner flag over and over again when you are aiming at the goal, is very precise shooting, but not very accurate. Hitting the ball somewhere different in the goal (top right, bottom left and so on) is accurate, but not necessarily precise.

DATA AND ITS CREATIVE PRESENTATION

One of the interesting things about science is that it often seems to convert everything to numbers. The speed of something becomes a number, and the taste of something can (with some thought) be converted to a number. Even colours (the brilliance and depth) can be described by assigning numerical values. It can be quite good fun to come up with 'taste' or 'colour' scales. Of course most numerical values are based on S.I. units of measurement (International System of Units) and these are adopted everywhere. Again, there is nothing wrong with children getting used to measuring in units by designing their own (for example distance by hand widths, volume by Smarties) but sooner or later the appropriate unit will need to be introduced. It is worth remembering which unit we use for a certain measurement as there are often mistakes made over this. Probably the most common is the unit used for the weight of an object. In conversation we will often say that something weighs so many kilograms, when actually the S.I. unit is Newtons, as weight is measured as a force; the kilogram is a measure of mass.

Graphs are a pictorial presentation of the collected data and they do afford an excellent opportunity for creative design. There are plenty of inventive ways to present data from traditional charts and graphs, to three-dimensional structures constructed from art materials, to 'living graphs' involving the children as the units. Of course with any graphical presentation the key components should really be observed, namely a clear title as to what it shows, that the axes are clearly labelled and that the S.I. Units (or children's units) are given and that in all cases the independent variable (remember, the one that the experimenter controls) is plotted on the x axis and that the dependent variable (the thing that the experimenter is looking for change in) is always plotted in the y axis. Just making that clear and consistent will be truly advantageous as the children move through science at school.

DRAWING CONCLUSIONS

The reason we do experiments is to provide evidence to help answer, or at least elucidate, a hypothesis that we normally set up before we start. We can take any data the experiment has provided us with and we can present it in a way that allows us to clearly see what has happened. Very often when we do this, of course, we find very little has actually happened! The important thing at this point is not to immediately think that the experiment has not worked. It usually has worked and you have provided some intriguing data. It just sometimes means that it's worked in a way that you weren't expecting.

This is a really important point, if you have reduced error as much as you can and you are assured that it would only be the changes in the independent variable potentially causing change in the dependent variable, then your data is valid. If you have found nothing happens, then that may be a really important finding. In science negative results are always more important than positive ones. It is a really important feature of science that we rule things out rather than rule things in. It is a perennial problem trying to convince enthusiastic children of this however.

Of course part of the process of looking at the results is that it can encourage further questioning not only of the process, but also of course, of the experimental design and this too is a really valuable focus for discussion. 'How could we have done this experiment in a different way?' is the sort of question that relies on creative thinking and eventually, action. The process allows children to see that science is actually a continuous process of design, experiment, results, conclusions and redesign.

BACK TO THE NATIONAL CURRICULUM

In September 2013 the UK Government published the new science programmes of study for Key Stage 1 and 2 to be introduced in England in 2014. It is a 32-page document and if you are a primary school teacher or are training to be one, you should be familiar with it. A simple frequency analysis of the document is quite illuminating. As one would expect the words 'science/scientific' are quite frequent, occurring 103 times. Following a science-based approach, the word 'question' occurs 52 times which is the same for the words 'observe/observing'. It can be assumed here that questioning and observing are then key features of science in Key Stages 1 and 2. Recording observations is referred to less with the words 'record/recording' occurring 25 times in total. The word 'data' occurs 19 times, 'conclusion/s' six times, 'presenting/presentation' only five, 'creative' three times (but in relation to creative uses of materials). Curiously, the word 'experiment' occurs only once. Words such as 'imagination', 'inspire', 'wonder', 'outside' perhaps not surprisingly do not appear in the document.

This simple word count, without context, is only provided to show at least how important the initial stages of observation, recording and questioning is in relation to the National Curriculum. One further aspect that is more positive in the context of this chapter is the following from the Science Programme of Study: Key Stages 1 and 2:

> teachers will wish to use different contexts to maximize their pupils' engagement with and motivation to study science

Investigation in a variety of contexts in primary science provides the best opportunity for children to develop scientific thinking and skills. It will be the teacher who will now need to identify these contexts. The opportunity is now there to be inventive and creative with science methods. Hopefully you will take it.

FURTHER READING

Feasey, R. (2005) *Creative Science: Achieving the WOW Factor with 5–11 Year Olds*, Abingdon, Oxon: David Fulton Publishers
This is an interesting book that while pre-dating the present changes to the primary curriculum provides some original ideas and approaches.

Winston, A. (2014) *Quilt Lab: The Creative Side of Science*. Lafayette: C & T Publishing
A short book about how to teach about science and maths using quilt-making. It provides some intriguing ideas.

Ofsted (2003) *Expecting the Unexpected: Developing Creativity in Primary and Secondary Schools*. London: Office For Standards in Education
Always worth knowing what Ofsted think about creativity.

Johnston, J. (2007) 'Creative science?', teaching, thinking and creativity, No. 22. Available at http://www.bishopg.ac.uk/docs/Profiles/Johnston_TTC22_pg42_47_Can_children_be_creative.pdf
This paper reviews what is meant by creativity and its implications for primary science teaching.

Leedy, L. (2006) *The Great Graph Contest*. New York: Holiday House
A small book about graphs for younger children.

Whitehead, N. A. and Bickel, C. (2002) *Tiger Math: Learning to Graph from a Baby Tiger*. New York: Square Fish
Popular children's introduction to drawing graphs.

Roden, J., Ward, H. and Ritchie, H. (2007) *Primary Science: Extending Knowledge in Practice*. Exeter: Learning Matters
Good guide for new teachers but Part 1 in particular is useful in relation to science enquiry.

Finally the Understanding Science website is an excellent resource. Available at http://undsci.berkeley.edu/

REFERENCES

Cornell, J. (1989) *Sharing Nature with Children II*. Nevada: Dawn Publications
Department for Education (2013a) Science programmes of study: Key stages 1 and 2 National curriculum in England. [Online] Available at: https://www.gov.uk/government/uploads/system/uploads/attachment_data/file
Department for Education (2013b) The National Curriculum in England. [Online] Available at: https://www.gov.uk/government/uploads/system/uploads/attachment_data/file/260481/PRIMARY_national_curriculum_11–9–13_2.pdf

CHAPTER 7

GETTING CREATIVE WITH TECHNOLOGY IN SCIENCE

Chapter aims

By the end of this chapter, you should be able to:

- Identify some of the potential applications of digital technologies to primary science teaching

- Recognize creative approaches in the use of digital technologies in science teaching

- Describe the ways in which digital technologies can be used to enhance the way in which pupils may work scientifically

In 2013 the UK spent £595 million on ICT (information and communications technology) in schools, given that 2014 will see in excess of £600 million spent, £1 billion will have been spent in two years (TES, 2013).

Spending on equipment in schools has increased considerably with the mobile computer market, which includes tablets and laptops, contributing to the highest rise. Demand for mobile devices has also contributed to the spending rise in the UK, with 260,000 devices bought by schools in 2013, a figure up from approximately 100,000 in 2012 (TES, 2013).

This huge and impressive expenditure has presumably led to a diverse and varied range of digital technologies being available in most schools. These may range from mobile devices to smart boards and even to the less physical presence of cloud computing and digital learning platforms for schools. However, despite this outlay in digital technologies the educational charity NESTA found that such investment had not yet 'resulted in radical improvements to learning experiences or attainment', (Nesta, 2012). Furthermore, Scotland's Science and Engineering Education Advisory Group (2012, p. 26) state that ultimately, it is the quality of teaching that determines what pupils learn, not the quality or availability of technology.

Technology has undoubtedly had profound impacts on the management of schools and the organization and planning of teaching. Schools may have public access websites, electronic registers, digital facilities and applications for monitoring progress, websites and managing budgets. Teachers look increasingly to online resources and will most probably store and organize increasing numbers of classroom activities, evaluations and reports on mobile devices. In this way, the profession is almost unrecognizable from 10 to 15 years ago. A transformation in the running and organization of schools perhaps, however, 'evidence of digital technologies producing real transformation in learning and teaching remains elusive' (Nesta, 2012).

The arrival of such technologies can present teachers with significant problems. The first and foremost is the time it may take to become familiar with the operating protocols. Once familiarized however, it also takes time to plan and integrate its effective use into the curriculum. There is an important point here. Technology alone will not have any impact on learning; it is best perhaps to think about what is an effective learning activity and explore how the use of digital technologies may further enhance that learning experience. In other words, not to see the technology as the central focus, but as additional to an already effective session and in this way continue to improve already successful learning. This also places the technology in a position where it is part of the learning process, not necessarily central to it. Too much onus on the use of technology, in some cases, may even detract from learning; where for example the technology becomes of more interest and demands attention rather than the actual topic being studied. The term 'transparent technology' is explained in Box 7.1.

 Time for reflection 7.1

I find television very educating. Every time somebody turns on the set, I go into the other room and read a book.

(Groucho Marx)

When you watch television you normally concentrate (or at least focus) on the programme that's being broadcast. We look and listen to follow a plot line, or a line of argument, or we may simply be looking at pictures or images. Television does have significant power to teach and inform as well as to entertain. However, what we rarely ever do when watching TV is to consider the technology that surrounds the images and programmes that we are watching. The technology is invisible. As such it doesn't get in the way of story lines or narratives. How can we use technology in science teaching (and teaching generally) so that it too becomes invisible so that we, and the children, can concentrate on learning? Only then do we focus on the learning, rather than the technology.

This is referred to as transparent technology. Transparent technology is technology that does not distract from learning.

CONNECTING LEARNING

Contemporary digital technology can provide a variety of ways to connect children in schools. They can connect to their teacher, or to other students, or to experts in particular fields. These may be real time using available tools such as Skype, or recorded on a blog, or YouTube. However, increasingly with social media applications these connections may promote dialogue. The children cease to be passive recipients of information, but become instead active in the discourse and may explore and interrogate ideas more effectively. The role of dialogue and discussion in enabling conceptual change and its central role in effective teaching and learning in science is stressed in Chapter 2.

Digital technologies not only allow for innovative ways of presenting information but also afford unprecedented ways of sharing it, not just within the school, but also with a worldwide audience. Through networking and bringing groups together it can also provide a context for the work that potentially enhances the perceived relevance of the study and so improves the learning experience for the children. Such dialogues can take place over time, across a variety of settings and topics, and even across different groups of learners, perhaps linking primary school children with university students or staff.

Collaborative work is also possible with national science organizations. For example, the Open Air Laboratories Project (OPAL) looks at a new topical science theme each year. The children are asked to carry out the field work and collect the appropriate data. Past surveys have included work on worm populations, air quality and tree health. By taking part schools are provided with dedicated survey packs and the children can upload their collected data to the OPAL website (http://www.opalexplorenature.org/). The preliminary sessions, supported by the surveys website and the relevant context of the fieldwork provides an opportunity to engage children in first-hand science research, one in which they can see the usefulness of their own work. OPAL is only one of such science-based projects and other suggestions are given at the end of this chapter.

DIGITAL TECHNOLOGY AND SCIENCE

Becta (2009) reported that ICT has fundamentally changed the ways in which scientists measure, handle data and access information. It also stated that it offers opportunities to extend work in the classroom and affords insights, possibilities and efficiencies that are difficult to achieve in other ways. Ofsted (2013, p.17) in its most recent report on schools successful in science reported about two-thirds of the schools visited used information and communication technology (ICT) for science, and about half of these did this effectively to support the teaching of science. Most commonly, this was through teachers' use of presentation software, including multi-media pictures and clips of scientific phenomena. In a small minority of the schools visited, the pupils used ICT regularly for internet-based research themselves. It was unusual, however, for the teachers to use ICT to record and process evidence from experiments. They recognized that opportunities were often missed to use technology to help in processing data from investigations and to give direct evidence to pupils of the underlying concepts.

BECTA (2009) suggested the main applications of ICT in science as:

- providing information
- supporting fieldwork
- assisting observation
- recording and measuring
- sharing data with others
- facilitating interpretation
- simulating experiments
- providing models or demonstrations
- enhancing publishing and presentation.

Additionally, Becta's *21st Century Teacher* (2010) offered exemplars on using technology effectively for teaching and learning in science for visualizing different concepts, collecting data and conducting experiments. It is interesting that even as technology makes rapid advances and changes, the applications of technology in enhancing science learning remain largely similar. Some of these applications will be discussed in more detail with consideration for newer technologies.

Science and technology are often seen to go hand-in-hand and in other countries they are formally linked together through the curriculum framework, for example in Northern Ireland where children study the 'World around us' through science and technology, history, and geography (CCEA, 2004). Gresnigt et al. (2014) offer a critical perspective on integrated curricula. Their international review considered the effects of integrated science and technology curricula in primary school. The reported effects were overall positive with students' motivation and appreciation of science and technology reported to have increased, and most projects reporting an increase in the time spent on science. In addition, the projects generally reported positive learning results in the domain of science and technology, as well as in the domains of mathematics and language, which involve knowledge as well as higher-order thinking skills. So there is research evidence to support an integrated approach to teaching science with technology.

The National Curriculum for England, 2014 (DfE, 2013) has recently seen a fundamental change to content moving from ICT towards what is described as computing science. The basic principles of computing are introduced very early with:

Children from:

- The age of 5 will be taught what algorithms are and how they are used in digital devices – they will also learn how to write and test simple programs and to organize, manipulate and store digital content.

- The age of 7, pupils will be taught to understand computer networks including the internet, and how they can provide a range of services, such as the world wide web.

Computer science has a far greater emphasis on the actual working of digital devices and can involve children in design and simple programming. There are a number of available devices, such as the Raspberry Pi, that will provide excellent sessions in simple programming. However, although there are potential opportunities to embed digital technologies in science sessions, it is important to do so not for the sake of simply introducing or becoming familiar with the technology, but to really enhance effective learning in science through sustained, creative approaches. Education Scotland (2013) report that in many schools design technology is a highly creative subject, particularly where digital skills are involved and so therefore has a particular scope for promoting creativity and learning in science. Additionally, in an earlier report on primary science, Murphy (2005) highlighted the use of ICT as a creative context for teaching science. However, this is where we note a word of caution. It is an important point that as part of the creative use of technology it becomes the medium through which learning takes place. This is an important distinction. To illustrate the use of digital technologies in science it is perhaps worth thinking of how we 'work scientifically'. In other words by looking at each stage of a science-based methodology we may identify ways in which this may be achieved.

DATA HARVESTING WITH DIGITAL TECHNOLOGY

Observation is a primary point in science and digital technologies may assist in a variety of ways. The internet is a powerful source of images that in themselves can enhance the learning experience. On a topic such as 'the solar system' the NASA website (http://www.nasa.gov/audience/foreducators/) provides astounding images of the planets as well as animations and interactive applications that allow you to explore the solar system as you move from planet to planet. The ESA website (http://www.esa.int/ESA) and other astronomy sites such as Red Orbit (http://www.redorbit.com/) all have fantastic image libraries, although private sites are prone to advertisements.

Interactive online applications such as Google Earth can be excellent teaching resources. Google Earth in particular has a number of tools that can be really useful in science teaching. The measuring tool for example allows a comparison of the relative sizes of natural features (such as the north/south extent of the Amazon rainforest compared to that of Great Britain). As distances can be measured from place to place, it may provide an excellent means of thinking about food miles. Children can simply measure and add up to calculate the distances that the component items of a meal have travelled. Returning to the solar system, Google Earth now also includes Google Mars and Google Moon, so that features such as craters and mountains on these different worlds may be measured and explored in high definition.

Furthermore, nearly all aspects of the National Curriculum may be enhanced and explored through the BBC website (http://www.bbc.co.uk/schools/) as it has fantastic sets of pictures and films. Children can see high definition images of animals and plants from around the world as well as images of prehistoric life and each image comes with a full description.

As powerful and as beautiful as such images are, they may not replace first-hand field observation as a learning experience. Cheap and robust digital technology may allow the children to have their own nest box cameras to observe nesting birds. There are a range of cameras manufactured today that are waterproof (to shallow depths) and may be placed in the school pond or in rock pools. They can produce a 'live' image that the children can see on a mobile device, or some can be set to take images at predetermined time intervals. If the camera is left in a rock pool and the images later run together, a simple time-lapse film may be generated demonstrating the movement that took place in the pool. There are dedicated and fairly cheap time-lapse cameras on the market.

Observation does not only imply the visual, for audio recording may be a useful. In different settings recording bird song is a way in which children can begin to explore ideas of habitat and animal association. Recording their observations in the field can also be effectively done through audio-recording devices or by digital cameras. These recordings may be structured or may simply be free images of objects that the children simply finding interesting or intriguing.

There are a range of digital microscopes designed for schools on the market that will interface directly to a mobile device and can produce quite effective images to adequate levels of magnification. Some are even small hand-held devices and the clarity and simplicity of their use is ever improving.

There are a range of relatively cheap digital devices including cameras, mobile webcams, movie cameras and so on, that can be used to enhance field and classroom observation that also afford children the opportunity to use the equipment and process the results in meaningful ways.

For more technical data collection there is a range of dedicated data loggers on the market and it is worth regularly checking out what is available as they have moved on in terms of ease of use and in relation to functions. Today, many include on-board graphing and wireless sensors will readily remotely interface with mobile devices over some distance.

There is also huge potential in using other hardware tools such as the Raspberry Pi computer for collecting data. These can be quite advanced, but there are growing uses for such simple and cheap tools in primary schools, both in terms of gathering data and also presenting it. The further reading suggestions at the end of this chapter will provide you with links to some interesting introductions to this hardware and its applications in schools.

Data harvesting is one thing, but working scientifically requires the focus of a question to answer or hypothesis to test. The recording of the process of investigation by film or by audio is one good way of enhancing the activity, the film could be divided into the relevant sections of introduction, methods, results and conclusions.

However, the analysis and presentation of data may also be effectively and creatively achieved through digital media.

PRESENTING RESULTS: CHARTS, GRAPHS AND INFOGRAPHICS

The creative use of digital media can really help to enhance sessions when ordering, exploring and analysing data. There are of course the easily accessible software applications that are common to most PCs, such as Microsoft Excel, that can produce charts and graphs of numerical data. Although, even with these standard applications it is worth spending some time exploring how to edit charts in terms of axis settings and text. However, for children, spreadsheet charts are somewhat static and are hard to see in context. The data are simply 'presented'. Pasting the charts into presentation applications such Powerpoint or Prezi allows slides that explain the activity to be included, show pictures or short films or soundtracks and may allow some limited animation of any charts or graphs.

There are however more interesting forms of so-called 'data infographics' tools that are increasingly appearing on the internet such as easel.ly and vizualize.me. Here the data can be put into context and symbols, and maps and pictures may be included to build up a poster of the results.

There is a variety of freely downloadable animation software applications, from stop-motion to explanations of producing RSA animate-style films (see Further reading). Animation presents a range of creative opportunities. Certainly graphs may be annotated, but not necessarily as two dimensional charts. Stop-motion software provides an opportunity for graphs to be made from anything from modelling clay, paper, or even people. Animation also allows processes such as growth of a plant, or the evolution of an animal to be demonstrated and through such presentations the learning and understanding may be reinforced. To enhance the data in a way that actively engages children and helps them better understand is the objective of what is ultimately a creative process.

DATA AND ANALYSIS

One further advantage of the internet is the fact that there is a great deal of open data available. These data allow children to explore issues and science using real data. Furthermore there are some excellent sites that also suggest ways of displaying data in really meaningful and creative ways. Learning to present and understand what charts and graphical representations of data mean is a key literacy skill in science and perhaps in wider educational contexts as well.

More sophisticated methods of analysis are of course also available. Microsoft Excel and other similar spreadsheet software can sum and mean numerical data, as well as a whole range of highly sophisticated analyses well beyond primary science.

The data collected by children may not be in numerical form, but this does not necessarily negate analysis. Data may be in word forms, where children might have written down key observations or memories of field trips, or it may be the text derived from searches for information on scientists. All text may be subjected to simple visual analysis by using 'word-clouds' generated from freely available online tools such as Wordle (http://www.wordle.net/). This particular site affords children the choice from a wide selection of designs and colours. There are many other sites, such as TagCrowd (http://tagcrowd.com/) that are perhaps less design-based, but do provide a more accurate visual representation as they ignore certain words (such as pronouns) and can be set to ignore others. There are wide ranges of such tools and links that are presently of varying degrees of ease of use and editing control. They are generally easy to use and do provide the basis for a good deal of follow-up discussion.

All forms of data need to be presented, whether numerical, visual or audio. Indeed, the presentation and communication of methods, findings and conclusions provides a perfect opportunity for creative approaches to this. Films, short documentaries, animations and webcasts are all possible using digital technologies. Of course price will be a significant constraint, so if you do have the facilities, you should really make the maximum use of them. Working scientifically involves designing inventive methods by which to collect and interrogate data and thereby answer questions. The research frontier uses digital equipment in nearly all phases of investigation and dissemination. For children's learning in science to be authentic, then perhaps, so should they.

CONCLUSION

Such is the rapidity of developments in contemporary digital technologies, any chapter that addresses its use in schools runs the risk of being out of date before it is published. The applications that are discussed here and the links that are provided are current, however, things are changing very rapidly. So rapidly in fact that it may seem impossible to keep up. This can be daunting for a teacher, particularly one who has the added challenge of integrating such technologies across subjects. Teacher confidence in using ICT in science was identified as a significant issue (Murphy, 2005, p. 45) in a report on primary science. However, it is important to remember that technology can enhance learning as part of the overall experience. The degree to which digital technologies contribute to that process is a decision of lesson design and planning.

The important thing however, is that its use, whatever it may be or in what form it takes, does enhance and improve learning.

Technology has the potential to provide opportunities for collaborative work that may help contextualize any research, through networking, that opportunity may be global, pairing students with those from different countries comparing findings or results, thereby developing a community of learning.

Digital technologies certainly offer potential for teachers to explain and demonstrate through images, animations or short films and they allow teachers to structure and to differentiate their lessons more effectively. They also offer the opportunity for children to carry out different forms of scientific explorations, through the use of remote, or hand-held cameras, sound recording and wireless sensors that transmit data to the classroom. They also present opportunities for the really creative presentation of results and conclusions that can be shared collectively online.

Science is grounded on enquiry, so the use of digital technology naturally fits with an enquiry-based approach to teaching and as such it does have very real potential in enhancing learning in science. However, the creative potential of such technologies and the possibilities that they present for children to network with others from around the world are considerable. Digital technologies in all their wide forms, increasingly provide exciting opportunities for effective and creative science teaching.

FURTHER READING

Nesta (2012) Decoding learning: the proof, promise and potential of digital education. [On-line]
    Available from http://www.nesta.org.uk/publications/decoding-learning (accessed 10.12.13)
This is also listed in the reference section of this chapter, but it is a really interesting report on the effectiveness of IT in schools, with great ideas on how to make it more so.

There is so much open data available that lets young people work with large and real data sets to explore science. There is a great deal of material in this series of blog posts: http://edu.blogs.com/edublogs/2011/03/data-reveals-stories.html
    Another one: https://www.google.com/publicdata/directory
    Some wonderful animated graphs of which some are science-related and some more political and could be used with older children can be found at http://www.gapminder.org/
    The collection from Becta and the ASE offers a range of case studies on the effective use of technology in primary science. While the case studies are a few years old, they give an excellent picture of the range and varied use of technology and the benefits of it in primary science. They are available from:
    ASE (2014) Becta Science Resources [Online] Available at: http://www.ase.org.uk/resources/becta-legacy-science-resources/Descriptions and ideas relating to available new hardware, that has exciting potential for primary schools are available at the following sites: http://www.briandorey.com/post/Raspberry-Pi-Solar-Data-Logger.aspx http://www.raspberrypi.org/archives/1620

REFERENCES

Becta (2009) Primary science with ICT: pupil's entitlement to ICT in primary science. Becta in association with the ASE [Online] Available at: http://www.ase.org.uk/documents/becta-ict-in-primary-science/

Becta (2010) The 21st century teacher: science. Using technology to enhance science teaching. [Online] Available at: http://www.ase.org.uk/documents/becta-the-21st-century-teacher-science/

Department for Education (2013) Science programmes of study: Key stages 1 and 2 National Curriculum in England. DFE-00182–2013

Council for the Curriculum Examinations and Assessment (2004) The world around us. The Northern Ireland curriculum. CCEA. [Online] Available at: http://www.nicurriculum.org.uk/key_stages_1_and_2/areas_of_learning/the_world_around_us/

Education Scotland (2013) Creativity across learning 3–18 [Online] Available at: http://www.educationscotland.gov.uk/Images/Creativity3to18_tcm4–814361.pdf

Gresnigt, R., Taconis, R., van Keulen, H., Gravemeijer, K. and Baartman, L. (2014) Promoting science and technology in primary education: A review of integrated curricula, *Studies in Science Education*, 50(1), pp. 47–84, DOI: 10.1080/03057267.2013.877694

Murphy, C. (2005) Primary science in the UK: a scoping study. The Wellcome Trust. [Online] Available at: http://www.wellcome.ac.uk/stellent/groups/corporatesite/@msh_peda/documents/web_document/wtx026636.pdf

Nesta (2012) Decoding learning: the proof, promise and potential of digital education. [Online] Available from http://www.nesta.org.uk/publications/decoding-learning (accessed 10.12.13)

Ofsted (2013) Maintaining curiosity: a survey into science education in schools. [Online] Available at: http://www.ofsted.gov.uk/resources/maintaining-curiosity-survey-science-education-schools

SEEAG (2012) Supporting Scotland's STEM education and culture. Science and engineering education advisory group. Second report. The Scottish Government. [Online] Available at: http://www.scotland.gov.uk/Resource/0038/00388616.pdf

TES (2013) [Online] Available from http://www.tes.co.uk/article.aspx?storycode=6358755 (accessed 10.12.13)

PART 2

CHAPTER 8

ART AND DESIGN AND CREATIVE SCIENCE

Chapter aims

By the end of this chapter, you should be able to:

- Explore the relationship between art and science education
- Explain the key role observation plays in developing science ideas and how art can support this
- Use a range of art techniques and methods to develop children's scientific attitudes, skills and understanding

INTRODUCTION

Art, craft and design embody some of the highest forms of human creativity. (Department for Education, 2013, p. 1) and in primary schools children are encouraged to be creative in the Arts domain of art, design, drama and music. Liu and Lin (2014) report the integrating of the arts and science curricula as one way to foster scientific creativity. In this chapter, we will be focussing on how art and design can contribute to meaningful and creative learning and understanding in science as well as enhance skills and attitudes.

Artists throughout time and from many different cultures have long used the natural world to inspire their work and document the world as they see it. Vincent Van Gogh's famous painting of the sunflowers is but one of his many depicting flowers. Other work includes irises and almond blossoms; emphasizing his particular interest in flowering plants and trees. Claude Monet dedicated a series of paintings to water lillies and his *Poppies in a Field* captures the beauty and simplicity of nature. Monet's *Corner of the Garden at Montgeron* captures the ever-changing nature of light and colour. More recently, nature photography has grown in popularity and is devoted to capturing natural elements such as landscapes, wildlife, plants and close-ups of natural scenes and textures. Textile artists also draw inspiration from the natural world and there are some beautiful and creative works of art in this style, for example Rembrandt's *Three Trees*. This is Rembrandt's largest and most striking etched landscape.

Not surprisingly, when we reviewed a comprehensive guide to teaching art in primary and secondary school (Hume, 2008), of the 30 or so activities which could be integrated with science, all but five were related to plants or animals in the natural world. What this chapter aims to do is to ensure that such integrated work is meaningful and focused on scientific outcomes, including developing knowledge and understanding across the science programme of study as well as skills and scientific attitudes.

SCIENCE AND ART ENQUIRY

Science education literature offers two contrasting approaches to creativity in the context of art (Kind and Kind, 2007). On the one hand, there is the acknowledgement that art is by nature a more creative subject, so by integrating art and science it allows science to be more creative. In this vein, it acts as a 'tool' for making 'the rational' science education more creative (p. 6). On the other hand, is the appreciation that art and science share similar creative processes, both in knowledge development and in the nature of the knowledge itself (p. 6). With regard to the latter, there is a strong link to investigation and enquiry, so long as the focus is not on finding a single correct answer. This type of approach to enquiry-based learning in science was discussed in Chapter 3 whereby the teacher had control over what the children were investigating and what the expected outcome was. This was contrasted with an open-ended problem-solving approach. This type of enquiry requires divergent thinking; allowing learners to follow various directions to arrive at alternative solutions. It is in this domain that art and science can share similar creative processes.

 Activity 8.1

Write down at least five attitudes or traits which you consider to be characteristic of being creative.

Now consider the following traits and group them as either scientific attitudes, artistic attitudes, both or neither.

Accept other points of view, adventurous, caring, cautious, confident, conforming, co-operative, critical, curious, decisive, determined, enthusiastic, flexible,

fun, hard-working, humble, imaginative, independent, intuitive, objective, observant, open-minded, optimistic, passionate, responsible, risk-taking, sensitive, serious, subjective, thoughtful.

Was there much overlap between science and art? Looking at the groups,
which one is most creative according to your list of creative attitudes or traits?
What does this say about your conceptions of creativity in science?

SCIENCE PROCESS AND ATTITUDES

Key scientific attitudes include curiosity, a respect for evidence, willingness to
change, flexibility and sensitivity. Ultimately, scientists have to be curious about
the world around them and about how it works. Children are naturally curious
and full of questions and it is important to encourage this. Evidence is the foundation for developing scientific knowledge and understanding and scientists have
to be prepared to change or review their ideas in light of new or alternative evidence. Finally, scientists should be sensitive to the natural and man-made environment when carrying out their investigations. This has an effect in the primary
classroom when studying plants and animals in the local environment. On a bigger scale, it is about scientists being ethical and moral in their work. Harlen (2006)
offers some useful strategies for developing attitudes to science in the primary
classroom.

Curiosity

It is in the first attitude, curiosity, that we see the strongest link to creativity and
art. Lunn and Noble (2008), in their research study, focused on re-visioning the
image of a scientist and by far the most persistent theme emerging from the
research was of the creative aspect of science. They also noted the recurrence of
the word 'wonder' in the narratives with the range of scientists interviewed:

> "Wonder" featured in the interview narratives as an aspect of the scientific
> enterprise. Describing an emotion excited by strange, novel, or impressive
> objects or occurrences, the noun 'wonder' is antithetical to the popular con-
> ception of the scientist as emotion free and lacking a spiritual dimension.
> (Lunn and Noble, 2008, p. 801)

It is this wonder, a feeling of amazement, at the natural and man-made world
and the plants and animals that live in it that drives science, art and creativity. The first step in the process of scientific enquiry is often an observation,
which then leads to a question. However, teachers need to help children to
raise questions from observations. One way is to encourage a questioning
environment in the classroom. Having lots of objects, including familiar ones,
for children to observe and time to observe them is important. Modelling curiosity and questioning are equally important.

Observation

Observation was highlighted as a potential first step in science enquiry as it is often questions and problems that arise from observations which lead to scientific investigations. Usually when we ask initial teacher education students what observation is, we get various definitions involving careful or purposeful looking, seeing, watching and these are indeed aspects of scientific observation. However, observation involves using all of the senses (where appropriate) not just the eyes. Touching, smelling, hearing and tasting as well as seeing the world around us should all be encouraged in the primary classroom. The foundations of scientific observation are developed in the early years and Ofsted (2012) note an example of good practice where a 'child-minder successfully enables children to enjoy experimenting with different types of art, textures and materials to expand their knowledge, interests and curiosity'. By using sight and touch to enjoy and create a broad range of art, children are beginning to develop their observation skills as well as encouraging curiosity.

However, our observations, and children's, are influenced by our experiences, existing ideas and expectations so they are not wholly objective. Such prior knowledge can affect what we choose to observe, what we actually observe, which observations we regard as relevant and which we deem irrelevant, and how we interpret them (Gunstone, 1991). Teachers need to be aware of this and consider this when planning observation experiences. For example, a typical observation lesson might involve observing snails. These are common molluscs and children are familiar with them. After allowing time for the children to observe the snails, we would then ask them to do an observational drawing. It is at this stage, we normally have to prompt them to only draw what they have actually observed. They will often draw more human features like eyes and mouth and draw a cartoon snail.

To avoid this and develop their observation, the children can use magnifying glasses or other tools to focus their observations. Allowing children time to observe is also important. This will allow them to move beyond the obvious observations and to note less obvious features. Figure 8.1 shows the role observation plays in both inductive and deductive enquiry in the primary classroom. Inductive reasoning is more open-ended and exploratory so is an appropriate process to support generative thinking and creativity. However, it should be recognized that these two processes are not mutually exclusive when investigating science. Indeed an initial observation, followed by further observation might lead to a tentative theory which then could be tested more rigorously through a deductive process.

It is in the observation phase of the enquiry process that art can really be a factor. By doing detailed observational drawing or painting, macro photography or modelling with clay, children can develop their observational skills and make observations which can then lead to scientific questions and investigations. Stephens and Walkup (2001) recognize that scientific illustrators must be expert at seeing detail and drawing accurately what they observe and must have a strong scientific curiosity and a keen interest in both art and science. When doing observational drawings it is important that children are encouraged to use the full space on the page. This allows them to capture more details. They should also be encouraged to annotate them. Macro photography is in essence close-up photography and has particular value when wanting to study the natural world

Inductive reasoning   **Deductive reasoning**

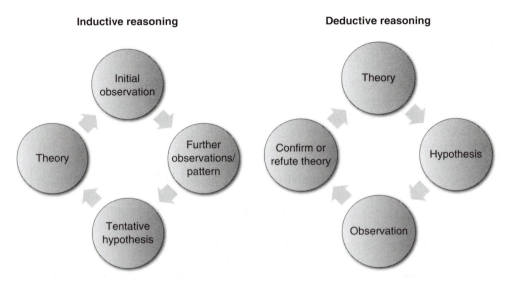

Figure 8.1   Scientific enquiry process – deductive and inductive reasoning with observation as a key role in both processes

close-up. The close-up allows us to bring the natural world back to the classroom for much more detailed and focussed observation. Modelling with clay is particularly useful when wanting to show texture in observations.

Further observations may also be required at the data collection stage, whereby careful observations of texture, colour, line, or pattern may be required. Noting similarities and differences are important, and children should be encouraged, in particular, as their observation skills develop, to note similarities. This is evidence of progression in observation. It is important that the learning stays focussed on the science objectives when integrating with art and design and this can be achieved by children predicting before making their observations and then explaining them afterwards. Gunstone (1991) suggested that the predict-observe-explain process makes tasks more minds-on.

Investigation

There are also opportunities to integrate art and design with science investigations. Working scientifically is a critical aspect of primary science and it should be embedded in all science lessons. Gompertz et al. (2011) describe an integrated activity where children had to design an area to encourage birds as part of a whole school gardening project. Over the course of the project the children made bird feeders, designed bird boxes and made periscopes (so they could observe birds from a distance). This is a wonderful example where art and design play a crucial role in enhancing the science learning experience.

Chapter 3 explored approaches to teaching science and enquiry and investigation are crucial aspects of this, particularly if we are trying to encourage creativity. Check out Activity 8.2 to challenge your creative ideas about using art when investigating science.

Activity 8.2

Table 8.1

Programme of study	Possible investigation
All living things and their habitats	Investigate a local habitat
Seasonal change	Investigate the changes, noting similarities and difference, in a chosen tree or plant cross each season.
Animals, including humans	Observe and investigate the similarities and differences between two mini-beasts e.g. snail and woodlouse or worm and centipede
Evolution and inheritance	Observe and investigate the similarities and differences between family members
(Use of) everyday materials	Compare and contrast different natural and man-made materials used to build a school
States of matter	Use a visit to the local park to explore the three states of matter
Rocks	Compare different kinds of rocks in the local area
Properties and changes of materials	Investigate a range of materials
Earth and space	Create a model solar system
Forces and magnets	Make a kite to investigate air resistance
Sound	Make a musical instrument which can produce high and low pitch sounds
Light	Investigate light and shadows using puppets
Electricity	Making an electric circuit to light a model of the classroom

- Choose one of the above areas of science and the suggested investigation. Decide on a learning objective for the investigation. Try to consider both concept and skills development.
- Now think about how you could link it to art and design; brainstorm your ideas and consider which medium would be best for the investigation: drawing, painting, photography, printmaking, sculpting or textiles.
- Map out the basic structure of a lesson/scheme.
- Consider how the art or design element contributes to the learning and development in science. If it doesn't, could you adapt the activity to do this?

Time for reflection 8.1

Is there opportunity for observation, using as many of the senses as appropriate? Would the children be working with a range of materials or in environments that encourage curiosity and questioning? Are the children getting the opportunity to

> work scientifically? Are they applying known skills and knowledge in different contexts? Are a variety of responses and outcomes possible from the investigation? Can the children follow their own lines of enquiry? Are the children evaluating their work? Are they communicating their ideas and findings in interesting ways?
>
> These are some of the elements that will raise the creativity level of the investigation.

Howard-Jones (2008) suggests that providing students with tasks that require the making of unusual connections will encourage generative thinking. The strategy of having to incorporate unrelated material in an outcome has often been used by teachers to stimulate creative thinking. He also refers to the artist Kurt Schwitters who famously created a collage from the contents of his wife's bathroom bin!

SCIENCE COMMUNICATION

When most people reflect on their experiences of science, they remember lots of writing. This is a fairly accurate memory and reflects the traditional way science is communicated. The familiar layout of aim, resources, method, results, discussion and conclusion allows scientists to share what they have done and what they found out, allowing others to repeat it and then refute or accept it. It is a transparent and objective account of the scientific experience. This tradition can be a positive experience for people who enjoy writing and like the structure of scientific writing. However, for others this is one sure way to turn them off science for good!

The study by Lunn and Noble (2008) focussed on re-visioning the image of a scientist. They quote Dr Wendy Nielsen, a research participant, who talked passionately and animatedly, using a series of colourful metaphors and descriptions, of 'slimy' and 'ginormous' seaweeds. This was in contrast to her writing and speaking science in a professional setting, where she follows traditional scientific conventions:

> I will talk extravagantly about things but when put you put me on paper I am very precise. I think it's a kind of a productive tension in the discipline…
> So it's not ginormous, its 5–7 meters, and it's not disgustingly slimy looking, it's a kind of greenish, greying at the edges. (Lunn and Noble, 2008, p. 801)

Luckily for us, we don't always have to communicate science in this precise way. While children can benefit from the experience of scientific report writing, there are lots of other ways that children can communicate their ideas and experience in science. Children can communicate through creative writing, for example a haiku poem; role play showing how magnets repel and attract; music such as writing and performing a rap. Subramaniam (2013) in a TEDx talk demonstrates using dance to explore the concept of water shortage.

Children can also communicate through collages, comic strips, diaries, drawings and models and this is where art and design can play a big part in supporting science as a creative subject. As mentioned earlier, writing can be a barrier to children's enjoyment and engagement with science. This is not surprising since as well as written language, children also have to contend with complex scientific language. Scientists communicate using a range of conventions, including specialized vocabulary, numbers, graphical representations, symbols and notations. While it is expected that children will develop this language as they progress through science, it should not be a barrier to them engaging in science and sharing their ideas. By allowing children expression of ideas in a variety of ways, more children can share and communicate their scientific ideas. In this way a creative and varied approach to communicating science is more inclusive.

Evagorou and Osborne (2010) describe how language is central in everyday life since it is one of the tools for understanding the world around us. Within classrooms, they recognize language as the principal means of communication. It is the tool to reflect upon our thoughts and share our experiences with others and is thus both a technology for transmitting information and a means for interpreting our experiences (p. 135). The latter point is critically important in science, whereby we make observations and attempt to interpret and make sense of them. By allowing children to explore their ideas and experiences through a range of media means that they can use language and modes of representations that suit them.

CONCLUSION

Mesure (2005) suggests that science teaching would benefit from adapting the artistic process of self-expression, including 'risking failure, taking leaps of faith and trusting in a more creative approach when the outcome is not at all certain' (p. 13). Kind and Kind (2007) suggest this might be a way of making teaching meet children's needs, while truly emphasizing creativity. The challenge, of course, is to ensure that the teaching still has science as a main focus rather than artistic expression. To achieve this, awareness of the characteristics of scientific creativity and clear goals for the learning outcomes are needed (Kind and Kind, 2007, p. 9). The characteristics of scientific creativity have been explored in Chapter 1.

Art is by nature a creative subject as is science, and this chapter has explored the role art and design can play in enhancing creativity in science, both as a tool and as a complementary process. The key role that observation plays in developing science ideas and the crucial role that art could play in this was discussed. The nature of science enquiry and investigation and opportunity for divergent thinking and exploring materials and objects was highlighted by working with a variety of art media.

FURTHER READING

Ainsworth, S., Prain, V. and Tytler, R. (2011) Drawing to learn in science, *Science*, 333, pp. 1096–7
In this short article, the authors put forward an argument for more drawing in science, highlighting a number of benefits, exploring five ways that drawing can enhance learning and teaching in science.

Klopp, T.J., Rule, A.C., Suchsland Schneider, J. and Boody, R.M. (2014) Computer technology-integrated projects should not supplant craft projects in science education. *International Journal of Science Education,* (36)5, pp. 865–86
In this paper, the authors recommend that room should be retained for crafts in the science curriculum to model science concepts. They report that more science content was found in craft products than technology-rich products in their study.

Root-Bernstein, R. and Root-Bernstein, M. (2013) The art and craft of science. *Educational Leadership*,70(5), pp. 16–21
This is an intriguing piece of writing which discusses the interactions that occur between the arts, crafts and sciences and makes a strong case for art-infused science education.

Subramaniam, K. and Padalkar, S. (2009) Visualization and reasoning in explaining the phases of the moon. *International Journal of Science Education*, 31(3), pp. 395–417
Subramaniam and Padalkar suggest that visualization is an important process in science learning, and point to the importance of developing among students the ability to work with diagrams.

REFERENCES

Department for Education (2013) Art and design programmes of study: Key stages 1 and 2 National Curriculum in England. [Online] Available at: https://www.gov.uk/government/uploads/system/uploads/attachment_data/file/239018/PRIMARY_national_curriculum_-_Art_and_design.pdf

Evagorou, M. and Osborne, J. (2010) The role of language in the learning and teaching of science, in Osborne, J. and Dillon, J. (eds) *Good Practice in Science Teaching. What Research Has to Say.* 2nd ed., Maidenhead: Open University Press

Gompertz, B., Hincks, J. and Hincks-Knight, R. (2011) Science and technology outside the classroom, in Waite, S. (ed.) *Children Learning Outside the Classroom From Birth to Eleven.* London: Sage, pp. 94–105

Gunstone, R.F. (1991) Reconstructing theory from practical experience, in Woolnough, B.E. (ed.), *Practical Science*. Milton Keynes: Open University Press, pp. 67–77

Harlen, W. (2006) *Teaching, Learning and Assessing science 5–12*. London: Sage

Howard-Jones, P. (2008) *Fostering Creative Thinking: Co-constructed Insights from Neuroscience and Education.* Bristol: Higher Education Academy Education Subject Centre ESCalate, p. 13

Hume, H.D. (2008) *The Art Teacher's Survival Guide for Elementary and Middle Schools.* 2nd ed., San Francisco: Jossey Bass

Kind, P.M., and Kind, V. (2007). Creativity in science education: perspectives and challenges for developing school science. *Studies in Science Education*, 43, 1–37

Liu, S-C. and Lin, H-S. (2014) Primary teachers' beliefs about scientific creativity in the classroom context, *International Journal of Science Education*, 36(10), pp. 1551–67

Lunn, M. and Noble, A. (2008) Re-visioning science 'love and passion in the scientific imagination': art and science, *International Journal of Science Education*, 30(6), 793–805

Mesure, S. (2005) Creativity in science: The heart and soul of science teaching, *Education in Science*, 214, 12–14.

Ofsted (2012) Good practice resource – inspiring children's creativity. [Online] Available at: http://www.ofsted.gov.uk/resources/good-practice-resource-inspiring-childrens-creativity

Stephens, P. and Walkup, N. (2001) *Bridging the Curriculum Through Art Interdisciplinary Connections*. Glenview: Crystal Productions

Subramaniam, S. (2013) Subathra Subramaniam, transcendence – turning people onto science through dance [Video file]. Retrieved from https://www.youtube.com/watch?v=nqvki2hSDzE

CHAPTER 9

CREATIVE SCIENCE THROUGH DRAMA AND STORYTELLING

Chapter aims

By the end of this chapter, you should be able to:

- Recognize the potential for storytelling in science to develop science attitudes, skills, knowledge and understanding
- Develop strategies for oral storytelling in and outside the classroom
- Summarize a range of drama techniques and describe how they might be used in the science classroom
- Defend the use of drama as an approach to science teaching and learning in the primary classroom

INTRODUCTION

Il était une fois …

… والأوان العصر وسالف الزمان، قديم كان،في ما يا كان

Der var engang …

Es war einmal …

Once upon a time, not in your time, not in my time but a time long ago …

The power of storytelling can capture the attention of children and adults alike with those simple words, 'once upon a time'. In many cultures, storytelling, often through song, chants and poetry, was part and parcel of daily life and was how history, morals and lore got passed from one generation or one community to the other. In fact, every human culture in the world seems to create stories as a way of making sense of the world. In old Ireland, a seanchaí, or storyteller, was a well-respected member of the community who was usually a servant to the chief of the tribe and kept track of important information for their clan. In African culture, stories were often created and told through the medium of dance and music. In Aboriginal cultures, children were told stories from a very early age; stories that helped them understand the air, the land, the universe, their people, their culture and their history. In England, 'wassail' refers to the ancient custom of visiting orchards, reciting incantations and singing to the trees in apple orchards in cider-producing regions of England to promote a good harvest for the coming year. We can recognize the long-term relationship between stories and our understanding of and connectedness to our world and the people that live in it (and these are only a few of examples from around the globe). These storytelling traditions are still in place today and many are witnessing a revival. Jonathan Gottschall (2012) in his book *The Storytelling Animal: How Stories Make Us Human* writes: 'We are, as a species, addicted to stories'.

Storytelling has always had a presence in the primary classroom and Daniel (2012) recognizes its potential across the curriculum. Some subjects by their very nature lend themselves to the tradition of storytelling and in the case of 'English' is a curriculum requirement in the 2014 National Curriculum for England (Department for Education, 2013, p. 21) as children should be taught to develop pleasure in reading, motivation to read, vocabulary and understanding by becoming very familiar with key stories, fairy stories and traditional tales, retelling them and considering their particular characteristics from Year 1. Scotland's Curriculum for Excellence encourages children from the early years to create their own stories and share these in imaginative ways (Education Scotland n.d.). Moreover, in the Irish Primary School Curriculum for English, there is an additional expectation that children will hear, discuss and react to local storytellers (DES/NCCA, 1999 p. 38). However, what of science? Is there room for story telling in the science curriculum and the science classroom? We argue an emphatic YES! and not just to provide a hook but to promote teaching for creativity.

Denning (2001) argues that storytelling plays an essential role in children's learning, it brings people together to experience a common perspective and stretches everyone's capacity to empathize with others and share experiences. Parkinson (2011) recognizes that storytelling helps children develop a wide range of skills and that they are marvellous starting points for teaching an art that can help them to pass on experience, train and use imagination, develop language skills, promote their own confidence, communication and creativity and much more. Storytelling and story making may also be essential catalysts for developing critical and analytical thinking skills. Recently, there is much research on using technology to enable, support and enhance children's creative storytelling. Daniel (2007) also advocates for storytelling in the primary classroom but recognizes the vital role teachers need to play as role models for storytelling.

So why use oral storytelling in science? Just as stories are used in English, history and other subjects in the curriculum, stories used in science can help develop scientific attitudes, language and skills as well as knowledge and understanding. Oral storytelling has particular power when considering environmental, local and global issues in science with its potential to extend children's ability to empathize with others and share experiences. Stories can act as wonderful lesson starters and are particularly effective when used as part of a sequence or scheme of work. They can capture the imagination and enthusiasm of the children and motivate them to achieve their science objectives. The key element in any subsequent work following storytelling will be the dialogue and discussion among the children. Chapter 2 recognized the importance of dialogue and discussion in identifying and supporting conceptual change. This chapter with its focus on oral storytelling and dramatic techniques which demand dialogue and discussion, has underpinning in this theoretical framework. When using drama and storytelling strategies you are also giving children that critical time to think, which is so often squeezed out of the busy classroom schedule and equally important, to share their thinking. Sharing their thinking and ideas in response to a drama or story is vital in enabling children to progress in their scientific understanding. Interestingly, in a study on primary science, Murphy (2005, p. 11) reported that female teachers were significantly more likely than male teachers to use role play and stories in their teaching of science. However, she also reported that teachers most often used discussion (91 per cent often used) and group work (84 per cent) as creative contexts for teaching science; whereas role play (10 per cent) and drama (8 per cent) were the least used contexts. Also the use of stories was more prevalent in Key Stage 1.

 Time for reflection 9.1 – Teacher as storyteller

What skills and techniques do you need to be an oral storyteller?

Hopefully at some stage during your initial teacher training or early experiences in the classroom you have told children an oral story. Think about one of these occasions. If you haven't, think about a time you read children a story (and please make it your goal to tell an oral story as soon as possible!). The following reflections and questions were adapted from de Rusett's *Guide to Storytelling* (2012).

Think about where and how you sat and where the audience sat when you told your story. Were there barriers between you and your audience? Could everyone hear and see you easily? It is important to let the audience know that storytelling is different from circle time or other activities by speaking slower and louder than normal.

When you told the story, did you give an introduction about where the story comes from? Was this your favourite story from your childhood? Was it a story you once heard and have adapted to make it your own?

(Continued)

(Continued)

How did you start your story? While 'once upon a time' is a classic story starter, think about other ways to start your story by considering the time, place and weather of the story.

Did you use simple facial expressions to show the feelings of the characters as they progressed through the story? Also, did you use your body and hands through mime and gesture to add more detail to the characters, situations or surroundings? Think about using your body to make yourself as big as possible when describing a character that may be physically big or big in personality, similarly as small as possible with a small or timid character. The way you hold your shoulders and head can convey a lot about the physicality and personality of the character.

Think about how you used your voice when you were telling the story. You have the power to control the pace and volume so use this to your advantage. Did you vary the pace and volume? Did you use different voices for different characters or to create sounds to support the story, for example, animal (a frog croaking), emotional (yawn), weather (rain) or happening (crash) sounds?

Did you pause at a particular point in a sentence or part of the story to create atmosphere and tension?

It is important the audience feel included and part of the story. Did you ask questions, such as 'do you know what happened next?', or use phrases that included the audience, for example 'as you know walking through woods can be scary but exciting …'.

Luckily the ability to structure a story, change pace and emphasize words, use gesture and facial expression and make eye contact are all things that we, as teachers, already have in our tool box. So next time you go to tell or read a story, please think about using these techniques and strategies … practice makes perfect!

Activity 9.1 – Tell a story

Have you got a favourite fairy tale? If so, collect examples from other cultures which can add further opportunities for learning. A popular and lasting one is *Cinderella* and there are so many examples of this story from many diverse cultures. *Mufaro's beautiful daughter* (Steptoe, 1987) is an African 'Cinderella' story; *Yeh-shen* is a wonderful 'Cinderella' story from China (Louie, 1996) and *Sootface* a Native American Indian 'Cinderella' story (San Souci, 2010). While these could also be used as picture books for story time as the illustrations are wonderful; the joy in children's faces as the familiar story is revealed but told in a land and with people and objects that are unfamiliar to them is worth all the time and effort in preparing the story and telling it orally.

This is a skill that can be honed outside of the classroom. Get a few friends or student teachers from your course together and have a go at telling your favourite story. Pick one that you know well. Identify the key stages in the story. Think about how you will start your story. Think of ways of adding simple gestures.

What words need emphasizing? What is the best way to sequence the story? Is there repetition of events or details? What way can you involve the audience? Don't be afraid to add your own detail! Before telling your story to your friends have a go at saying it out loud a few times yourself, ensuring you have included the key stages. Over time it will get easier and a lot more enjoyable to tell a story without the comfort blanket of a picture book or other book.

 ## Activity 9.2

Consider the following objectives and guidance for the 2014 National Curriculum for England (Department for Education, 2013)

Table 9.1

Year	Statutory guidance Pupils should be taught to:	Non-statutory guidance
Year 4	Recognize that environments can change and that this can sometimes pose dangers to living things.	Pupils should explore examples of human impact (both positive and negative) on environments such as the positive effects of nature reserves, ecologically planned parks or garden ponds, and the negative effects of population and development, litter or deforestation.
Year 6	Identify how animals and plants are adapted to suit their environment in different ways and that adaptation may lead to evolution.	They should also appreciate that variation in offspring over time can make animals more or less able to survive in particular environments, for example by exploring how giraffes' necks got longer or the development of insulating fur on the Arctic fox. Pupils might work scientifically by: observing and raising questions about local animals and how they are adapted to their environment; comparing how some living things are adapted to survive in extreme conditions, for example cactuses, penguins and camels. They might analyse the advantages and disadvantages of specific adaptations, such as being on two feet rather than four, having a long or a short beak, having gills or lungs, tendrils on climbing plants, brightly coloured and scented flowers.

Visit your closest library or bookshop and evaluate what stories could support science teaching such as environmental themes or stories that consider evolution and inheritance. It will be worth the time in finding some key stories that have strong connections with these themes. If you need help getting started, Anne Dolan (2012) explores the possibility of using picture books to help student teachers devise strategies for encouraging children to imagine the future through dialogical engagement in general and through the use of literature circles in the primary classroom in her book *You, Me and Diversity, The Potential of Picture Books for Teaching Development and Intercultural Education*. Consider

(Continued)

(Continued)

exploring some of these picture books and choose one that best supports one area of science. Extend this by telling one of these stories orally outside, using your techniques practised earlier. This would work particularly well if you are considering an environmental theme. The power of this oral storytelling can further children's connectedness with the natural world and situate their ideas and experiences in a local context.

Traditional picture and fiction stories provide a rich and diverse resource for teachers and their children, however it is also important to encourage children's own story creating. Valkanova and Watts (2007) describe a research study that involved digital storytelling in science, where children had to produce a short three-minute film (edited from 40 minutes) to show to family and friends what they had learnt in science. The research aspect involved analysing the type of talk throughout the process and the nature of the stories. Some groups chose to tell *a* story rather than simply tell *the* story of what they had learnt. 'This was a strategy several groups used, allowing the medium of video film and visual construction to free their talk. In such situations the medium was used as a vehicle for inventive thinking and communication' (Valkanova and Watts, 2007, p. 801). There were also instances indicating how children played with stories to make sense of their ideas and knowledge. This links strongly with the notion of assimilation of knowledge, see Chapter 2. Kelly and Cutting (2011) describe a storytelling activity which combines elements of history and geography, with strong links to science. In this, children are told a story about a great dragon who lives in southern England and none of the King's people are brave enough to fight it until a young girl steps forward. This brings her an adventure with wizards, pirates and witches as she encounters a series of challenges which help her ultimately to defeat the dragon. The science learning here was helping the witches make a potion to put the dragon to sleep requiring the young girl to do some simple plant identification. These are just some examples of the use of storytelling in science.

DRAMA IN SCIENCE

As with storytelling, the use of drama in English to explore stories, events and character is common in primary school curricula. Additionally, it is typical for primary-aged children to also study drama as a subject in itself, so what of using a creative medium such as drama in the science classroom?

A range of drama and literacy approaches have been used to teach science in the past. Brock (1999) describes the use of drama, story and role play in a multi-sensory environment to negotiate and solve scientific problems. Kaplan (1993) showed how a drama activity could be used as a springboard into a science investigation. Puppets have also been strongly advocated for in the science classroom (Rollnick et al., 1998; Keogh et al., 2006) and in recent years with great effect (Simon et al., 2008). Simon et al. (2008) reported puppets having an impact in three distinct ways: on the nature of the discourse in both teacher–child and child–child interactions, on the engagement and interest of children, and on teachers' beliefs and practice. Watts (2001) describes three benefits of using poetry in the science classroom including giving children a chance to 'play with words and toy with language' encouraging students to play creatively and imaginatively with science concepts and ideas, especially when ideas are 'half-formed'. Ødegaard (2003) uses similar arguments to justify the inclusion of drama in school science, showing examples for how this may be used to increase students' learning of science concepts and their understanding of the nature of science and science in society. A strategy to foster critical and creative thinking in the secondary science classroom is a 'structured controversy'. This involves students in discussions and debates which address more than one side of an issue and require students to back arguments with evidence and reference to consequences (DCSF, 2008). Pennick proposes that science teaching that uses provocative questions and creates a safe environment for exploring, risk-taking, experimentation, and speculation, can help improve students' creativity (1996, cited in Lee and Erdogan, 2007). Additionally, the notion of creativity was expressed explicitly in the 1999 National Curriculum for Science in England and Wales, 'that science is about thinking creatively to try to explain how living and non-living things work, and to establish links between causes and effects' (DfE, 2011).

Cremin (2009) argues that drama offers children the chance to engage creatively in fictional-world-making play. Such play, whether in the role-play area or in classroom drama, involves making and shaping worlds, investigating issues within them and returning to the real world with more understanding and insights. Mantle of the Expert (MoE) is one such drama technique that we can use effectively in the science classroom. It is based on the principle that treating children as responsible experts increases their engagement and confidence. MoE encourages creativity, improves teamwork, communication skills, critical thought and decision making (Drama Resource, 2013). A problem or task is established and the pupils are contracted-in or 'framed' as an enterprise – a team of experts using imaginative role play to explore the issue. The children may be involved in mimed activities, improvisation, research or discussion. While the focus is on the enquiry process, it can often lead to real outcomes such as writing letters, printing leaflets or selling products. The teacher's role is to guide the drama, stepping in and out of role as necessary, providing encouragement and motivation to the experts. The children perceive a real purpose for learning and discovering together in an interactive and proactive way. This provides them with skills and knowledge they can apply to their everyday lives.

Mantle of the Expert involves a reversal of the conventional teacher-student relationship in which the students draw on the knowledge and expertise of the teacher; instead the teacher assumes a fictional role which places the students in the position of being the one who knows or is the expert in a particular branch of knowledge (Heathcote and Herbert, 1985, p. 173). MoE has real potential in science and Luke Abbott (2013) shares his experience of working with teachers in Ramallah, Palestine to develop their skills in MoE in science. He describes an example where 'a scorpion centre' is set up having identified a problem. The problem started from the notion that if a child was stung by a scorpion 'You might have to go all the way to Jericho Town for a doctor and if it's a child, the child might die on the way.' The teachers in this case suggested a centre in the local town that could deal with scorpion bites and where people could also study them. This allowed for Mantle of the Expert where the teachers could play the part of scorpion experts, researching, developing and running the centre. Abbott then takes on the role as someone who will pay $100 for every yellow scorpion found. This led into discussion around ethics, morality and the place of science in the environment. He argues that this supports the science units on 'Ourselves', 'Habitats', 'Local animals', 'Growth and growing' and 'Similarities and Differences'. For further information on this, read the article in full. Additionally, for further ideas on considering controversial issues in science, see Chapter 13.

There are a range of other drama techniques that can be used in the classroom. These include:

- Improvisation – Improvisations allow children to produce short performance pieces (movement and/or dialogue) which have not been previously rehearsed, scripted or planned.

- Hot-seating – For this, the teacher or child is in role in the hot-seat, where they are questioned by children in the class. The role might be a character from fiction, a historical character, a famous person or an imaginary person.

- Freeze-frame – Freeze frames are still images or silent tableaux used to illustrate a specific incident or event.

- Conscience or decision alley – This strategy is used as a way of exploring thoughts, underlying issues or dilemmas of a character at a particular point in a story.

- Flashbacks and flash forwards – In this, children are asked to improvise scenes or freeze-frames which take place seconds, minutes, days or years before or after a dramatic moment. This enables the exploration of motivations and consequences.

- Role play – In role play, children and the teacher step into particular role(s) and suspend belief.

- Forum theatre – A scene, usually indicating some kind of negative behaviour or attitudes, is shown twice. During the replay, any child in the audience is allowed to shout 'Stop!', step forward and take the place of one of the characters, showing how they could change the situation to enable a different outcome.

- Teacher-in-role – The teacher assumes a role in relation to the children.

- Thought tapping/tracking – A technique for examining the private thoughts of characters at particular moments.

- Story telling – This can involve the teacher telling stories or the children sharing their stories.

See the recommended further reading for more information on these and other drama techniques suitable for use in the primary science classroom. Some of these are also explored in the following case example.

Activity 9.3

Think of a favourite story from your childhood. Now brainstorm as many links to science as possible considering all elements of science. Some links may seem tenuous but keep going and more appropriate and effective links will be found. Here are some of the stories I like to use when teaching science with one or two suggestions of strong links to science:

The Three Little Pigs – Materials and their Properties

Wall E – Materials, Recycling, Care for the environment, Green plants

Peter Pan – Light and shadows, Day and night, Ourselves

Case example

Finding Nemo, Disney Pixar's 2003 animated movie about the journey a timid clownfish takes to bring his son Nemo home after he is captured in the Great Barrier Reef and taken to Sydney. This story lends itself wonderfully to the study of marine biology, considering living things and their habitats, food chains, food webs, etc. and also the study of controversial and environmental issues. This is an example of a primary science lesson using *Finding Nemo*.

Introduction

Teacher creates some excitement. Who has seen the movie? Who were their favourite characters? Why? The chances are most children will have seen it, if not, re-tell the story orally with some pictures to support.

Activity 1: Freeze-frame and thought tapping

Teacher prepares a fact file on 6–8 of the characters from the movie. These can be adapted to allow for differentiation across the primary age phase. In groups of 4–8 (depending on class size and age), each child is given a fact file and in their groups they discuss their character and the information given on the card – appearance, diet, adaptations, survival strategies, etc. After five minutes of discussion, the children in their groups do a freeze frame of their characters living under the water. The teacher then goes around the groups and does thought tapping – this is a technique for examining the private thoughts of characters at

(Continued)

(Continued)

particular moments. In this example it could involve questions like 'Are you worried about where your next meal is coming from', 'How do you survive when you've got big predators like Bruce (a shark) around?' or 'Why do you like to position yourself on the seabed?'. The teacher can model and encourage the use of scientific words through effective questioning and dialogue with the children.

> I wear a snorkel and mask and as teacher-in-role pretend to be swimming and taking photographs with an underwater camera taking in all the marine life around me ... and of course reacting appropriately when I see Bruce the Great White Shark!

Activity 2: Modelling

Staying in their characters, the children then create food chains or food webs (depending on their ability). This provides opportunity to again encourage and use scientific language. The teacher can purposely omit key elements, such as a primary producer. In a marine habitat for example, turtles mostly eat seagrasses and so a food chain with a green sea turtle, like Crush in *Finding Nemo* needs to have seagrass. With the other main aquatic producers, phytoplankton and algae, it can provide an introduction to discussion on photosynthesis and one of the seven life processes, respiration.

Activity 3: Conscience Alley

When we've done this lesson with our students, initial teacher education students, it is typical for someone to quote Bruce, the Great White Shark: '*I am a nice shark, not a mindless eating machine. If I am to change this image, I must first change myself. Fish are friends, not food*'. This is a great opportunity to do some structured controversy!

Through a conscience (or decision) alley, a means of exploring a character's mind at a moment of crisis and of investigating the complexity of the decision they are facing, the decision of whether Bruce should eat fish or not is considered. To do this, the class divides into two groups and forms two lines facing each other. One side come up with reasons to eat fish, while the other group comes up with reasons for not eating fish and should offer alternatives. It is useful to give each group a few minutes to come up with ideas. Either the teacher or a child then walks very slowly through the alley. As they pass each child, they give them one reason why they should or shouldn't eat fish. By the time the teacher or child has reached the end of the alley they should have made a decision. It is important that the reasons for the decision are shared and discussed. Furthermore, there is opportunity here for the teacher to steer the discussion towards eco-systems and how they are naturally balanced. This allows for discussion to then follow on controversial issues such as over-fishing, dolphin-friendly fishing and whaling. Some links to the 2014 National Curriculum for England have been identified (see Figure 9.1).

Purpose of study: They should be encouraged to understand how science can be used to explain what is occurring, predict how things will behave, and analyse causes.	
Scientific knowledge and conceptual understanding: Pupils should be able to describe associated processes and key characteristics in common language but they should also be familiar with, and use, technical terminology accurately and precisely.	
Working scientifically	
Freeze-frame and thought tapping	Lower KS2: using straightforward scientific evidence to answer questions or to support their findings
Modelling	Upper KS2: using simple models to describe scientific ideas
Conscience alley	Upper KS2: identifying scientific evidence that has been used to support or refute ideas or arguments
All living things and their habitats	
Freeze-frame and thought tapping	Y2: identify that most living things live in habitats to which they are suited and describe how different habitats provide for the basic needs of different kinds of animals and plants, and how they depend on each other
Animals, including humans	
Modelling	Y4: construct and interpret a variety of food chains, identifying producers, predators and prey
Conscience alley	Y3: identify that animals, including humans, need the right types and amount of nutrition and that they cannot make their own food; they get nutrition from what they eat
Evolution and inheritance	
Freeze-frame and thought tapping	Y6: identify how animals and plants are adapted to suit their environment in different ways and that adaptation may lead to evolution.

Figure 9.1   Mapping of the *Finding Nemo* drama activities against the 2014 Primary Science Curriculum for England

CONCLUSION

In this chapter we have considered using storytelling and drama as creative approaches to science teaching. The power of storytelling has real implications in the classroom so why not utilize it in the science classroom. Stories provide relevance and purpose to the science activity and this ensures progress is made and outcomes are meaningful to the children. Through story-telling and drama children can situate themselves in experiences that enable them to empathize with others. This has real potential when considering local and global themes, particularly environmental issues. Using techniques like Mantle of the Expert, teacher-in-role or puppets, the children's thinking, methods and results can be challenged in a positive learning environment.

FURTHER READING

Daniel, A.K. (2012) *Storytelling across the Primary Curriculum.* Abingdon: Routledge.
This book is a rich resource for those who want to explore in depth the theory and practice of storytelling in the primary classroom.

Dolan, A.M. (2014) *You, Me and Diversity, The Potential of Picture Books for Teaching Development and Intercultural Education.* London: Trentham Books.
In this research-based book, Anne Dolan offers clear and concise guidance on using picturebooks in the primary classroom for teaching children about development education and promoting intercultural understanding. While only a few of the examples have direct relevance to science, the approaches suggested can be successfully applied to relevant picturebooks with science related themes.

Baldwin. P. (2009) *The Primary Drama Handbook.* London: Sage
This is a comprehensive guide to drama in the primary classroom, which as well as offering tips on using drama, also provides a key insight into the key role drama can play across the curriculum.

REFERENCES

Abbott, L. (2013) More stories of science and mantle of the expert from Jericho. Mantle of the Expert. [Online] Available at: http://www.mantleoftheexpert.com/articles/more-stories-of-science-and-mantle-of-the-expert-from-jericho/ (accessed 29.06.13)

Brock, A. (1999) *Into the Enchanted Forest: Language, Drama and Science in Primary Schools.* Stoke-on-Trent: Trentham Books

Cremin, H. (2009) *Teaching English Creatively.* Oxford: Routledge

Drama Resource (2013) Mantle of the expert. [Online] Available at: http://dramaresource.com/strategies/mantle-of-the-expert

Daniel, A.K. (2007) From folktales to algorithms: developing the teacher's role as principal storyteller in the classroom. *Early Child Development and Care*, 177: 6–7, 735–50

Daniel, A.K. (2012) *Storytelling across the Primary Curriculum.* Abingdon: Routledge

Denning, S. (2001) *The Springboard: How Storytelling Ignites Action in Knowledge-era Organizations.* Boston, MA: Butterworth Heinemann

DCSF (2008) Developing critical and creative thinking: in science. Department for Children, Schools and Families. 00054–2008DVD-EN [Online] Available at: http://webarchive.nationalarchives.gov.uk/20130401151715/https://www.education.gov.uk/publications/eOrderingDownload/Developing%20critical%20and%20creative%20thinking%20-%20in%20science.pdf

Department for Education (2011) Science: Sc1 scientific enquiry. [Online] Available at: http://www.education.gov.uk/schools/teachingandlearning/curriculum/primary/b00199179/science-/ks2/sc1

Department for Education (2013) The National Curriculum in England. [Online] Available at: https://www.gov.uk/government/uploads/system/uploads/attachment_data/file/260481/PRIMARY_national_curriculum_11-9-13_2.pdf

Department of Education and Science/National Council for Curriculum and Assessment. (1999) *Primary School Curriculum. English language.* Dublin: The Stationery Office

De Rusett, W. (2012) Storytelling techniques, hints and tips. [Online] Available at: http://www.grtleeds.co.uk/storytelling/wendy.html

Dolan, A.M. (2012) Futures talk over story time. *Primary Geography*. Sheffield: Geographical Association, 78(2), 26–17

Education Scotland (n.d.) Curriculum for excellence: literacy and English. Experiences and outcomes.[Online] Available at: http://www.educationscotland.gov.uk/Images/literacy_english_experiences_outcomes_tcm4–539867.pdf (accessed 31.07.13)

Gottschall, J. (2012) *The Storytelling Animal: How Stories Make Us Human*. Boston: Houghton Mifflin Harcourt

Heathcote, D. and Herbert, P. (1985) A drama of learning: mantle of the expert. Theory into practice. *Educating through Drama*, 24(3), (Summer, 1985), pp. 173–80

Kaplan, H. (1993) *Projects for Science and Technology with Drama*. London: Franklin Watts Ltd

Kelly, O. and Cutting, R. (2011) Understanding places and society through history and geography outside the classroom in Waite, S., 106–18–105

Keogh, B., Naylor, S., Downing, B., Maloney, J. and Simon, S. (2006) Puppets bringing stories to life in science. *Primary Science Review*, 92, pp. 26–8

Lee, M.K. and Erdogan, I. (2007) The effect of science-technology-society teaching on students' attitudes towards science and certain aspects of creativity. *International Journal of Science Education*, 29(11), pp. 1315–217.

Louie, A-L (1996) *Yeh-Shen. A Cinderella story from China*. London: Puffin

Murphy, C. (2005) Primary science in the UK: a scoping study. The Wellcome Trust. [Online] Available at: http://www.wellcome.ac.uk/stellent/groups/corporatesite/@msh_peda/documents/web_document/wtx026636.pdf

Ødegaard, M. (2003) Dramatic science. A critical review of drama in science education. *International Journal of Science Education*, 39(1), pp. 75–101

Parkinson, R. (2011) *Storytelling and Imagination: Beyond Basic Literacy, 8–14*. New York: Abingdon

Rollnick, M., Jones, B., Perold, H. and Bahrc, M.A. (1998) Puppets and comics in primary science: the development and evaluation of a pilot multimedia package. *International Journal of Science Education*, 20(5), pp. 533–50

San Souci, R.D. (2010) *Sootface. An Ojibwa Cinderella Story*. Logan: Perfection Learning Corporation

Simon, S., Naylor, S., Keogh, B., Maloney, J. and Downing, B. (2008) Puppets promoting engagement and talk in science. *International Journal of Science Education*, 30(9), pp. 1229–48

Steptoe, J. (1987) *Mufaro's Beautiful Daughter. An African Tale*. New York: Lothrop Lee & Shepard

Valkanova, Y. and Watts, M. (2007): Digital story telling in a science classroom: reflective self-learning (RSL) in action. *Early Child Development and Care*, 177: 6–7, 793–807

Watt, (2001) Science and poetry: passion v. prescription in school science? *International Journal of Science Education*, 23 (2) pp. 197–208

CHAPTER 10

SUSTAINABILITY AND PRIMARY SCIENCE

Chapter aims

By the end of this chapter, you should be able to:

- Introduce some ideas around the concept of education for sustainability
- Provide a framework approach to teaching some of these ideas in science
- Provide some ideas for developing your own ideas and approaches

---

SCIENCE, SUSTAINABILITY AND THE 2014 NATIONAL CURRICULUM FOR ENGLAND

In 2000 the National Curriculum Handbook made 29 references to sustainability. The 2008 Primary National Curriculum made 17 references to it. In 2013, despite protestations and petitions at the time, sustainability was removed in terms of direct reference from Key Stages 1 and 2 of the 2014 National Curriculum for England (DfE, 2013).

Given that one objective was to reduce the curriculum to detail the 'essential knowledge' in the prescribed subjects, the absence of 'sustainability' indicates that the government in 2013 at least does not recognize it as essential. The concern of course, is that the perceived fall in the priority that sustainability has been afforded may stall the significant progress that has been made. However, this need not be the case. Additionally, the rationale for reducing the content of the National Curriculum was to make sure that it would 'not absorb the overwhelming majority of teaching time in schools'. This in turn would allow individual schools a certain degree of freedom to develop their own curricula and additional programmes of study and to develop approaches to learning that would be complimentary to these.

Its presence in primary education settings will now depend much more on the commitment of individual staff and staff teams to design and develop opportunities for its inclusion, rather than the statutory insistence of government. Design often requires some degree of creative thinking and recognizing appropriate points where some of the basic concepts of care for the environment may be included. The teaching of primary science affords significant opportunities for this.

MOTIVATION IN A TIME OF CRISIS

If you need any motivation for thinking about including aspects of environmental and sustainability education you may want to just consider further some of the issues that were mentioned in Chapter 1 when we talked about how we live in a time of science.

> It was the best of times, it was the worst of times, it was the age of wisdom, it was the age of foolishness, it was the epoch of belief, it was the epoch of incredulity, it was the season of Light, it was the season of Darkness, it was the spring of hope, it was the winter of despair.

In this quote from *A Tale of Two Cities*, Charles Dickens famously addressed the paradoxical characteristics of periods of revolution. Although addressing the political and social upheavals of the French Revolution, how far can we apply these sentiments to the technological and scientific revolution that we are presently experiencing? Despite the undoubted positives of modern life, we have to ask at what cost has this come?

Table 10.1 shows a series of graphs for a number of environmental indicators. There is a large amount of data displayed but you don't have to look too closely at the graphs just to get an idea of the direction in which the trend is moving; all these indicators suggest rapid increase. Some are positive and indicate economic improvement, but the environmental guides suggest things are getting worse across a wide range of parameters. Not only that, but many seem to be getting worse ever more rapidly.

David Orr (1994) famously wrote about 'The Problem of Education' over 20 years ago, pointing out that given the worsening state of the planet we still educate our children while studiously ignoring a growing environmental crisis. Subsequently we now have significant, extensive and irrefutable evidence warning of the declining state of the planet (Stern, 2006; IPCC, 2013) and the need to foster greater sustainability is an avowed international educational aim. The last ten years in fact has been the UN Decade for Education for Sustainability. Certainly there have been really impressive and successful sustainability educational initiatives in the UK and the primary sector in particular has really come to embrace sustainability

Table 10.1 These graphs and representations of them have become known collectively as the 'Great Acceleration'. More are available at: http://www.igbp.net/4.1b8ae20512db692f2a680001630.html

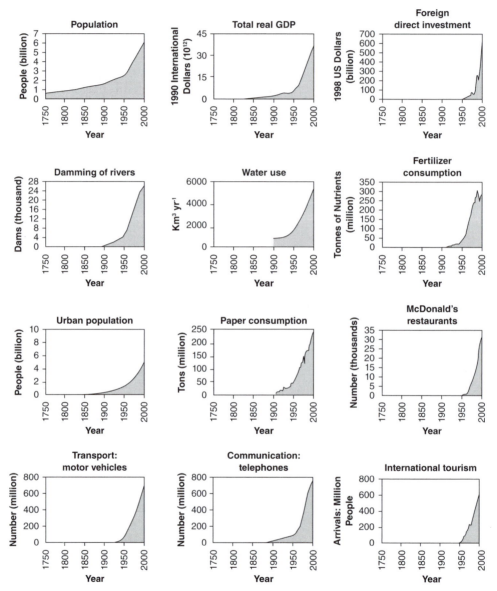

They were produced from Steffen et al. (2004) *Global Change and the Earth System: A Planet Under Pressure (IGBP)*. Springer-Verlag: Berlin, Heidelberg, New York

issues. Critics of environmental and sustainability education are however likely to suggest that progress remains too slow (Saylan and Bloomstein 2011).

However complex the issues of sustainability are, the need to address them and the ways that we explore, explain and respond to them should interest anyone involved in teaching children in general and in particular anyone interested in teaching science to children.

THINKING ABOUT THE FUTURE

One of the great problems of teaching today is that we are trying to prepare children for a future that is uncertain. Beyond the certain knowledge that the future is going to be different, we don't really know in what ways.

In 2001, Headley Beare wrote an introductory chapter to the book *The Future School* that concerned a five-year-old called Angelica. It started:

> Hello I am Angelica I am 5 years old. I really don't know much of a past. In fact, I am the future! … My world is already very different from the one you have grown up in.

The chapter goes onto describe the changes that will take place throughout Angelica's life. You can perhaps imagine the changes in the world that a child who will grow up in the twenty-first century, and whose own children will know the twenty-second century, will see. At the conclusion of an extensive set of future predictions as to the nature of the future, it poses these challenging questions:

> So, do you know what to teach me? Do you know what I need to learn? And do you know how to teach me? Are you confident that you can design a curriculum which will equip me to live in my world.

> My name is Angelica. I am 5 years old. And I am sitting in one of your classrooms today. (Beare, 2001)

Thinking about the future is really very difficult because we live in uncertain times, but how we do see the future is vital in education, for the simple reason that we are teaching the people who will be living in it? One aspect of the future must be an understanding of issues relating to sustainability and resilience. Children in your class will need a skills set that will allow them to live in a very different world from today. To give precise answers to Angelica's questions is difficult (though interesting to consider). However, something of an answer was written even before the question was asked when author and futurist Alvin Toffler wrote:

> In times of change learners inherit the earth; while the learned find themselves beautifully equipped to deal with a world that no longer exists.

It may be the sense of wonder about the world that scientist and conservationist Rachel Carson saw in children that ultimately promotes not only a desire to learn, but also a desire to continue to learn. As teachers we have this task and perhaps in science we have the means.

WHAT IS SUSTAINABILITY AND HOW DO WE EDUCATE FOR IT?

The most widely used definitions of the term 'sustainable development' remain those based closely on that of the Brundtland Report (1987) namely:

> Sustainable development is development that meets the needs of the present without compromising the ability of future generations to meet their own needs.

You might have seen this quote, or very similar ones before. You may also be aware of the considerable criticisms it has attracted over the years, particularly in relation to the term 'development'. Despite these issues, it is worth carefully considering, as there are two integral points within the definition that are useful. First, sustainability that clearly deals with meeting 'needs'. These are explained in the report as referring to basic needs. Second, it emphasizes the responsibility we have to reduce the negative impacts that we are having on the world around us.

When developing science-based sessions that take ideas of sustainability as a core aspiration we can use these two ideas as a focus. Teaching science sessions that have components that directly consider (or may provide the basis for extended work on) 'needs' or that relate to people's impact on the environment are part of a science of sustainability.

NEEDS: DEVELOPING IDEAS AND APPROACHES

The idea of what is needed for life can be clearly explained in science sessions. Indeed, the word 'needs' appears several times throughout the Science Programmes of Study (DfE, 2013). At Key Stage 1 for example, children should be introduced to:

- The basic needs of plants and animals.

- The basic needs of animals, including humans for survival (water, food and air).

- How different habitats provide for the basic needs of different kinds of animals and plants and how they depend on each other.

- Asking questions about what things animals need for survival and what humans need to stay healthy; and suggesting ways to find answers to their questions.

- Identifying that animals, including humans, need the right types and amounts of nutrition.

A creative approach to this would be to relate these points to the wider environmental or sustainability considerations. The basic needs of animals include the basic needs of humans, the utilization of our environment may provide those needs, but we should take great care to preserve it. Our needs for health include 'clean' water and 'clean' air. We can consider our food, in terms of where it comes from, how is it grown? In later sessions they could consider the impact of food production and ways of lessening adverse influences on the wider environment.

Indeed, when thinking about basic needs it is not too long before food has to be considered and a popular way of thinking about food is through the idea of 'interconnectivity' (see Activity 10.1) and of course food, not least through the biology of its growth and production, can be an effective way to introduce a whole range of science concepts.

 ## Activity 10.1

Most high-street supermarkets display food produced from all over the world, even common fruit and vegetables come from surprising places. A simple example is that of apples, as only just over 30 per cent of apples sold in the UK are produced in the UK. Another 30 per cent plus comes from EU countries such as France and Italy, but the other 30 per cent (approx.) comes from such diverse locations as New Zealand and Brazil (DEFRA, 2012).

One commonly used method to stress this to children is the so-called 'apple meditation' first suggested by the Centre for Eco-literacy in California (USA) where children are given an apple and asked to think about the journey that the apple had been on. Who picked it, who packed it, who transported it, even who planted the original tree? The story is long and adventurous, but stresses the distances involved. When the child tastes the apple, stories of the sunshine that the apple has stored can be told alongside questions such as where did the water in the apple juice come from? Often imported apples are hybrids and growing on from the seed therefore is not an option, but planting an apple tree and measuring its height against the children's in a 'growth race' not only helps them connect with food, but can provide some really interesting data to plot over time at intervals across the year (or years if done with an early years group).

A whole range of contemplative, creative and hands-on activities relating to food and the environment are available at the Centre for Eco-literacy website at http://www.ecoliteracy.org/

In fact, at Key Stage 1 of the 2014 National Curriculum (DfE, 2013) there is a significant component of ecological education. This not only deals with the observation of plants and animals but also states that children should be 'beginning to notice patterns and relationships'. Understanding ecological relationships and seeing ourselves as part of the natural world is an essential component of environmental education and the promotion of sustainability. Not only is it a key part of the National Curriculum, it should be a key part in all aspects of our work if we are really interested in preparing children for a secure and sustainable future.

Food, water, and clean air are also all themes that can be developed for the 'needs' part of the so-called Brundtland definition, but what of the limits to our impact?

IMPACT ON THE ENVIRONMENT AND INTERCONNECTIONS

Basic ecology and ecological principles have a significant role at Key Stage 1 and 2. This is advantageous for us when helping children to make connections. Ecology is, after all, primarily the study of relationships.

> The principal focus of science teaching in lower key stage 2 is to enable pupils to broaden their scientific view of the world around them. They should do this through exploring, talking about, testing and developing ideas about everyday phenomena and the relationships between living things and familiar environments, and by beginning to develop their ideas about functions, relationships and interactions. (DfE, 2013)

In fact it is not so much understanding relationships that is essential, but rather the inter-relationships that are key here. Put succinctly by John Muir when he said 'Everything is downstream to everything else'. Another helpful framework when considering impacts on the environment are Commoner's 'Four Laws of Ecology'. These are given below:

 Time for reflection 10.1

Read through the following so-called Laws.
  Commoner's 4 Laws of Ecology

1. Everything is connected to everything else.
2. Everything must go somewhere. Nothing disappears. There is no 'waste' in nature and there is no 'away' to which things can be thrown.
3. Nature knows best. Humankind has fashioned technology to improve upon nature, but such change in a natural system is, says Commoner, 'likely to be detrimental to that system'.
4. There is no such thing as a free lunch / Nothing comes from nothing. Exploitation of nature will inevitably involve the conversion of resources from useful to useless forms.

  For primary science the first two laws are probably most appropriate. Does your planned curriculum address these? How might you demonstrate that the first two laws relate to human activity? Is this reflected in your planned curriculum?

The first two of Commoner's Laws at least provide a good starting point to base sessions on or around the interconnected nature of ecology. It would be a missed opportunity if at some point ideas of human influence were not at least discussed. For sustainability education, the idea of our actions having inevitable implications elsewhere in the environment is vitally important. It is one of the key concepts that children will need to take with them into the future.

EXAMPLE-BASED APPROACHES

The WWF resource publication *Linking Thinking* (2005) is a useful starting place to help teachers think about how we can think and develop ways that help us understand the interconnected nature of the world around us.

One interesting activity that is provided is the simple picture of a tree, with the question, 'What is this?' This is intriguing as although your initial response may be 'It's a tree' you are asked to consider what else could it be? This is where children's creativity and imagination can be employed in all sorts of ways.

- It's a home – for who?
- It's a food source – for who?
- It's the tip of the iceberg
- It's a city
- It's a climbing frame
- It's an oxygen factory

The value of the tree is now seen as something beyond the individual organism. It is not only seen as a central part of a food web, but as a habitat in itself, an essential part of an ecosystem. A study of the tree through close observation, will reveal all sorts of ecological science principles, but may also promote a sense and understanding of the importance of interconnectivity with and within the environment. Developing science skills such as observation and recording are perhaps somewhat redundant without thinking carefully about what has been seen and making links and connections to other ideas. Making connections is in fact as important to scientific enquiry as it is to issues of sustainability. Far from being opposed, they are really complimentary.

The most popular way of thinking about sustainability and introducing it into the classroom curriculum is through the simple use of drawing comparisons and parallels to other processes or effects. For example, when children are looking at the basic needs of plants, it will become apparent that plants will take up water from the soil and will also lose water to the air and that they grow by taking up nutrients from the soil, but return them to the soil when they rot down and decompose. This of course clearly demonstrates that the recycling of materials (nutrients and water) is an essential characteristic of the natural environment but it may also provide a valuable opportunity to mention the practical problem of 'recycling' of waste materials produced by us.

A session on recycling need not move away from a science perspective. Activities relating to waste may involve sorting waste materials (the materials are always clean for obvious reasons) and as the topic of magnetism is a requirement in Year 3 of the national curriculum, magnets may be actively employed in the classroom to help sort different materials. Even if it is only separating paper clips from sand, it introduces the idea of recycling being a feature of the human environment.

Materials that may compost can be added to a compost bin (composting makes an excellent study in its own right, particularly in terms of volume reduction, heat generation, habitats for soil fauna, soil production). Other waste materials may be re-used and recycled having been identified and actually utilized.

Materials can be reused by producing pencil holders from empty plastic bottles, art mobiles, flower pots, bracelets and so on. Such activities are both imaginative and creative, but perhaps we need to tread lightly here, as there are only so many pencil holders that you can make and art mobiles will hang for a while (usually collecting dust) and then what do you do with them? We run the risk of recycling rubbish into rubbish if we are not careful.

Care also needs to be taken with the use of case examples of problems or issues. At a primary level we need to avoid the promotion of what amounts to a 'science of doom'. What we actually want is a science of hope and possibility. Complex socio-scientific issues such as pollution or conservation may be appropriate for older children, however we can still promote a sense of environmental stewardship in younger children through the promotion of so called 'ecological thinking' and this can start at a very early age.

Ecological thinking is concerned with the interrelationships between things, after all ecology is the study of relationships and concepts such as food webs and ecosystems are fundamental to it. We can see ourselves as being in a complex economic, environmental and social web of relationships.

Other 'interconnected' approaches do tend to involve food, as this can be an entrée not only into the geography of food production, but also into the science of growing food. A school garden (or a few grow bags, or pots) is probably one of the greatest single teaching resources in primary science in terms of potential for science teaching. There is not enough room in this chapter to discuss in full the activities relating to science that one could carry out in such an environment, but their importance just as a habitat for insects and earthworms shouldn't be underestimated. From simple bug hunts, to the nature of soils, to composting, growing plants and even food, such outdoor spaces are fertile, outside laboratories, so-called Green Lab. They should be treated as such.

One further and important aspect of such areas however is that they also afford a direct physical contact for children and the natural world. They allow children a sensory experience and this in itself is an increasingly important component of sustainability education.

One further aspect is using the work of scientists to explore science ideas. The National Curriculum names some in the guidance sections, but for a less European, more gender-balanced and environmental approach, the work of scientists such as Rachel Carson, Vandana Shiva and Jane Goodall could prove to be an interesting insight, not only to the practical work of these scientists, but may allow the opportunity to show that scientists do care passionately about the environment.

GOING FURTHER, GOING DEEPER

One characteristic of most ecological science at least is its need to be taught outside. Although not explicit in talking about teaching science outside, the National Curriculum at Key Stages 1 and 2 does talk a good deal of providing 'experience' of observation and that children should 'experience different types of scientific enquiry, including practical activities'. Given that field work forms the basis of much practical science, teaching at least part of the science curriculum in the natural environment should be seen as essential (a point we will return to in the next chapter). Ideas relating to teaching science outside are addressed elsewhere in this book, however, it is worth noting here that there is an increasing emphasis on learning outside the classroom. This is due to a wide range of influences which are discussed in Chapter 11 but one of these is the different type of pedagogical approaches that such different environments provide.

Carrying out science activities outdoors is not only a generally enjoyable experience for children, but also affords opportunities for so called 'emergent environmentalism' (Palmer, 1998) in other words the experience has wider and potentially more profound learning outcomes. Certainly the outdoors provides opportunity for activities that we strongly associate with science. Exploring, observing and investigating are most evident. We can for example search for mini-beasts and look at the different habitats that we find them in. Children can be genuinely excited and motivated during such activities but equally focused and often fascinated by close observation of behaviour of such creatures. This in turn can lead to science-based discussions or a greater appreciation on the child's part of habitats, food webs and life cycles, which in turn can be further explored. Of course, allied to these activities there are more learning outcomes, such as working with others, developing observational skills, using and improving communication skills, through verbal or written description or by sketching and drawing.

However, there are other forms of learning that may also take place. Children gain other benefits from contact with animals of any kind. Having first observed they have less trepidation and will often have greater confidence around them. Confidence is important in science as it is promoted by close observation but such close engagement and consideration can also be an emotional experience for children. In science we tend to wince whenever the terms 'emotion' or 'feelings' are mentioned, but actually any person with a science background will tell you that the practice of science is a terrifically emotional roller coaster. To ignore that, particularly when working with children, is really to misunderstand an important (though not much talked about) characteristic of modern science. If we accept that emotional engagement is an important part of science then we open up to a very wide range of different teaching and learning approaches.

Joseph Cornell is the name most closely associated with the development of more 'emotive' outdoor learning strategies. The activities outlined in his highly influential books *Sharing Nature With Children, 1 & 2* (1979 and 1989) set out to help children acquire a deeper appreciation of the natural world through learning that is both sensory and empathetic. These approaches, and variations of them, are widely used in outdoor learning and in environmental education, but have a great deal to contribute to teaching primary science. They are used to highlight certain ecological principles, they use the close observation of nature, they attempt to promote an empathy with living things and ultimately aspire to help children engage more deeply with the natural environment, broadly along the lines of what E.O. Wilson (1984) famously described as *biophilia*, the promotion of a love of nature. That's pretty important in the study of environmental science at least.

Gompertz et al. (2011) describe a variation and combination of these approaches known as 'earthwalk' activities. Once again, some of the language used with these approaches is not normally associated with science. Activities called 'Hug a Tree' with broad outcomes that 'brings us into harmony with our natural surroundings' (Cornell, 1989) would not normally be regarded as part of a schools-based scientific investigation. However, these activities promote very close observation (the basis of much of Key Stage 1, Years 1 and 2 (Department of Education 2013)) but also promote an understanding that observation in science is not only visual but can (and does) involve a range of other senses such as touch, listening, taste, etc. The 'earthwalk' activities and their specific use to science are well detailed by Gompertz et al. (2011).

Furthermore, children are naturally inquisitive; they ask questions based on their own observations. In this sense, they are 'natural' scientists. As teachers we can use this natural propensity for questioning. However, here we do need to help children ask the appropriate questions. At Key Stage 1 throughout Years 1 and 2, statutory requirements for children include the ability to observe closely, the capacity to ask simple questions and to perform simple tests (Department of Education 2013, p. 6). In other words our task as teachers is to help focus the observations, however made and to help children formulate questions (or 'best guess' hypotheses that were discussed in Chapter 6) that they can then think of ways of testing.

Asking questions is the first stage of developing investigative skills that will allow the child to plan and design ways of exploring further.

Of course science and sustainability issues can be easily promoted outdoors and certainly the allied ideas of deeper environmental engagement can be fostered, however, when we talked earlier of the broader aims of sustainability we suggested that changes in behaviour needed to be environmental, social and economic. In other words sustainability is not just about the natural environment, it concerns the whole school.

THE WHOLE SCHOOL APPROACH

The whole school approach to sustainability essentially concerns acting on our concerns for the future. It suggests that schools need to adopt practices that reflect the values that it promotes. In other words putting into practice what they preach. It concerns integrating curriculum, pedagogy and practice with operational aspects such as governance, organization and finance. Therefore, the values and ideas taught are constantly reinforced by the wider practice of the school. Sterling (2001) describes it as '… working to make the educational institution a microcosm of the emerging sustainable society, rather than of the unsustainable society'. Read through Time for Reflection 10.2.

Time for reflection 10.2

Think of a school that you have had recent experience of. How near was it to a whole school approach? Think about the following questions:

- Was any energy utilized by the school produced from alternative sources?
- What attempt was there to conserve heat, light and electricity?
- How did most staff travel to work?
- Were children actively involved in the management of the school?
- How often did/had the school carried out an environmental audit?
- How often did the children work outside?
- How often was 'sustainability' a theme in lessons?
- How would you rate 'sustainability' at the school in terms of curriculum, management, commitment and staff behaviour?

In this way science is not seen as a separate subject, but rather is integrated fully within the curriculum and as such may be tempered, enhanced and contextualized by such an approach.

The WWF and London South Bank University surveyed a number of schools between 1994 and 2004 and concluded that 'knowledge and understanding of sustainable development issues was relatively high, but this was not resulting in people changing their behaviour to make their actions and choices more sustainable' (WWF, 2006).

Further research identified that behavioural change was hindered by fragmented approaches, a lack of participation and school practices that clearly did not follow on from what the children were being taught and the values that were being promoted.

The best way to see how such approaches are realized in schools is through the WWF website on the whole school approach. Here you will find a whole range of CPD resources, case examples and practical suggestions that explore the idea, both theoretically and practically.

http://www.wwf.org.uk/what_we_do/working_with_schools/resources/whole_school_approaches/

David Orr (1994) argues that education has to transform not only the substance and processes of the formal curriculum and the purposes of learning but also how educational institutions and educational buildings work.

However, let's not lose sight of the science here.

CONCLUSION

We began this chapter by talking about how we live 'a time of science' and yet have ended it by talking about relationships, environmental behaviour and even school management.

You may be wondering about this! In our defence it is rather indicative of the whole area of sustainability. In the WWF *Linking Thinking* publication (available at the earlier WWF web address) Stephen Stirling suggests joining two points with a line to demonstrate their relationship. The line would normally be a two-way arrow. He then suggests doing the same with three points and then multiple points. The result is a series of complex relationships not unlike diagrammatic representations of ecosystems and it is this holistic approach to teaching that Education for Sustainability really requires if it is not to become an additional (and detachable) add-on in schools.

Primary science is in an excellent position to promote this, as we are interested in the characteristics of observed phenomena, but equally, if not more interested in relationships. Our integrated ecological approach in science is ahead of the curve in many ways.

We have mentioned a number of times the importance of the natural inclination of children to ask questions. However, we have to ask ourselves as teachers, how sustainable are our behaviours and how sustainable are the practices of the schools we work in.

How contradictory would it be to encourage children to engage with nature if we don't? How hypocritical is it to promote a sense of responsibility for the environment if we don't share it?

At the beginning of this chapter we asked you to consider the profound environmental issues that the world faces. If we are to educate children to navigate these problems and to build a world that is sustainable then good science teaching is vital. Science, for all its faults, has the potential not only to afford a sense of rational problem solving, but a science of sustainability which also allows for perhaps a more affective engagement with the wider world around us and promotes possibilities for the future. At primary level we need to avoid a science of doom, but rather we need to promote a science of wonder and one of hope and one that looks to the future.

FURTHER READING

Davis, J. (2010) (ed.) *Young Children and the Environment. Early Education for Sustainability.* Cambridge University Press: Cambridge
An Australian perspective, but still relevant to developments in England.

WWF (2005) Linking thinking: new perspectives on thinking and learning for sustainability.
A really good, freely available resource to help staff develop ideas around sustainability and is available from http://www.eauc.org.uk/wwf_linking_thinking_new_perspectives_on_thinking_

Some very good online staff development resources are also available at http://www.tes.co.uk/sustainability-whole-school-teaching-resources/ and at http://www.esf.education.ed.ac.uk/
There is further discussion and resources on the Association for Science Education site. Available from http://www.ase.org.uk/resources/scitutors/professional-issues/education-for-sustainable-development/

Further CPD resources are available at http://www.wwf.org.uk/what_we_do/
working_with_schools/resources/whole_school_approaches/

REFERENCES

Beare, H. (2001) *Creating the Future School.* New York: Routledge

Brundtland Report (1987) *Our Common Future. The World Commission on Environment and Development.* Oxford: Oxford University Press

Cornell, J. (1979) *Sharing Nature with Children.* Nevada: Dawn Publications

Cornell, J. (1989) *Sharing Nature with Children II.* Nevada: Dawn Publications

Department for Education (2013) Science programmes of study: Key stages 1 and 2. National curriculum in England. DFE-00182–2013

Department for Environment, Food and Rural Affairs (2012) Statistics at Defra. Available online from https://www.gov.uk/government/organizations/department-for-environment-food-rural-affairs/about/statistics

Gompertz, B., Hincks, J. and Hincks-Knight, R. (2011) Science and technology outside the classroom, in Waite, S. (ed.) *Children Learning Outside the Classroom. From Birth to Eleven.* London: Sage Publications, pp. 94–105

Intergovernmental Panel on Climate Change (2013) Climate Change 2013: The physical science basis. Available from http://www.climatechange2013.org/images/report/WG1AR5_ALL_FINAL.pdf

Orr, D. (1994) *Earth in Mind: On Education, Environment and the Human Prospect.* Washington: Island Press

Palmer, J. (1998) *Environmental Education in the 21st Century: Theory, Practice, Progress and Promise.* London: Routledge

Saylan, C. and Blumstein, D. (2011) *The Failure of Environmental Education (And How We Can Fix It).* Berkeley: University of California Press

Steffen et al. (2004) *Global Change and the Earth System: A Planet Under Pressure (IGBP).* Berlin, Heidelberg, New York: Springer-Verlag

Sterling, S. (2001) *Sustainable Education: Re-visioning Learning and Change.* Totnes: Green Books

Stern, N. (2006). Review on The Economics of Climate Change (pre-publication edition). Executive Summary. London: HM Treasury

Wilson, E.O. (1984) *Biophilia. The Human bond with Other Species.* Cambridge, MA: *Harvard University Press*

WWF (2005) *Linking Thinking: New Perspectives on Thinking and Learning for Sustainability.* Available online from http://www.eauc.org.uk/wwf_linking_thinking_new_perspectives_on_thinking

WWF (2006) Living Planet Report. Available online from http://awsassets.panda.org/downloads/living_planet_report.pdf

CHAPTER 11

TEACHING SCIENCE OUTSIDE THE CLASSROOM

Chapter aims

By the end of this chapter, you should be able to:

- Introduce some of the motivations for promoting science outdoors
- Consider some of the evidence of the benefits of studying science outside the classroom
- Suggest ways of using creative teaching methods to promote effective scientific enquiry

---

INTRODUCTION

We couldn't be inspired with a love of the natural world, we couldn't grow up as fully rounded young people unless we spent time out of doors. Not just an occasional trip tacked on at the end of the summer but integrated properly into every subject that we were learning ... I don't believe that any of us can grow up properly in this country unless we've had the chance to feel and have communicated to us direct the passion for the natural world that the best teachers can bring. I'm so glad that the new national curriculum ... [had] such a firm emphasis of giving children that knowledge, and knowledge they can only really grasp if they are educated out of doors.

(Michael Gove, Secretary of State for Education (January, 2014))

For those interested in the promotion and implementation of outdoor learning, such comments from the Secretary of State for Education can certainly be seen as a positive affirmation. In the 2014 National Curriculum (DfE 2013) the 'firm emphasis' that is referred to only really begins to appear beyond primary Key Stages 1 and 2 for until then the only direct references made to outdoor education are in relation to the physical education programme. However, at this point it is worth remembering that the 'slimmed down' 2014 National Curriculum is now seen as the guideline for essential knowledge rather than its more prescriptive precursor. This provides a significant opportunity for teachers and for schools to develop their own approaches and methods for delivering the statutory outcomes in what the National Association for Environmental Education has called 'one of the greatest opportunities for truly inspirational education … Learning outside the classroom provides a dazzling opportunity to help contextualize the new National Curriculum at both primary and secondary levels, wrapping real world meaning around dreary lists, and making learning more memorable and inspirational' (NAEE, 2012).

If you have been in teaching for some time you may find the term 'opportunity' something of a well worn euphemism for 'more work'. Taking children outside can sometimes undoubtedly be troublesome, occasionally even the simple logistics of moving a group of children can prove problematic. This combined with the varied issues (time, cost, risk assessment) that tend to rise up before, during and after trips can sometimes be seen as simply too much hassle.

So, the first question must therefore be, why bother?

Time for reflection 11.1

Read through the following:

In September 2012, a global meeting of conservation leaders worldwide adopted a resolution recognizing the importance of the 'Child's Right to Connect with Nature and to a Healthy Environment'. The International Union for Conservation of Nature (IUCN) resolution called for this to be included within the framework of the United Nations Convention on the Rights of the Child.

In June 2011, the Coalition Government published the Natural Choice, a White Paper that included the recommendation 'to strengthen the connections between people and nature' (Defra, 2011, p. 44).

In 2012 the Natural Environment White Paper (4th Report) stated 'that Defra set a firm target for increasing public engagement with nature, such as the percentage of children of primary school age regularly engaging in nature activities'.

Children spend so little time outdoors that they are unfamiliar with some of our commonest wild creatures. According to a National Trust survey, one in three could not identify a magpie; half could not tell the difference between a bee and a wasp; yet nine out of ten could recognize a Dalek. (Moss, 2012)

Learning outside is a proposed right of the child. The government has genuine concerns about connecting people and nature as do academics.

Reflect on your own motivation for using, or not using the outdoors.

GOING OUT TO THE INDOORS

Before going further, it is important to point out how there are different meanings to learning outside the classroom. School trips are still common, although increasingly perhaps subject to financial pressure. Such trips out, commonly to zoos, aquaria, museums or science centres, are significant events. They also provide important and varied learning experiences for the children. Careful planning in relation to timings relative to the curriculum and working closely with the receiving institutions may enhance these visits significantly. Often such institutions have education teams, pre-prepared resources and planned activities that can be both generic or bespoke. They are undoubtedly valuable and worthwhile, however, outdoor learning is just that. It may involve as much planning and resource development, but provides a very different set of learning opportunities and therefore requires a different set of learning approaches.

WHY OUTDOOR SCIENCE LEARNING TODAY?

Broader considerations

Ideas relating to the importance of children learning outside are not new and have a provenance that includes writers such as Rousseau, Montessori and Kolb among many others. However, in the contemporary context there is a growing concern as today children, in the UK at least, now appear to spend significantly less time outdoors outside school hours than previous generations and as a result, their direct experience of their environment and the wide benefits that such contact seemingly provides is much reduced.

It is probably a truism to say that our childhood world was very different from the one our parents knew as children. Every generation seems to know a singular childhood world and on that basis change seems natural, as it is inevitable. However, perhaps it is the pace of change, particularly in technology, that seems disconcerting. The digital recreational choices children have available to them are as legion as they are seemingly enjoyably addictive. For those of us interested in science and technology of course, we can admire the astonishing technologies that have come together to produce these machines and the impressively rapid improvement in graphics and sound quality that are their hallmark. As teachers however, we may be a little uneasy about the attraction of home entertainment. Certainly, over the last few years statistics have begun to emerge relating to children's play patterns. For those who promote outdoor play (and learning) they make poor reading. Sigman (2012) estimated that in the UK by the age of 10 the average child has access to five screens; that children in the UK spend more time in front of screens than they do at school and this in turn has led to growing concern, not only about the changing nature of play, impact on sleep patterns, exercise and attention span, but that children are simply not going outside anymore.

For some time this trend has been identified as also relating to the dissatisfaction with, or simple lack of, appropriate outdoor play areas (Valentine and McKendrick 1997) and from increasing parental concern over children being potentially at risk if they are outside alone and unsupervised. No matter how much reassurance one can offer in terms of the very low risk, parents are increasingly reticent to let their children play outside.

The author Tim Gill likens the loss of children playing unsupervised in parks and green spaces to a human equivalent of Rachel Carson's *Silent Spring*. The loss of young children from public spaces is like the loss of songbirds. The future is even more worrying for as Sigman (2012) points out, children today, by the time they reach the age of 80 years, will have spent 17.6 years, nearly a quarter of their lives, in front of screens.

The suggested general advantages of outdoor learning to children are overwhelming and as such are perhaps too numerous to consider in detail when the focus of this is on using the outdoors for learning science specifically. However, in brief, the learning advantages that outdoor settings provide for primary aged children are well reviewed by Waite (2011) and the broad benefits for physical health and social development are detailed in Every Child Outdoors (RSPB, 2010). The benefits of the outdoors in relation to behaviour and mental well-being are also extensively reviewed by Bird (2007) and Bowler et al. (2010).

Even a cursory glance through the published literature shows broad and sometimes unqualified agreement, that outdoor learning is a good thing. Indeed, even the Office of Standards in Education (Ofsted) in 2008 published a report that found overwhelming evidence that outdoor learning not only contributes significantly to raising standards but also enhances the quality and depth of learning. By 2010 Ofsted wanted to see through the school inspection framework 'substantial opportunities for children to learn outside the classroom' and that learning outside provides for an 'enjoyable and enriching education' (Ofsted, 2010).

In a rare convergence of agreement, the Secretary of State for Education, Ofsted and health and educational researchers agree on the significant advantages of outdoor learning. You should not need much more convincing for the overall advantages, but what of science teaching?

EDUCATIONAL ADVANTAGES OF LEARNING SCIENCE OUTSIDE

In 2010 Ofsted suggested that learning outside adds something to the learning experience and that outdoor learning is generally enjoyable. Improving the enjoyment of children learning may be reason enough, but for the teaching of science there are other important elements to consider. For example, imagine that you were carrying out a class and that somehow you could throw a switch and the walls and ceiling of the room would withdraw leaving you effectively outside. Would you continue to teach the same activity that you had originally started, or would you adapt your approach to take into account the new learning opportunities that were now presented to you?

The question here is how does teaching science vary between indoor locations and outdoor settings? Probably the most obvious characteristic is lack of physical confinement and the opportunity to move and to explore. There are parallels here with learning opportunities. Science-based observations are equally unbounded in outside settings. Children can clearly see things in context, the habitats of insects and arthropods, orientation of flowers relative to light and wind direction. These brief examples (more become apparent in the field) show not only how children can be encouraged to make the interconnections that were discussed in Chapter 10, but also can begin to be encouraged to think ecologically. To observe at first hand the influence of the physical environment on living things and how living organisms interact with one another, could certainly be an effective way of learning. However, unconfined environments may also provide too much stimulus. So much is going on and there can be so many distractions and so much excitement that getting the children focussed and closely observing what you want them to look at can sometimes present problems.

Here we can learn a good deal from the work of environmental educators such as Joseph Cornell. In *Sharing Nature With Children II*, he proposes and develops an approach to outdoor learning that he calls 'Flow Learning'. It is worth considering in more detail, particularly as one of the great things about the approach is that rather than diminishing the children's excitement at being outside, it exploits and focuses it. When children go out into a playground or a park or any open space, their excitement is such that they often will need to run around and holding them back can be quite a problem. By adopting the Flow Learning approach you actually utilize that excitement.

It is easy in education, where we are surrounded by theories of learning, to lose track of simple truths, one of which is that going outside often feels like an adventure and science is about adventures. Children do not have to go far to experience the excitement of adventure and enquiry, a sense that has a direct lineage to the sense of wonder experienced by Charles Darwin, Mary Leakey or Jane Goodall. The excitement of exploration, no matter how local and on what scale should not be underestimated.

Of course another consideration relates to the nature of scientific enquiry. Science after all concerns the world around us. It asks questions relating to observed patterns and relationships, form and function, space and time. These observations for young children need a context for them to be acknowledged as relevant and teaching science outside can help to provide such a perspective. Earlier we suggested that observing organisms allows them to apply ecological ideas by seeing them happening in the real world. In some ways, ecology and biology lend themselves to the outdoors, however, so do physics and chemistry. Physical science can easily be brought outside and a context provided. For example, going outside on cold, frosty days is an excellent way of noticing the different states of matter in relation to water. Such a short expedition on a cold day would allow so many different learning opportunities. Of course traditionally a good deal of the so called earth sciences lend themselves to outdoor learning. Soil, water and the search for insects and arthropods can be fun and can be easily developed and implemented. This certainly fits in with curriculum content such as life processes and living things. In fact one might even consider if this section is easier to teach outside than in. It takes perhaps a little more thought to develop strategies that help to explain the more physical sciences, such as chemistry and physics, but this can be a highly creative and rewarding exercise.

Ideas and resources for science activities are plentiful on line, but of course there are other advantageous aspects to outdoor science. Not least of these are developing links with organizations in the wider community. Conservation groups such as the Wildlife Trust, or the Woodland Trust are always worth contacting relative to outdoor science, both in terms of potential access to safe locations and for ideas around activities that the children can carry out. There may also be local environmental companies and organizations that would be willing to help and to get involved.

Using the outside as the basis for science work can also allow further parallels to be drawn to how science research is commonly conducted. The children can, in a non-competitive sense, be organized into teams to conduct their investigations. Each team could carry out the same investigation using similar or even different methodologies, particularly useful if the children have designed, or at least helped design these methods. Later they may come together to share their results. This would be an effective way of looking at precision and accuracy and beginning to think about the importance of 'replication' in science. Alternatively each team can take on one part of a wider investigation, building up a picture of a process or habitat. 'Working scientifically' is the phrase used in the National Curriculum and of course teams often carry out science research and progress is made through sharing the results. Increasingly 'working scientifically' implies working in teams and sharing results.

Furthermore, results from some science-based research takes time to gather. Long-term experiments allow data to be built up and can be returned to over the years as the children pass through the school.

 Case example 11.1

At Embercombe near Exeter in Devon a number of outside, science-based activities are offered that combine both the children's imagination and clear science principles. Simple, long-term observations on tree growth were carried out by children planting saplings, much smaller than themselves. Having measured the height of 'their' tree and their own height at the time of planting, the children have returned each year to measure and compare their own growth predictions to what has actually happened.

Further information concerning their work in promoting outdoor science may be found at: http://www.embercombe.co.uk/

THE IMPORTANCE OF THE OUTDOORS IN SCIENCE

In the last few years, outdoor learning has also been increasingly seen as a means of promoting and fostering an emotional connection between children and the natural environment. At times this may seem slightly opposed to the mindset that we often associate with science, namely the rational and the reductionist. However with young children even when teaching science we really should consider the importance of imagination and creativity. They are essential for good science practice. There is no reason at all why such approaches should not be used in science teaching.

The outdoors provides an enormous number of opportunities for visual observation and as important as that is, it also affords a whole range of other sensory experiences. Touch, smell, sound may all be engaged in science work and as such perhaps help to rebalance a visual bias that indoor science tends to promote. Using different senses, beyond the visual to appreciate the environment and such observation (not necessarily visual) is of course a basic skill in science.

 Activity 11.1

There are a range of sensory observation methods that can be used with children in science lessons.

Touch can be used on different tree bark. Can children eventually identify the trees by touch?

Careful listening, even in urban areas, allows birdsong to be heard, direction and even distance to be estimated. How does cupping their ears change things?

Why do flowers smell? Does the smell vary between them?

Can the children identify different fruits from smell and taste?

Try to place these in the context of the science programme of study, particularly as a way of promoting identification.

The outdoors also facilitates creative activities such as drawing and sketching. Again, these are basic skills in science that we should encourage, not only as a means to get accurate depictions of a particular plant, or animal or feature, but also as a mechanism for really close observations. It is from these observations of form, that ideas of function can be discussed and then looked for. At this level of teaching we can really benefit by not differentiating between science and art.

Other outdoor approaches include empathetic games and activities that allow children to experience a so-called 'deeper engagement' with the natural world. For those with a science background, it is easy to baulk at these ideas as having anything much to do with science. However, there is a whole range of concepts and relationships that can be introduced and explored through them.

One further and important point here concerns our responsibilities as teachers and as individuals interested in science and it relates to the opening paragraphs of this chapter. As we discussed, the world is indeed a very different place today, but today's generation of young children in your class will know the late twenty-first century and their children will live in the twenty-second. Today's generation of children will need to face up to challenges that not only threaten the survival of other species, but quite possibly even our own. In other chapters we talk about the science of sustainability and here we perhaps also need to consider that promoting a closer relationship between the outdoors and children is something that may also promote not just a deeper understanding of the world but also a sense of care and stewardship. In the past, science has at times seemingly been held partly or solely responsible for much of the damage that the planet has sustained. Helping children to appreciate the world may well play some part in promoting an environmentally ethical science. 'Working scientifically' is an important part of the new Primary Science Programmes of Study (DfE, 2013) and is described thus:

'Working scientifically' specifies the understanding of the nature, processes and methods of science for each year group.

Teaching about ethics in science is increasingly seen as part of simple science literacy, therefore promoting ethical approaches to even the observation of living things outside, however small, is actually appropriate.

Finally, science is not an indoor activity and it is perhaps a misunderstanding of science and certainly a stereotype that science is an indoor subject. Scientists are just as likely to work outside on occasion as they are inside. If we are to parallel the methodology of science, then we should at least pay some regard to its practice.

At a recent conference concerning digital technologies and teaching, one presentation concerned using 'second life' technologies in teaching and involved a demonstration of how children could navigate around a 'roam anywhere digital world'. The presenter argued that learning took place in a more informal way, with the student being actively encouraged to explore this new world. If they saw a tree in the distance they could simply go up and examine it more closely. This would get them acquainted with the world they were in.

What would be the response if a young child had seen a real tree in the school playground and had wandered out to observe it more closely?

 Time for reflection 11.2

I won't deny I've been engaged in violence, even indulged in it. I've maimed and killed adversaries, and not merely in self-defence. I've exhibited disregard for life, limb and property and savoured every moment. You may not think it to look of me, but I have commanded armies and conquered worlds and though in achieving these things, I've set morality aside. I have no regrets. For though I've led a double life, at least I can say I have lived.

Do not underestimate the power of PlayStation.

The above is part of a monologue (some spoken by young children) from a recent television advert. Given the power of such advertising, it is not surprising that children increasingly play indoors. How far, if at all, do you think that this leads to a disassociation with the natural world?

This is an important point as science is all about exploration, exploring observations, reactions and explanations. Good science questions involve such exploration. No matter how interesting virtual worlds become and how lifelike the impressive graphics appear, digital environments lack the physicality of the outdoors.

A good question for you to ask yourself in terms of your own commitment is how often are you and the children in your class outside in an average week. One thing that is essential is our own reaction to being outside. If we want children to want to be outdoors, then we need to show how much we want to be out there as well. Too often, it is easy to talk about the outside, but to be put off by the time and to some degree, inconvenience of actually taking children out. The more children go outside the better they get and the faster they become at getting prepared. How long would it take your class to get outside?

Being outdoors is in many ways one huge science experience. Science is often described as asking questions about the world around you; well, where better to ask those questions than out in the world?

CONTEMPORARY OUTDOOR LEARNING

Several years ago if you had visited an outdoor education centre the chances were you would have seen tanks of pond water with the associated flora and fauna, collections and findings of natural objects, hand lenses, microscopes, perhaps even simple graphs from experiments that had been carried out. Today, you are as likely to see boxes of blindfolds, flexible mirrors, dressing up clothes and on the walls, pictures and poems drawn or written by the children.

Many general outdoor learning approaches attempt to 'engage' children in the environment and of course there is nothing wrong with this. The preferred teaching methods that are widely used frequently involve creative and inventive sensory activities such as 'earthwalks' and those events allied to 'flow learning' (Cornell, 1989). As we have seen, these are valuable approaches that may be utilized in encouraging children to look more closely at the environment and to use other means of 'observation' beyond the visual.

Likewise, we can also look at employing the creative arts to help children look carefully and to record and think about what they are seeing, or hearing. In an environmental education context, these are methods that try to promote affective learning, in other words they try to elicit behavioural change in children (and adults). Contemporary research in outdoor education has produced a significant literature relating to affective 'engagement' with the environment, some even address methods for 'measuring love of the environment' (Chawla and Cushing (2007); Perrin and Benassi (2009); Duerden and Witt (2010); Ernst and Theimer (2011); Okaty (2012); Callado et al. (2013)).

Indeed, the term '*biophilia*', first used by Wilson (1984) to describe a love of nature, is commonplace in outdoor education and phrases such as 'promoting a love of the environment' and 'immersive' and 'deep engagement' are frequently used with impunity but rarely (if ever) interrogated. Such approaches are no longer on the margins of outdoor or environmental education but rather commonplace in the mainstream.

There is certainly nothing wrong with promoting a love of nature, it is something that as teachers we should aspire to. However, we do perhaps need to tread a little lightly here. Encouraging the use of children's imaginations and promoting empathy when it comes to wildlife is not necessarily a bad thing. However, as positive as we may think the promotion of children's imagination is, it does need to be focussed. We may use these outdoor education techniques to engage children (not that they seem to need it most times) and to introduce and to focus attention, but we also need to clearly framework these techniques in a science-based approach. The methods used may be a creative and effective ways of promoting observation and reflection, even their explanations can be imaginative, but it will lose its value to science teaching if, eventually, it is not tempered by the rational.

CONCLUSION

In writing a chapter about teaching science outside the classroom, in a book about creativity in science, it is hard in some ways to conclude that children's imaginations need at some point to be reined in. However, imaginative involvement in designing experiments and evaluating them remains a vital aspect of 'working scientifically'. Indeed, in 2013 the Ofsted Report into science education found that:

> Invariably, achievement was highest where pupils were involved in planning, carrying out and evaluating investigations that, in some part, they had suggested themselves. (Ofsted, 2013)

Furthermore the outdoors as a medium for teaching science was also highlighted, for where schools:

> embraced outdoor learning and used their outdoor learning areas to teach environmental science; again, these on-site examples allowed pupils to experience science in action, regularly and at first hand. (Ofsted, 2013)

Teaching science outside the classroom provides such a range of effective and exciting learning opportunities. It also provides involvement that hopefully engages children in looking, thinking and most importantly experiencing the world around them.

FURTHER READING

Outdoor Science: A co-ordinated approach to high-quality teaching and learning in fieldwork for science education. ASE and Nuffield. Available from http://www.nuffieldfoundation.org/sites/default/files/files/ase-outdoor-science-report.pdf

This is an interesting report on the importance of outdoor science for effective teaching.

Louv, R. (2010) *Last Child in the Woods: Saving Our Children from Nature-deficit Disorder.* Atlantic Books: London
In this important book Louv argues that childhood and children are put at risk if deprived of outdoor play.

Ideas and resources are plentiful in Beeley, K. (2013) *50 fantastic ideas for Science Outdoors.* Featherstone Education
More resources are available online from the ASE at http://www.ase.org.uk/resources/outdoor-science/
Also, there are resources available from the British Science Association at http://www.britishscienceassociation.org/creststar/outdoors-active
More resources may be found here: http://www.pinterest.com/gusliz/outdoor-science-activities/
Finally, practical ideas can be found in the 'Outdoor Explorer' books by Sandy Green (2013)

REFERENCES

Bird, W. (2007) Natural thinking. A report for the Royal Society for the Protection of Birds, Investigating the links between the natural environment, biodiversity and mental health. [Online] Available at: http://www.rspb.org.uk/Images/naturalthinking_tcm9–161856.pdf

Bowler, D., Buyung-Ali, L., Knight, T. and Pullin, A.S. 2010 The importance of nature for health: is there a specific benefit of contact with green space? CEE review 08–003 (SR40). Environmental Evidence: www.environmentalevidence.org/SR40.html

Chawla, L. and Flanders Cushing, D. (2007) Education for strategic environmental behaviour. *Environmental Education Research*, 13(4), pp. 437–52

Collado, S., Staats. H. and Corraliza, J. (2013) Experiencing nature in children's summer camps: Affective, cognitive and behavioural consequences. *Journal of Environmental Psychology*, 33, pp. 37–44

Cornell, J. (1989) *Sharing Nature with Children II*. Nevada: Dawn Publications

Department of Education (2013) Science programmes of study: Key stages 1 and 2 National Curriculum in England. DFE-00182–2013

Department for Environment, Food and Rural Affairs (2011) The natural choice: securing the value of nature. [Online] Available at: https://www.gov.uk/government/uploads/system/uploads/attachment_data/file/228842/8082.pdf

Department for Environment, Food and Rural Affairs Committee Natural Environment White Paper Fourth Report of Session 2012–13, Volume I. Available online from http://www.publications.parliament.uk/pa/cm201213/cmselect/cmenvfru/492/492.pdf

Duerden, M.D. and Witt, P.A. (2010) The impact of direct and indirect experiences on the development of environmental knowledge, attitudes, and behavior. *Journal of Environmental Psychology*, 30, pp. 379–92

Ernst, J. and Theimer, S. (2011) Evaluating the effects of environmental education programming on connectedness to nature. *Environmental Education Research*, 17(5), pp. 577–98

Gove, M. (2014) Reaching into the outside. 10 future priorities for field studies and outdoor learning providers. Selected sections from the speech by Michael Gove MP, Secretary of State for Education

Moss, S. (2012) Natural Childhood. National Trust UK. [Online] Available at: http://www.nation altrust.org.uk/document-1355766991839/

NAEE (2012) The new National Curriculum offers opportunities for LOtC. [Online] Available at: http://www.naee.org.uk/node/163

Ofsted (2008) Learning outside the classroom. How far should you go? Reference no: 070219 [Online] Available at: http://www.ofsted.gov.uk/resources/learning-outside-classroom

Ofsted (2010) Transforming education outside the classroom: responses from the government and Ofsted to the Sixth Report of the Children, Schools and Families Committee, Session 2009–10. [Online] Available at: http://www.publications.parliament.uk/pa/cm201011/cmse lect/cmeduc/525/52504.htm

Ofsted (2013) Maintaining Curiosity: a survey into science in schools. Reference No: 130135. [Online] Available at: http://www.ofsted.gov.uk/resources/maintaining-curiosity-survey-sci ence-education-schools

Okaty, J. (2012) The effectiveness of outdoor education on environmental learning, appreciation, and activism. FIU electronic theses and dissertations. Paper 791. http://digitalcommons.fiu. edu/etd/791

Perrin, J. and Benassi. V. (2009) The connectedness to nature scale: a measure of emotional con- nection to nature? *Journal of Environmental Psychology*, 29, pp. 434–40

RSPB (2010) Every child outdoors. Children need nature. Nature needs children. [Online] Available at: www.rspb.org.uk/childrenneednature

Sigman, A. (2012) Time for a view on screen time. *Archives of Disease in Childhood*, 97(11), pp. 935–42

Valentine, G. and McKendrick, J. (1997) Children's outdoor play: exploring parental concerns about children's safety and the changing nature of childhood. *Geoforum*, 28(2), pp. 219–35

Waite, S. (2011) (ed.) *Children Learning Outside the Classroom. From Birth to Eleven*. London: Sage

Wilson, E.O. (1984) *Biophilia. The Human Bond with Other Species*. Cambridge, MA: Harvard University Press

CHAPTER 12

THE SCIENCE OF HEALTH AND WELLBEING

Chapter aims

By the end of this chapter, you should be able to:

- Introduce the idea of health being a component part of the environment
- Explore ideas of wellbeing
- Discuss ways of including aspect of wellbeing in the study of primary science

INTRODUCTION

As long ago as 2004, the National Healthy Schools Standard argued that encouraging the health and wellbeing of pupils in schools provided genuine educational benefits. If pupils feel happier and more motivated, this enhances their learning experience and the promotion of social and emotional wellbeing encourages greater inclusion and improves behaviour and attendance (National Healthy Schools Standard, 2004). Subsequently, organizations such the Children's Society (2013), UNICEF (2013) and the National Children's Bureau (2013) have all identified child wellbeing as key social priority. However the Education Act (2011) re-aligned Ofsted's role so that it would no longer pass critical judgement on health and well-being policy and the only reference in the subsequent National Curriculum for England Framework (DfE, 2013) to the term wellbeing is in relation to 'national' wellbeing.

However, the fact that child wellbeing has no formal place in the primary national curriculum (2013) should not relegate its importance at the school level. Indeed,

> We recognize and applaud the important and valued role schools have always played in supporting the wider health and wellbeing of every child in their care. We have every expectation that this vital role will continue as teachers recognize the need to deal with individual circumstances which can block a child's readiness to learn and their ability to succeed. (Department for Education (2010) The Importance of Teaching White Paper)

Again, it is worth remembering that the 2014 curriculum now stands as an outline framework. The priorities and emphasis on issues such as wellbeing are now the responsibility of schools. The position of ideas pertaining to wellbeing within the taught curriculum is therefore one of design and the science programme of study may provide opportunities for its inclusion.

In contrast to wellbeing, a cursory glance through the National Curriculum for England (2013) demonstrates that 'health' is now strongly associated with the science programme of study in Years 2, 3 and 6. There are some appropriate references to health in the physical education programme. However, the emphasis is now on the science programme to explore concepts of health, both in terms of environmental and human health. Given that health and wellbeing are often quite difficult to separate, the science programme of study may therefore provide a coherent, intriguing and important opportunity to explore both.

 Time for reflection 12.1

These are statements taken from the National Curriculum for England (2013) for the Science programme of study.

- All living things have certain characteristics that are essential for keeping them alive and healthy.
- Asking questions about what humans need to stay healthy and suggesting ways to find answers to their questions.
- They might research different food groups and how they keep us healthy and design meals based on what they find out.
- Pupils should learn how to keep their bodies healthy and how their bodies might be damaged – including how some drugs and other substances can be harmful to the human body.
- Pupils might work scientifically by; exploring the work of scientists and scientific research about the relationship between diet, exercise, drugs, lifestyle and health.

Science has a predominant role in the promotion of health in the National Curriculum. Look at the extracts above and consider the opportunities that this provides for integrating science across other areas of the curriculum.

CHILD HEALTH ISSUES

2012 was a memorable year for sport in the UK. London hosted both the summer Olympics and Paralympics in which Great Britain won rafts of medals, but there were also notable successes in football, cricket, golf, cycling, even tennis. The UK, from the point of view of elite sport at least, presented a national image of health, fitness and vitality.

Of course that is only part of the picture and subsequent data from a range of sources dealing with children's health and wellbeing, in particular, suggests a different trend. For example, Public Health England in 2013 suggested that 18.9 per cent of children in Year 6 (aged 10–11) were obese and a further 14.4 per cent were overweight. For children in Reception (aged 4–5), 9.3 per cent were obese and another 13.0 per cent were overweight. As the report concludes, these data suggest that over a third of 10–11-year-olds and a fifth of 4–5-year-olds are either overweight or obese. Indeed, the UK has one of the highest child obesity rates in Europe (Public Health England, 2013).

The publication of these data has resulted in the use of somewhat dramatic terms such as 'the obesity epidemic' and 'Generation XXL'. While it is important to bear in mind that, as the data suggest, the majority of children are not overweight but it is still a worrying trend.

While complex geographic, economic and social parameters appear to influence the distribution of child obesity, two primary drivers in otherwise healthy children are the combination of poor diet and lifestyle, with the latter particularly relating to lack of sufficient exercise. Before looking at ways in which the science curriculum can address some of these issues, it is important, now that the decision for curriculum design and emphasis is schools based, to consider wider aspects of child health in learning contexts.

While research is limited in relation to child body weight and academic performance there is some evidence linking childhood obesity with an adverse impact on the child's cognitive development. There is also evidence that suggests that children who are overweight are more likely to have higher rates of absenteeism and increased visits to hospital. Further work also identifies a link to health problems, such as a higher incidence of heart disease in later life.

The literature does however, clearly establish a relationship between physical activity and academic performance.

Getting children to be active, particularly outside, has undoubted advantages and science can provide a good focus. However, before we consider some of the practical applications, there is one other aspect to health that we need to consider.

HEALTH AND BEHAVIOURAL ISSUES

There is now a substantial body of research evidence that supports the idea that children's behaviour generally as well as behavioural disorders, such as Attention Deficit Hyperactivity Disorder (ADHD), are improved when children are involved in activities outdoors. There is a 30 per cent improvement the symptoms of ADHD if those activities are in a green space, rather than an urban site or playground. However, any outdoor activity appears to show an improvement when compared to indoor activities is a significant issue affecting up 10 per cent of school children. Indeed,

> Children increase their physical activity levels when outdoors and are attracted to nature ... All children with ADHD may benefit from more time in contact with nature ... (Bird, 2007)

There is a significant relationship between natural environments and low levels of ADHD symptoms (Kuo and Taylor, 2004). An earlier study in 2001 evaluated parents' perceptions of their child's ADHD symptoms in 'green', 'ambiguous' and 'not green' settings, and found that 85 per cent of parents rated 'green' settings as the conditions in which their child's ADHD symptoms were less severe (Taylor et al., 2001).

Teaching outdoors, appears to improve children's behaviour generally and for those with behavioural disorders in particular, it provides the opportunity for the children to exercise, or at least be less sedentary and it can provide the basis for 'hands-on' active learning in science (see Chapter 11).

HEALTH AND SCIENCE AT KEY STAGES 1 AND 2

When considering a multifaceted subject such as health, at times the divide between people and their environment is difficult to distinguish as they are often inter-related or inter-dependent in some way. However, the way we approach studying the world and often the way curricula are organized, we can, without care, produce artificial divides.

Healthy environments and science

The 2013 science programme of study is produced at least, in a way that has separate sections on plants and animals. Too often perhaps, this translates to an approach to delivery rather than a guideline of content.

Healthy environments are those where all aspects, both plant and animal, living and non-living, operate successfully as an interrelated whole. A healthy environment includes healthy plants, healthy animals and healthy people. It is important to breakdown the compartmentalization in teaching science, particularly environmental science and to emphasize that interdependence and the interrelationships between things that this promotes, are the real drivers for environmental health.

In the first instance children should be able to recognize that all living things have requirements for health. In the Year 2 programme of study: 'Living things and their habitats', children will be introduced to basic ecological concepts, exploring habitats and being encouraged to recognize the interdependence of organisms through food chains and food webs. The idea of interdependence is of course an excellent way of introducing the way in which ecosystems adjust and self-regulate, but also how the food web can be easily disrupted and how small human impacts may have profound implications.

Games involving the physical construction of webs when each child takes the role of a plant or animal in that web and then removing, one plant or animal causing the web to collapse are well used, but still enjoyable ways of introducing this idea. Indeed, when it comes to healthy environments many of the activities traditionally used in environmental education are, once again, potentially of great use here and can be used effectively to introduce a range of ecological concepts.

Healthy schools

In the early stages of the programme of study for science, in Years 2 and 3, there is a statutory requirement for children to describe simple food chains, but the guidance notes also suggests that children should be introduced to the idea that all living things have certain characteristic requirements that keep them healthy. From exploring what keeps plants healthy, to what keeps humans healthy is an interesting transition and is explored in the national curriculum. Integrating observations made around plant growth and eventually human health are easier to make if the plants grown are edible. Only small spaces are needed either for the construction of a school vegetable garden, or for the introduction of plant containers.

The educational, recreational and outdoor opportunities that school gardens may afford make them invaluable teaching resources. The learning opportunities and benefits that they present are already well documented (Passy and Waite, 2011). For science teaching at least, some form of growing area should be looked at as an essential resource.

The idea of growing edible plants in school gardens is now well established and there is a wide range of online resources that are freely available. In the UK the Royal Horticultural Society (RHS) runs campaigns to promote school gardening and supports others such as 'Bake Your Lawn'. Here the idea is that children sow $1m^2$ of ground with wheat (the seed can be provided) that they then grow, harvest and mill. With the resulting flour they bake a loaf of bread. There are significant learning opportunities for science (both plant and human) from such an activity that are, of course, further enhanced by the benefits derived from the children being outdoors.

Also school gardens are a good way of developing an integrated environmental approach. Looking at the interdependence of organisms, they provide a source of living organisms for the children to study in science sessions, can tie in parents and the wider community through their construction and maintenance and may simply provide a quiet green space for children and staff.

Of course, much of the children's (and the teachers') day may not be based outside the classroom, but health issues can still be discussed indoors. What are the human requirements for a healthy indoor environment? This is an interesting question and even a research topic for children. Aspects such as light and space are equally important for plants and people. As a professional teacher you should be in a good position to consider what would constitute a healthy classroom.

 Time for reflection 12.2

The healthy classroom

We can teach about the science of health in a classroom, but perhaps we need to consider a more holistic approach that includes the indoor environment. What in your mind would constitute a healthy classroom?

Consider each of these headings in relation to your own class, or one you might be using.

Is the class big enough? Are there sufficient spaces for ease of movement and for activities such as 'circle time'? Are there quiet areas for children to work? Is there sufficient light? Is there sufficient ventilation? Look at the walls. Is there too much 'stuff' on them? Is the room tidy? Are there any plants in the room?

Does it feel like a healthy environment?

A wider approach to a healthy school might include looking at the different way people arrive, whether by walking, cycling (both staff and students) and the science behind how that promotes health. Diet, health and exercise are all important aspects to the science programme of study and the overall approach to these issues from the school reinforces their importance and can provide a range of wider learning opportunities. However, looking more specifically at the nature of human health can also provide a hands-on, participatory approach to science education.

LEARNING ABOUT HUMAN HEALTH SCIENCE

A familiarity with the conditions that promote healthy plant growth may be followed by work on human growth and what we require to remain healthy. By Year 3 the emphasis moves away from the needs of water and food, towards more sophisticated ideas of nutrition.

Nutrition and nutrients are difficult concepts. However, during growth children develop instinctive ideas and beliefs to help them understand the world around them. When trying to teach about health, in relation to nutrition, for example, such preconceived ideas and notions need to be considered. Authors argue that a child's ability to learn about such concepts improves if educational materials are specifically designed to take into account children's developing ideas.

One example that they provide relating to nutrition involves the nature of nutrients. The idea is difficult for young children, particularly as children in Key Stage 1 commonly have a view of matter that is continuous. In other words the subdivision of an apple would result in ever smaller pieces of apple, as opposed to the constituent parts. Here Gripshover and Markham (2013) use the fact that young children understand mixtures: recognizing, for example, that water into which sugar has been dissolved still contains sugar, thereby explaining nutrients to the children by analogy thus: 'Nutrients in food are like sugar dissolved in water. You cannot see nutrients just like you cannot see the sugar, but they are there' (Gripshover and Markham, 2013). This approach also allowed the role of blood as a transport mechanism to move nutrients around the body to be explained. Nutrients then can become the basis of identifying similar foods as the basis of the idea of food groups and for healthy eating:

> food contains diverse, invisible nutrients that are extracted during digestion and carried around in the blood. This constitutes quite an achievement and demonstrates that young children can benefit from a curriculum that capitalizes on their developing intuitive theories. (Gripshover and Markham, 2013)

In Year 2 there is a statutory requirement for children to know about different types of food, but only by Year 3 is it suggested that children explore and research different food groups. Again, this is quite a difficult concept as the food groups do contain disparate types of food that would certainly not appear to be related. Eggs and beans in proteins, milk and fish in fats, fruit and bread in fibre may seem difficult to understand why they are in the same groups. Exploring the reasons in simple forms, such as eggs and beans being early stages of growth, may go some way to helping explain.

Certainly the development (and consumption) of healthy menus based on the science of nutritional requirements can be productive and again there are a number of helpful resources online to help develop this and these are listed in Further reading at the end of the chapter.

Exercise is the other component of health that can be explored. In the same way that there are different food types, the effect of different exercise types can be explored. Effects of exercise may be studied in relation to pulse rate, with children recording their heart rates, plotting recovery times. Measuring body temperature after exercise not only introduces an important aspect of science, namely, that 'no change' can be really intriguing but can also lead to discussions on how the human body regulates its temperature. This in turn can progress to looking at how other animals regulate theirs.

Physical exercise may very well be within the physical education programme of study, but it can also provide a range of integrated science-based activities.

Naturally, not all science has to involve activity. The characteristics of relaxation are one aspect of health that children can also learn about. What happens to your heart rate when you are calm? Can you reduce your heart rate by making yourself calm? These are intriguing questions that children may benefit from researching.

One final aspect of children's health that is sometimes overlooked concerns sleep. It is recognized that sleep has an important role in the development of the brain (Kelly et al., 2013) and it is therefore important for children to get enough sleep as their bodies grow and mature.

There is also a significant amount of evidence now to suggest sleep also plays an important role in children's day-to-day ability to function. Lack of sleep makes it much harder to concentrate and thereby reduces cognitive ability (Bub et al., 2011).

Increasingly, evidence suggests that an appropriate degree of sleep is just as important for children's development as the previous discussions on healthy eating and exercise.

WHY WELLBEING?

In 2011 a survey asked more than 3,000 children (between 6–12 years of age) across Europe the question, 'How do you imagine the future?' While new technologies were certainly described (flying cars, a particular favourite) the overwhelming response was a future that was at 'peace' and where new technologies would improve our social wellbeing. When the question was extended to, 'What do you hope for the future?', a world at peace was still the primary response, followed by responses alluding to a healthy environment (Young Internet, 2011)

These then are the over-riding future priorities for children, peace, wellbeing and a clean environment. Further concerns are illustrated by a survey on child worry. It suggests that concerns over conflict, isolation, relationships with family and friends and social and environmental issues appear to be among those areas that most concern children (Young Internet, 2011). If peace, relationships, wellbeing and a healthy environment are seen as the most important criteria for the future, science would appear to be well positioned. Making science relevant from what children see directly affects them.

Health and wellbeing are of course linked in many ways, but whereas health generally concerns physical health, wellbeing tends to refer to the less well-defined areas of psychological wellbeing and relates to more elusive concepts such as happiness and contentment. A clear explanation of what is meant by wellbeing is contained in the Children's Society's Good Childhood Report (2013). In the report they point out that there are two approaches, namely those that are subjective self-evaluations of wellbeing (known as 'hedonic') dealing with issues such as how happy or content people feel and those that address personal development and actualization. These ideas owe much to human psychologists such as Maslow and Brunner and are generally known as 'eudaimonic' and refer to psychological wellbeing.

One further and vital aspect of child wellbeing is that of child protection. In 2010, the Department for Education made a key change in replacing 'every child matters' with 'help children achieve more'. At the time of writing, there is a suggestion that child protection policy and the role of teachers may change. However, the ideas of the Every Child Matters agenda remain apposite at present and despite the change in title, for teachers of course, every child does matter and will continue to do so.

In the context of our care for children of course, measures and surveys of illusive concepts such as wellbeing can always be criticized but it was hard to ignore the 2007 UNICEF Report Card 7 that put the UK at the bottom of the child wellbeing league table. By the more recent UNICEF Report 11 (2013) the UK's position had improved but the outcomes of even this latter survey makes difficult reading for anyone in the UK with responsibility for the wellbeing of children. Its findings underline the need to consider aspects of the wellbeing of children in schools and here certain aspects of science teaching, particularly in some of the teaching sessions and environments may provide opportunities for this.

HEDONIC WELLBEING AND SCIENCE

How do you know if you are feeling happy? How do you know if someone else is feeling happy? These are questions that we may use to begin to think about the physical characteristics of feeling happy. Likewise, the opposite questions relating to the physical characteristics of sadness or any emotion is an interesting starting point. Children may be asked to draw the faces of friends pretending to look happy or sad. What emotional characteristics can they recognize through such observation? Data can be collected from simple questions such as 'what things make you happy?' and these can be collated and displayed graphically. Some care needs to be taken when dealing with emotional responses, so it is good to 'act out' the expressions and to use suggested 'what makes you happy' categories. However, the topic of happiness is important and one that we can analyse by working scientifically.

Another area might be environmental preferences. For those who like to be outdoors, what is good about being outside? What are the best points? Fresh air, space, a sense of freedom? What might encourage those who may not like the outside to go out? Again, these ideas can be brought together, perhaps presented and discussed in terms of what we need for our own health. Of course, this may in turn lead onto further sessions on what other animals may need.

Looking at human needs in relation to the environment is one way to get children to consider not only their own physical health, but also the wider implications of how certain environments will promote other less well-defined responses such as making us feel good, less well described perhaps, but no less important an observation, particularly in the context of science.

In fact feelings are an interesting area to explore. In Chapter 11 we talked about the importance of carrying out observations outdoors. We pointed out that scientific observation does not have to be visual. It can be based on any of our senses. For example, how does the smell of cut grass, or chocolate make you feel? How does rain on your face make you feel? There is a simple way to answer the latter question out and that is to go out in the rain!

Observations of changing seasons, spending time looking at the world outside, noticing subtle changes in how trees or other plants may look across the seasons. Children could take pictures of a local tree each month, or monthly pictures of the skyscape over the school. These sorts of activities can be used as the basis of science sessions on plants or seasons, but also allow children some deeper emotional engagement with the environment. That in itself may be an important part of their overall sense of wellbeing.

Furthermore, there is another aspect to such approaches perhaps best summarized by Hodgson and Dyer (2003) when they say in relation to the outdoors and wellbeing:

> Teachers today are under intense pressure to produce academic excellence and there is a very real danger that some of the most important elements in the development of well-balanced individuals are having to be neglected. You have the opportunity to redress the balance. We promise you it's fun for YOU and the children. (Hodgson and Dyer, 2003)

OTHER FORMS OF WELLBEING

Earlier we mentioned aspects of wellbeing that look more to psychology, that are broadly categorized as eudiamonic. These have a broad range of characteristics but address issues such friendships, confidence and self regard. They tend to be related to mental wellbeing and the UK-based organization 'Youngminds' (www.youngminds.org.uk) produce some excellent resources that address these issues in broader ways.

However, there are ways in which science sessions may be of use in developing ideas of friendship, support and compassion. In Chapter 14 we discuss two relevant points, how remarkably physically similar humans are, something that we sometimes forget in celebrating difference, and the evolutionary advantages of compassion and friendship as aspects of fitness for survival. A really important point here is that humans are incredibly social animals. We live in close proximity to each other and aggression (despite what may appear in the news) is actually quite rare. Ideas for working together, caring for one another and having empathy with other human beings, wherever they may be, has an ecological basis and a part of our biological make-up that has made us so successful. This of course may be difficult to demonstrate practically, beyond looking at other social animals, but nevertheless it is an important message and one that is a core principal in human ecology.

FURTHER READING

UNICEF (2007) Report Card 7. Child poverty in perspective. An overview of child well-being in rich countries. [Online] Available at: http://www.unicef.org.uk/Images/Campaigns/Report%20card%20briefing2b.pdf
An interesting report, particularly for how low children in the UK score.

Ipsos Mori (2011) Children's well-being in UK, Sweden and Spain: the role of enequality and materialism. A qualitative study. [Online] Available at: http://www.unicef.org.uk/Latest/Publications/Ipsos-MORI-child-well-being/
Again an interesting report with some interesting discussions and approaches.

Gutman, L.M. and Feinstein, L. (2008) Children's well being in primary school: pupil and school. Wider benefits of learning Research Report No.25 [Online] Available at: http://eprints.ioe.ac.uk/2050/1/Gutman2008Children.pdf

Some still relevant discussions of well-being in primary settings.

A wide range of resources are also available on-line. Some links are provided below:
http://www.crickweb.co.uk/ks2science.html
http://www.teachingideas.co.uk/themes/keepinghealthy/
http://www.educationscotland.gov.uk/learningteachingandassessment/learning
acrossthecurriculum/responsibilityofall/healthandwellbeing/

REFERENCES

Bird, W. (2007) Natural thinking. A report for the Royal Society for the Protection of Birds, investigating the links between the natural environment, biodiversity and mental health. [Online] Available at: http://www.rspb.org.uk/Images/naturalthinking_tcm9–161856.pdf

Bub, K.L., Buckhalt, J.A. and El-Sheikh M. (2011) Children's sleep and cognitive performance: a cross-domain analysis of change over time. *Developmental Psychology*, 47(6), pp. 1504–14

Children's Society (2013) Good childhood report. [Online] Available at: http://www.childrenssociety.org.uk/sites/default/files/tcs/good_childhood_report_2013_final.pdf

Department for Education (2010) The importance of teaching. The Schools White Paper. [Online] Available at: https://www.gov.uk/government/uploads/system/uploads/attachment_data/file/175429/CM-7980.pdf

Department for Education (2013) The National Curriculum in England Framework Document. [Online] Available at: https://www.gov.uk/government/uploads/system/uploads/attachment_data/file/260388/MASTER_final_national_curriculum_11_9_13_2.pdf

Great Britain. Education Act (2011) Chapter 21. [Online] Available at: http://www.legislation.gov.uk/ukpga/2011/21/pdfs/ukpga_20110021_en.pdf

Gripshover, S.J. and Markman, E.M. (2013) Teaching young children a theory of nutrition. Conceptual change and the potential for increased vegetable consumption. *Psychological Science* 24(8), pp. 1541–53

Hodgson, J. and Dyer, A. (2003) *Let Your Children Go Back To Nature*. Milverton, Somerset: Capall Bann Publishing.

Kelly, Y., Kelly, J. and Sacker, A. (2013) Changes in bedtime schedules and behavioral difficulties in 7 year old children. *Pediatrics*, 132(5), pp. 1184–93

Kuo, F.E. and Taylor, A.F. (2004) A potential natural treatment for attention-deficit/hyperactivity disorder: evidence from a national study. *American Journal of Public Health,* 94(9), pp. 1580–86

National Children's Bureau (2013) *Tackling Child Poverty and Promoting Children's Wellbeing: Lessons from Abroad*. London: NCB. [Online] Available at: http://www.ncb.org.uk/media/892335/tackling_child_poverty_1302013_final.pdf

National Healthy School Standard (2004) *Promoting Emotional Wellbeing through the National Healthy School Standard*. Department for Education and Skills. [Online] Available at: http://www.nice.org.uk/niceMedia/documents/promoting_health_wellbeing.pdf

Passy, R. and Waite, S. (2011) School gardens and forest schools, in Waite, S. (ed.) *Children Learning Outside the Classroom From Birth to Eleven*. London: Sage, pp. 162–175

Public Health England (2013) Child obesity. [Online] Available at: http://www.noo.org.uk/NOO_about_obesity/child_obesity

Taylor, A.F., Kuo, F.E. & Sullivan, W.C. (2001) The surprising connection to green play settings. *Environment and Behaviour*, 22(1), pp. 54–77

UNICEF (2013) Report Card 11. [Online] Available at: http://www.unicef.org.uk/Images/Campaigns/FINAL_RC11-ENG-LORES-fnl2.pdf

Young Internet (2011) How do young children imagine the future? [Online] Available at: http://www.goodbeans.com/files/2012/01/Future-Survey-Press-EN.pdf

CHAPTER 13

TEACHING CONTROVERSIAL ISSUES IN SCIENCE

Chapter aims

By the end of this chapter, you should be able to:

- Understand why some issues are controversial in science teaching and how controversial issues present opportunities for teaching and learning

- Have some ideas around the approaches that you might adopt in dealing with some of these issues

- Have the confidence to deal with issues that may be culturally sensitive.

- Appreciate broader learning that can take place through the study of controversial issues in science

- Consider your own influence and position relative to some issues and strategies around 'teacher views'

INTRODUCTION

To an extent there will always be something of a contradiction in teaching, primarily because we are often ridiculously busy. From the day-to-day running around, preparing classes, sorting out the children to the administration preparation for inspections and reviews. Time is not exactly at a premium. With this in mind, it is understandable that we sometimes concentrate on the 'immediate' and perhaps overlook the long-term and deeper aspects of some of our teaching.

The organization of a trip to a zoo or to an aquarium normally means that just seeing the animals or the fish is probably enough. Such visits certainly provide a great deal of material for science teaching before, during and after the event, as well as plenty of cross over into other areas of the curriculum. Possibly it's too much for us to consider the ethics of keeping wild animals in captivity, or perhaps the validity of conservation claims, or whether perhaps you could achieve the same learning outcomes on a school-grounds bug safari hunt.

If you do find the time to sit down and consider the more controversial areas of present day science you may well come up with something of a media-driven list. That list will of course be contextualized by both time and location. For example, in the 1970s, research into assisted fertilization led to the development of in-vitro fertilization (IVF) techniques and these were seen as highly controversial. Press reports of 'test tube babies', giving an entirely false image of the process did not help to placate concerns and in 1985 there was a Parliamentary Bill that proposed to ban the procedure. Yet today IVF is an available assisted fertility method that over 48,000 women went through in 2011 in the UK and although it is still opposed by the Catholic Church it is perhaps not seen as controversial as it once was. That is not to say that this is the case elsewhere and this is an important part of teaching certain areas of science. What may seem uncontroversial in one place would be prohibitively so elsewhere. Furthermore, as the research into fertility treatments has developed, new techniques and new research avenues have opened up. Recently, the UK government gave support to a procedure known as 'mitochondrial transfer' where the mitochondria from a healthy female donor is combined with the nucleus of the mother and sperm of the father to prevent genetic diseases being passed with the result that the embryo (and eventually the child) will contain genes from three people. Some see this as a major step forward in the eradication of certain genetic diseases, though others may see it as a step nearer to so-called 'designer babies'. The point for us to consider here is that new technologies and techniques provide new and very often complex ethical dilemmas and challenges for established value systems.

This is not new of course. In science we have a long history of controversy, from suggesting that the Earth was not at the centre of the universe, to suggesting that the diversity of life on Earth was driven by natural selection. The latter example remains controversial in many parts of the world today, including in some communities in the UK. This poses the question as to what actually constitutes a controversial issue?

How we identify these issues can cause a problem. One was the 2011, NESTA survey of teachers in the US. The survey provided a list of 18 science topic areas and the teachers were requested to specify if they had experienced any pressure from the wider community not to teach about any of the prescribed areas. Of the 275 respondents, nearly half had experienced resistance to teaching about the age of the Earth. Even more, nearly two-thirds, had faced opposition to teaching evolution. These intriguing results underline some of the primary issues relating to the teaching of science. It may be that the theory of evolution appears equivocal in detail to many, as there are different views and perspectives within evolutionary biology that to scientists make it an interesting and fertile area of discussion.

Techniques used in dating the age of the Earth on the other hand, use a suite of refined laboratory methodologies that allow replication and verification. It is difficult to be critical of the results of these methods. Although error is always present, it is difficult to see how these highly refined protocols and endless replication could be so inaccurate that one could scientifically accept that the Earth was only 6,000 years old. Yet it would appear that stating that, based on the results, could be seen as controversial.

This then is the difficult issue. Controversy is contextualized by social and cultural considerations, the stronger the opposition to an idea within a community the more controversial that idea will become, eventually coming to be seen as offensive, seditious and even threatening.

Time for reflection 13.1

Harwood and Hahn (1990) have suggested that controversial issues are those that 'deeply divide a society, that generate conflicting explanations and solutions based on alternative value systems'.

  Think carefully about this statement in relation to science. Now consider the following questions:

- Does a 'society' have to be divided for there to be a controversy over a scientific finding or stance? Can such divisions occur at finer levels of definition, say at community level? If so, what is the most important influence?
- Is science a 'value system'? When they talk of 'alternative value systems' what do they mean?

This is a problem for teachers because, depending on the context, nearly any subject or topic could be seen as controversial or offensive, but as a result we are simply careful as to which books we read or resources we use. However, in science that is considerably more difficult. Science is a method of examining the world that is evidence based. Challenging that evidence is part of the scientific process, which is why we publish our methods (so others may replicate the work) and encourage critical engagement with our results.

In fact, criticality is a key aspect of science. In science, theories and laws are based on evidence, observed, produced or calculated. We interrogate the methods we've used and are always critical of our findings, but eventually the evidence will become quite irrefutable at which point you may have to accept that the world is round. People are of course free to continue to believe that the Earth is flat. Few scientific principles are enforced legally (unlike some religious ones). However, to do so is to simply ignore the overwhelming evidence, rather than to challenge it. One may simply not believe in gravity rather thinking that the surface of the Earth is just slightly sticky. In the same way you may believe that the world is only 6,000 years old and that natural selection is not the explanation for the diversity of life on the planet. When people say they don't believe in evolution they do so by ignoring the prodigious evidence.

Science is often at a disadvantage in that it is often mistakenly perceived as dealing in absolutes and irrefutable facts. Of course science does not. It is quite the opposite; for as we discussed earlier it is more likely to deal in probability. One of the great problems that science faces is its strength. As science is not about certainty, it constantly doubts itself. That's a good thing. The assuredness of certainty is actually intellectually rigid and infertile. Doubt on the other hand, is much more fertile and nutritious in terms of ideas and challenges. It seems curious perhaps to talk of doubt as a real strength, but until you understand how doubt is a core principle of science and see that as its strength, you haven't really 'got' science yet.

One of the key questions then is how do we teach about controversial issues without causing controversy. Is such an approach feasible?

Most strategies need to be fair to science. Too often perhaps we let evolution be described as 'just a theory and there are other explanations'. This is entirely incorrect. We need to remind ourselves here that there are no other overarching scientific explanations for the origin of species beyond natural selection. That is not to say that other explanations cannot be considered, nor are necessarily wrong, but rather every alternative explanation beyond evolution has little or no basis in science and needs to be considered outside of science lessons.

The importance of this has recently been heightened by the inclusion of evolution in the 2014 National Curriculum (DfE, 2013). This document is a tacit example of how evidence supports a theory. Children in Year 6 will learn about the form and formation of fossils. Later they can use these to look at how the form of animals and plants has changed over time. The fossil record, of course, is one of the sources of evidence for evolution. Having recognized change, the next step is to think about how these changes occur. It is not really possible to adequately explain such variation without some consideration of natural selection. Children are to be encouraged to think about how animals have become adapted over time to suit their environments (the example given is an investigation into how the giraffe's neck got longer). It also suggests that children could find out about the work of paleontologists such as Mary Anning and how Wallace and Darwin developed their ideas on evolution. Furthermore, all schools in England must teach evolution as a 'comprehensive and coherent scientific theory'.

State-funded faith schools in England will also have to deliver this component of the primary curriculum so a consideration on how to go about this is timely and apposite.

 Time for reflection 13.2

Consider the following points:

- Has science and the science that you have studied ever really undermined your beliefs, or reinforced them?
- Do you think that your own values may influence your teaching of science?

- Would it be acceptable for a child to leave your class on geology and rocks, despite evidence to the contrary, believing that the Earth is 6,000 years old and that people co-existed with dinosaurs? If not, would you try to persuade them otherwise?

SEEING CONTROVERSIAL ISSUES IN SCIENCE AS AN OPPORTUNITY

Teaching about certain topics can be a source of concern and anxiety and it is entirely understandable to think about simply circumnavigating controversial issues and teaching science as a process using 'safer' topics. However, the National Curriculum in England includes a number of controversial issues (such as evolution and sex education) that need to be taught, so avoidance now may be impossible. It is something as teachers that we have to get used to.

In fact, some would argue that science teaching is actually enhanced by using such issues as it can promote dialogue between the teacher and children and between the children themselves if handled appropriately and can be an interesting way of introducing the uncertainties of the scientific process. Not only that, but a range of other skills relevant to science may also be encouraged.

Before we look at the science skills that may be developed, it is important to remember that more direct teaching styles are not particularly appropriate when it comes to examining topics that may be deemed controversial. Direct instruction on how and what to think has little to do with good science or good education. The teaching approach therefore must be very carefully considered.

For your children to really gain from looking at controversial issues, there must be a type of teaching approach that encourages discussion and expression. However, children will need to acquire the confidence to express their views openly and to be able to do so with security and assuredness that such opinions are part of a wider discussion and that others may not agree. Indeed, using some of the creative approaches discussed in the second half of this book could be instrumental to this. Role play, drama or pictorial art may have much to offer here through role play in debates, or small dramas based around historical controversy, or by using visual representations of different ideas and views on the classroom wall.

In a process that is well described (Harwood, 2006 cited in Oxfam, 2006) each stage of any science investigation has different learning outcomes. However, the study of more contentious issues, such as evolution and natural selection, may provide additional opportunities. The following is not a definitive list of outcomes, but is certainly teaching around which these issues should allow:

- Creative thinking relating to experimental designs to demonstrate adaptation – such a process introduces to the children simple means of reducing error and thinking through how other variables may influence the results.

- Careful observation and noting can be especially important here. Looking carefully at the changes in fossils over time.

- Asking questions that originate from observation and data.

- Children then require reasoning to develop justifications for explanations based on their own evidence and from making inferences from their data.

- Contradictory views allow for an interrogation of the veracity of methods used and the way data was collected.

- Seeing their work in context and in relation to the work of others, such as Darwin or Wallace.

- Finally, it is through the expression of their ideas, in whatever form that may take, verbal, pictorial or diagrammatic, that they learn to discuss and exchange views.

Some of the above are not unique to the teaching of controversial issues and can be achieved through the creative delivery of any part of the curriculum. However, using these issues does provide an opportunity to allow for intriguing discussion and a sense of personal expression that other areas would perhaps struggle to provide.

POINTS FOR PRACTICE

There are a range of approaches open to teaching and exploring contentious issues in science and these methods should also help children develop a range of other relevant and requisite skills. Different topics may require different approaches, some may be best suited for pictorial or diagrammatic work and others may be better suited for discussion. However, when you are thinking about the method to adopt you will also need to consider the broader skills and values that you wish the children to learn or consider. For example you may consider the following:

Group work

The children work in 'research' teams, each child with a specialist role. The teams could even be working on different parts of the same problem and then report back at the conclusion of the session. This allows the children the opportunity of working together, but also evaluating their own results in relation to those of others. They can also see the importance of looking at different types of evidence and how this builds to present a coherent theory. Of course it also allows them to see that not all evidence may be valid, thereby promoting questioning skills.

Visual media

Making a 'research' documentary. Using mobile media to record events and views as a means of looking at different ideas through simulated interviews. The interviews could also be with adults beyond the classroom. Again, the children are thinking about questions and becoming familiar with and confident in questioning.

THE IMPORTANT ROLE OF DISCUSSION

Reporting findings is an important part of science practice but when it comes to discussing suggestions and inferences around potentially controversial issues the teacher's role becomes vital.

Here, a common criterion of any approach is one that promotes balanced views and this is no doubt important and originates from the liberal view that children make their own decisions and that the teacher, given their position of authority in the classroom, could easily influence the children's view. One discussion that invariably takes place is how the teacher's own personal views, values and beliefs should be placed in this type of teaching and there are a variety of positions that you might want to consider taking in any discussion. Any of these approaches can be useful, but as with any teaching style, their effectiveness depends on the topic, the context of the work and the age of the children. Something that is often overlooked, but is probably the most important consideration here is the teacher's discretion and working knowledge of the group's dynamics. Every group is different in a variety of subtle, and not so subtle, ways. The complexity of personalities, friendships, confidence, ability and maturity will often mean that the teacher needs to rely on their own evaluation of what the group can reasonably be expected to cope with. This is a decision, as in all teaching situations, that need not be made in isolation. The guidance and advice of colleagues should always be sought if there are doubts, but the teacher will ultimately need to make the decision.

In terms of the approaches that may be considered, Harwood (cited in Oxfam, 2006) has identified six possible standpoints.

 Activity 13.1

Read through the following approaches. We have provided an advantage and disadvantage to each. Think about these carefully, can you add more?
    The approaches that may be adopted are:

Committed

The teacher will clearly state his or her own views to the children.
    Advantages: It is an open and honest statement and could lead to interesting wider discussions as to why they hold that view.
    Disadvantages: Bias and possible promotion through predisposition to certain ideas and beliefs.

(Continued)

(Continued)

Objective or academic

The teacher provides, as best as possible, an account of as many different perspectives as is reasonably possible, but remains neutral themselves.

Advantages: All things considered and potentially no overt bias.

Disadvantages: Is it possible to consider all views? Indeed, are all equally worthy of consideration? Covert bias is possible through the selection of accounts and emphasis placed on them.

Devil's advocate

The teacher deliberately adopts contrary views for the sake of debate and discussion.

Advantages: It allows all views to be thoroughly tested and questioned.

Disadvantages: Is any true consensus reached? There is a danger of simply promoting children to respond along the lines of 'So what is the answer then?'

Advocate

The teacher adapts the Devil's advocate approach. Once the different views have been discussed they state their own position.

Advantages: How the teacher has come to that decision in itself is an interesting way of introducing to children how methods of evaluation may be influenced by personal beliefs.

Disadvantages: May provide disproportionate validation of the teacher's views as opposed to others, so possible bias again.

Impartial chairperson

Here the pupils provide their own views and the teacher may facilitate a discussion. However the teacher only facilitates the events and does not offer their own views.

Advantages: The group develops skills in articulating their views and presenting an evidence-based argument.

Disadvantages: Takes considerable skill to allow those less articulate to express their views with confidence. Debates can often be won by personality and performance rather than careful consideration.

Declared interest

The teacher states their own view and then all other possible views and interpretations attempting an unbiased presentation.

Advantages: The pupils may be able to interpret and evaluate ideas, knowing that there are different interpretations that may be equally valid.

Disadvantages: Again, care needs to be taken so that the teacher's view is given greater credence than the alternatives.

This is not a definitive list of approaches and we could perhaps add:

Adoptive position

The teacher places himself or herself beyond the dialogue by using certain phrases to identify different positions and views, such as 'If I were a scientist I might say...' or, 'People who disagree with the scientists might think that ...'
Advantages: Objective delivery of varied viewpoints and interpretations.
Disadvantages: It is still the teacher who selects the views and as such still may afford bias.

Of course it is not only the teacher that may adopt contrary positions when it comes to interpretations and issues. Creative pedagogies discussed elsewhere in this book such as role play and drama would be ideally suited.

Presenting a 'balanced' argument is often seen as a reasonable approach, but the trouble is that those with different perspectives will interpret balance differently. Ultimately, bias is very difficult to eradicate and whether it is possible, or even desirable, particularly in a contemporary multi-ethnic society is worth questioning. All of these approaches are good ways for children to really gain from looking at controversial issues and they are all based on a type of teaching approach that encourages discussion and expression. However, children will need to build the confidence to express their views openly and to be able to do so with security and assuredness that such opinions are part of a wider discussion and that others may not agree.

Of course the issue with science is that evidence can be interpreted in different ways. It is easy to misunderstand a science principle, such as the erroneous idea that a vacuum cleaner 'sucks' up a piece of paper, especially if the initial evidence might suggest that it does just that! It is not too difficult to demonstrate that the paper gets pushed into the vacuum (demonstrate the principle using water rather than air) it is much more difficult to demonstrate evolutionary change over time based on observation. Sometimes the changes in the form of a fossil may be due to stages in a creature's life cycle, rather than to any evolutionary process, in that the young may look very different from adults. All of these ideas are open for discussion and as such mirror the scientific world. Scientists of course have the chance to put their ideas forward for discussion and often an academic debate or discourse ensues. Of course during these debates it is the work that is criticized, not the person or team (that is why science papers are written in the third person if you've ever wondered) and it is vitally important that mutual respect and the ground rules of debate are strictly followed. Appropriate group behaviour is an important consideration here, as everyone needs to be sufficiently confident to give his or her ideas. Responses to misbehaviour are as important as letting a disparaging remark go unchallenged could be seen as condoning the sentiment.

Finally, it is important to remember the limitations of science. Science is one way of trying to understand the world around us and however powerful its methodology, it is only one way of trying to understand. One of the key aspects of science (as we saw in Chapter 6) is that we set hypotheses that are clear testable statements, normally taking the form of a prediction, for example, 'The water level will rise if we put some pebbles into the beaker' or 'The water level will rise if we put some sugar cubes in'. From such statements a definitive answer may be derived. These are very simple examples but the principle for all scientific hypotheses remains the same. Questions such as 'Do rocks have emotions?' or 'Does water like salt?' cannot be definitively answered. They can certainly be asked, but they would need to be rewritten for a scientific methodology to be designed to attempt any kind of response. This of course means that science can only answer the right type of question. This is often seen as a problem for science and it is certainly a limiting factor in its application. For some, the answers to the types of questions that science cannot answer may be found elsewhere, sometimes through simple belief.

CONSIDERING WIDER VALUES IN CONTROVERSIAL ISSUES IN SCIENCE

A final characteristic of teaching around controversial issues in science is the opportunity that it affords to promote not only academic skills in articulating ideas and building confidence, but that it also allows us the chance to promote certain values that are important in the practice of science.

Science is often said to aspire to be value free in that it deals objectively with results and evidence. Of course that is not necessarily the case. Science as a methodology values certain characteristics of practice such as accuracy and precision and inversely 'de'values unsubstantiated claims or exaggeration. We also have certain values that influence our ethical practice and those in turn may be shaped by cultural and societal influences. Of course other values in science are the ones placed on it by society and these at times may be contradictory. For example as of June 2013 the Large Hadron Collider at Cern has cost £2.6 billion. If we are concerned with values in science there is probably not a great deal to discuss relating to the research at Cern, but what of the wider ethical considerations of this research? Given the context of the unlikely achievement of the eight UN Millennium Development goals (including the eradication of extreme poverty and hunger) by 2015, what and whose 'values' does the LHC project actually present and represent? When we talk about values in science we need to think about whose values. Contemporary governments will fashionably say they value science, increasingly because of its potential contribution to the economy, others may value it for perceived wider intellectual and academic benefits. The vitally important value relating to science of course is the value that you put on it as a teacher.

Teaching controversial science topics is also an effective way of promoting values with children. Respecting other people's views yet learning how to question them in ways that are productive to both parties is one. In multi-ethnic and multi-faith societies where there are so many different belief and value systems, such an approach is vital. Learning how to take turns in presenting ideas and how to carefully listen to others are not skills exclusive to science, but are part of the critical nature of it, in the same way that teamwork, sharing results and being self-critical and self-doubting are also features of modern science practice.

CONCLUSION

Progress in modern science has been astounding. Progress in biomedical science in particular has been nothing short of revolutionary. For in a little over a hundred years, life expectancies in high-income countries such as the UK have all but doubled. In fact science has provided us with what amounts to a second life. However these new advances not only change our behaviour, but they have challenged the way we see the world. To end as we began, there is nothing new in this. Science has always challenged our worldviews. Sometimes this has been painful in the extreme when it has challenged belief, tradition and convention. Yet this is the nature of science, to question the expected, to defy orthodoxy and to be the instigator of change, however imperceptible that change may be. It is inevitable that at times it will promote controversy, but to avoid this and take the uncontested route in teaching means that whatever it is you teach, it is not science.

FURTHER READING

Troyna, B. and Carrington, B. (1988) (eds) *Children and Controversial Issues: Strategies for the Early and Middle Years.* Lewes: Falmer Press Ltd
Rather dated now, but still a good resource for ideas and approaches.

Oxfam (2006) Teaching controversial issues. Global citizenship guide. [Online] Available at: https://www.oxfam.org.uk/~/media/Files/Education/Teacher%20Support/Free%20Guides/teaching_controversial_issues.ashx
Referenced below as well, this short document is an excellent introduction to the topic and provides good links to other on-line resources.

Oulton, C., Dillon, J. and Grace, M.M. (2004) Reconceptualizing the teaching of controversial issues. *International Journal of Science Education,* 26(4), pp. 411–23
For an overview of science and its contribution to teaching controversial issues.

Wooley, R. (2010) *Tackling Controversial Issues in the Primary School: Facing Life's Challenges with Your Learners.* Routledge: Abingdon
Most resources look at teaching controversial issues in secondary school settings. This is an interesting look at the topic with specific reference to primary education.

REFERENCES

Harwood, A.M. and Hahn, C.L. (1990) Controversial issues in the classroom. [Online] Available at: http://www.ericdigests.org/pre-9218/issues.htm (accessed 09.07.13)
Oxfam (2006) Teaching controversial issues. Global citizenship guide. [Online] Available at: https://www.oxfam.org.uk/~/media/Files/Education/Teacher%20Support/Free%20Guides/teaching_controversial_issues.ashx (Accessed 19.07.13)
Department of Education (2013) Science programmes of study: Key stages 1 and 2 National Curriculum in England. DFE-00182–2013

CHAPTER 14

A SCIENCE OF EQUALITY

Chapter aims

By the end of this chapter, you should be able to:

- Review the issues of equality in relation to science
- Consider the contribution that science can make to achieving greater equality
- Suggest that the practice of good science is the practice of a science of peace and equality

---

INTRODUCTION

> Modern science has vindicated the natural equality of Man
>
> (Benjamin Disraeli in *Sybil, or The Two Nations*)

This chapter deals with equality and diversity. These are issues that have become integral to all sectors of education, not just in the modern primary school, and all teachers and educationalists are, or at least should be, committed to their promotion. In fact such promotion has become a major part of modern social educational thinking and as such has been the subject of much review, research and policy advancement in recent years. As teachers, or trainee teachers, you will certainly recognize this. Indeed the Teachers' Standards that apply to all teachers and define the minimum level of expected professional practice comments that the values of 'individual liberty and mutual respect and tolerance of different faiths and beliefs' should be upheld (DfE, 2011). However, as profound as such ideas and concepts are, how often do we address them when teaching science? Indeed, how many science-based CPD or INSET events have you attended where they have been discussed, let alone been the subject of suggested science activities? These fundamentally important aspects of modern education are seemingly not readily associated with science teaching. This is quite surprising because in fact science and its practice does have a good deal to offer when it comes to thinking about and promoting issues such as equality and diversity in our teaching. The new curriculum in science may also present us with future possibilities.

 Activity 14.1

Read the quotes below and think carefully about your responses to the questions.

Science and art belong to the whole world, and before them vanish the barriers of nationality.

Johann Wolfgang von Goethe

Racism, as we would characterize it today, was explicit in the writings of virtually all the major anthropologists of the first decades of this century, simply because it was the generally accepted world view. The language of the epic tale so often employed…fitted perfectly an imperialistic view of the world, in which Caucasians were the most revered product of a grand evolutionary march to nobility.

Roger Lewin

The enchanting charms of this sublime science reveal only to those who have the courage to go deeply into it. But when a woman, who because of her sex and our prejudices encounters infinitely more obstacles than a man in familiarizing herself with complicated problems, succeeds nevertheless in surmounting these obstacles and penetrating the most obscure parts of them, without doubt she must have the noblest courage, quite extraordinary talents and superior genius.

Carl Friedrich Gauss

- What do these three quotes suggest to you in relation to equality and science?
- Do we teach science in a way that suggests that it is a Western tradition?
- Are we ever in danger of inadvertently perpetuating myths and misconceptions about people through the way in which we teach science?
- Do you agree that certain members of the wider community still have to work harder to succeed in science, or is such discrimination a thing of the past now?

If we are committed to equality of opportunity it really is of great importance that we interrogate our own teaching practices in science to make sure that we are not inadvertently promoting, through implication or otherwise, any tacit forms of discrimination. It is not unusual for schools to dispense with resources that promote racial or gender stereotyping and we should undoubtedly do the same with science resources. However, the problem is with what do we replace them? Try putting the phrase 'famous scientists' into an online bookstore. Now count the number of women, or the non-Western faces, that appear on the front covers. It won't take long. In a six volume series of conversations with famous scientists published in the twenty-first century the front covers show the 218 participants (Candid Science Series I-VI). Only 17 are woman and with very few exceptions, the male scientists are exclusively of European origin. It's probably not the publisher's fault, for how many living woman scientists can you name? How many famous African scientists, historical or contemporary can you think of? Perhaps in science teaching we need to be particularly sensitive to these issues, as unfortunately the practice of science still reflects these inequalities that we oppose and are trying to counter. The National Curriculum Review in Science (DfE, 2013) suggested autobiographies of scientists; all the examples were white males. Indeed, in the text of the 2014 National Curriculum (DfE, 2013) nine scientists in total are mentioned; nearly all are white males and only two, at the time of writing, are still alive! Of the suggested names on the new science programme of study, Mary Anning (d. 1847) is the sole female representative. The very least we can do is select our case examples judiciously.

This is quite curious as actually science has a good deal to offer in terms of promoting both diversity and equality and hopefully the next section will help to identify some of the ways we can realize this through our thinking, planning and practice.

EQUALITY AND SCIENCE: WHAT DOES IT MEAN?

In the National Curriculum science programme of study, one of the key skills that pervades most of the year levels is the student's ability to observe and then to categorize based on those observations. Whether it is the similarities and differences between living plants and animals or between inanimate objects such as rocks and other materials, it is through such close observations that children go on to make broad groupings and eventually classifications. This, of course, reflects the practice of most branches of science and observation is a key skill.

 Time for reflection 14.1

In the now replaced National Curriculum (1999) Key Stage 1, Sc2 Life processes and living things under variation and classification stated that, 'pupils should be taught to recognize similarities and differences between themselves and others and to treat others with sensitivity'.

> This has been removed from the 2014 Programme of study.
> Does 'working scientifically' not involve such sensitivities?
> What strategies might you adopt to promote sensitivity to people's observed physical differences?

When it comes to the observation of themselves and of others, physical differences are generally easy to identify as they tend to be most obvious be they height, gender, hair colour or skin colouration. Identifying differences is an important part of science observation and is clearly intriguing for children. Even beyond the classroom, physical differences between people can be captivating and interesting for them. Visitors to schools from different countries or different ethnicities coming in to talk to children about their culture will sometimes appear both wonderfully exotic and exciting to children. We all have these stories.

Children are intrigued by differences and we, as scientists, characterize by it. Race, ethnic origin, nationality, gender are all terms that we are familiar with, and indeed at times we have a legal obligation to record it, but perhaps we need to remind ourselves that none of these are science terms. Indeed, in science not only is there uncertainty over their meaning but some terms such as 'race' are simply not recognized as having any scientific foundation.

This is a really important point, for the concept of 'race' is a sociological term, and has little basis in science.

Of course in the past, the scientific community has been less considered. The impact of the false and defective science has been appallingly profound. The consequences of providing a bogus scientific credibility for genetic discrimination and selection were ultimately realized in the death camps of Nazi Germany. This devastating legacy still haunts science and in particular modern genetics and genetic research today. It is a period of science history that we often tend to overlook or forget, but it is important for us as science teachers to remind ourselves of the risks and dangers associated with stressing the differences between people and the sensitivity with which we have to approach the science of people.

A Science of Equality

Despite the great diversity of people on the planet, it is modern genetics that is providing evidence of our similarities rather than our differences, as one of the most revelatory findings of genetic research has been the almost species-defining characteristic of human genetic uniformity. For example, the Human Genome Project (Chow-White, 2009) found 99.9 per cent of the human genome to be identical between individuals. This is quite astounding. Indeed, one of the defining features of the human genome is its startling lack of variation between individuals. We are incredibly similar. Very few genes control our physical variability. In fact skin colour is controlled by just twelve of our twenty thousand genes (Quillen, and Shriver, 2011).

Given these startling similarities at a genetic level, have such findings been used to repudiate and directly challenge dogma? Do we use them at all in science education?

Of course we need to recognize that the negative social forms of discrimination between people is something very distinct from identifying simple visual differences and has highly complex, multi-layered origins that do not simply start nor stop with a branch of biology. However, as scientists, perhaps we could do much more to combat percipient discrimination based on colour, ethnicity or gender, especially in challenging the sort of exclusivity that so often appears to be based on pseudo-science and myth. After all, we always argue that science is based on rationality and evidence and the evidence suggests that it is our similarity, not our differences that defines us in a scientific sense. Given that nearly 88,000 cases of racist bullying (including name calling and physical abuse) were reported in UK schools between 2007 and 2010 (Talwar, 2012) and that each year during this period there was an increase in the number of reported incidents that some large metropolitan boroughs witnessed a 40 per cent increase. Everyone involved in education has a role to play in confronting this issue including science educators. Perhaps one of the most effective and direct challenges to racism will be our genome; after all we are seemingly all equal under a microscope.

Not surprisingly, children are of course aware of physical and visually identifiable differences between people from an early age (Njoroge et al., 2009) and those differences need to be explored and discussed to avoid the development of misconceptions and misunderstanding that may form the basis of future negative discrimination. It would be naïve to suggest that teachers teaching science in primary schools can counter discrimination solely by using science topics, but we must be aware that we do need to tread carefully. Classification is based on both difference and similarity. Looking at differences between the physical characteristics of people is an important activity; it is vital to note those differences, not only in a science sense but also in a way that allows us to explore, understand and appreciate different ethnicities and different cultures. What we need to avoid is any opportunity to discriminate on physical difference. In other words, all animals show differences; zebras have different stripes and leopards have different patterns of spots, but we hardly notice the differences, simply recognizing the particular animal. The similarities between people are, in fact, far more striking than any superficial difference. That's the science-based message.

 ## Activity 14.2

There have of course been previous debates about multi-ethnic science and there has been much discussion as to what it actually means. What kind of activities could you design to promote similarities between people?

We can count similar characteristics and perhaps compare the results, but can we design something that goes beyond physical characteristics? That might consider the similarity of emotions such as sadness, happiness, love? Perhaps through facial expressions?

Activities that stress the positive aspects of humanity and that are universal can be seen as something that 'classifies' us.

SCIENCE AND CULTURAL IDENTITIES

Using similarities in simple physical appearance is one thing, but children may also identify differences in relation to ethnicity and culture. Such distinctions are properly celebrated in schools, and usually beyond the scope of science activities, but they do not have to be.

Schools will, for example, invite members of different ethnic communities to talk about their lives and beliefs. On occasion they may bring in food for the children to taste, or talk about their families. This is good practice and plays an important part in showing how different people live in different ways. The different foods may seem wonderfully exotic and different but of course there are the considerable similarities of dietary requirements. The same food groups are used over and over again and it is generally only the preparation that varies.

In 'Science in Primary Schools: the Multicultural Dimension' (1991) Alan Peacock discusses a range of scientific activities that can be carried out in relation to everyday aspects of different cultures and ethnic groups. He suggests topics such as food, particularly different types of bread that can be examined under hand lenses, to find similarities and differences. Fruits can be examined and compared likewise. He suggests making 'ethnic' musical instruments. Utilizing religious festivals particularly those involving water and light are also suggested as interesting ways of using science in different contexts.

SCIENCE AND SIMILARITIES IN EMOTION AND BEHAVIOUR

Another area of similarity between people that can be explored with children which is perhaps not drifting too far away from science *per se*, is the concept of the similarities of emotional experiences and responses. There are many examples of powerful universal emotions, not least of which, for example, could be a parent's love of their child or children. Such collective emotions clearly transcend culture and ethnicity. Not only do we all look the same, but we also feel the same and respond emotionally in similar ways.

When we think about behaviour and emotional responses we perhaps categorize them as psychology rather than science. We certainly may not instantly consider the contribution that modern ecology can make. Yet the subject of ecology is the study of the relationships between living organisms and one of the characteristics of our species, and perhaps contrary to what we may believe, is that we are very social creatures. Far from being violent, aggressive and destructive, we live in close proximity, share limited, and finite resources. Despite the wars and armed conflicts being regularly shown on television news footage, such events are actually remarkably rare. The London Underground or the trains in Mumbai during the Friday rush hour is a great example of how 'social' we actually are; that number of individuals in such close proximity and nothing (much) untoward happens.

Furthermore, as a species, we clearly exhibit biological altruism. Sam Harris (2012) has recently argued that such altruism, the simple fact that we help each other and exhibit highly levels of compassion, is because we are empathetic creatures and we demonstrate this all the time in our day-to-day behaviour. We look after our elderly and our infirm and increasingly this behaviour is seen as being one of our great evolutionary advantages. The idea of 'fitness for survival' is so frequently (and to be fair, understandably) misunderstood, in that it has something solely to do with strength, or physical and mental prowess. Of course in reality, our co-operation, compassion and indeed our biological altruism are contributing evolutionary behaviours that have underwritten our evolutionary superstardom. Having opposable thumbs is one thing, but our ability to care and to empathize are arguably as important; but how many times do we make this scientific point? The teaching of basic science in the classroom does have the potential to contribute something to anti-discrimination strategies and we, especially as science teachers, perhaps need to recognize and develop these ideas further in terms of stressing the science of similarity and the science of altruistic human ecology.

 Time for reflection 14.2

'We have so far to go to realize our human potential for compassion, altruism, and love.' (Jane Goodall, *Harvest for Hope: A Guide to Mindful Eating*)

'We want excitement and adventure; we want routine and security. We want to have a large number of sexually attractive partners, and we also want those we love to love us in return, and be utterly faithful to us. We want cute, smart children who will treat us with the respect we deserve. We want to be surrounded by music, and by ravishing scents and attractive visual objects. We don't want to be too hot or too cold. We want to dance. We want to speak with the animals. We want to be envied. We want to be immortal. We want to be gods.
  But in addition, we want wisdom and justice. We want hope. We want to be good.' (Margaret Atwood, *In Other Worlds: SF and the Human Imagination*)

- Jane Goodall seems to suggest that we are innately compassionate and loving. Do you agree with that?
- Is Margaret Atwood suggesting the same?

A 'WORLD SCIENCE', RATHER THAN 'SCIENCE AND THE WORLD'

The nature and story of science is often depicted as one of 'progress' and as such we can promote a sense that it moves forward. We do tend to 'look backwards' at the history of ideas, of how they came about, the people who carried out the experiments, worked on the problems and eventually discovered the answers or developed the theory. The problem, of course, and this is widely recognized, is that we run the risk of often portraying this undoubtedly important history of science as (if not uniquely) one that is predicated on the work of long-dead, white, male, Europeans (with an occasional North American). This, of course, is a completely inaccurate picture of scientific development. We may recognize this but how many times is the contribution of Islamic science discussed in class? Its influence on physics, mathematics, medicine and astronomy (and a whole range of other areas) is well documented, yet how often do we turn to it in our teaching? The great African civilizations built cities, irrigated land and studied the stars and yet are rarely referred to in science histories. Indeed, as Briffault as early as 1919 recognized:

> The debt of our science to that of the Arabs does not consist in startling discoveries or revolutionary theories, science owes a great deal more to Arab culture, it owes its existence ... What we call science arose in Europe as a result of new spirit of enquiry, of new methods of experiment, observation, measurement, of the development of mathematics, in a form unknown to the Greeks. That spirit and those methods were introduced into the European world by the Arabs. (Briffault, 1919)

The point here is that it would not change our understanding of biology, chemistry or physics. However, it would help to provide evidence that science is not uniquely European but is quite clearly multi-ethnic in origin, development and practice and it remains so. To imply anything else, even unintentionally, is simply bad history, let alone bad science teaching. Good practice involves different examples of science developments in different countries at different times.

MAKING SCIENCE RELEVANT TO ALL

Dillon and Manning (2010) suggest that science should be delivered in a way that encourages children to think and act scientifically by addressing topics that are relevant to them. Of course few would disagree (why would they, given the alternative stance?) but the more difficult question that we have to consider is what topic areas are relevant to children and young people in schools? This idea of relevance is one that is regularly put forward in literature concerning science education, but the key question here is whether we know what these areas are. There is a distinct paucity of research that actually explores this, particularly pre-adolescent children's perspectives (Sargeant, 2010). Some suggest science may be best taught through topical issues, a socio-political science for example (Eastwood, 2012) where present environmental issues are examined. However, perhaps we could look at other areas that are actually more directly relevant, for when we consider what is relevant to children, studies of their personal worries are probably the most sensitive indicator and successive studies in this area show children's major concerns to be related to personal relationships, such as friendship and separation, health and death and coming to personal harm (Silverman et al., 1995; Bernstein, 2002). Wider issues concern war and environmental disasters. For older children (9–14-years-old) their future relating to careers and money are increasingly cited (Ofsted, 2008).

Children's concerns about being 'different' in a variety of ways, both physically and culturally, within the school environment are important. Making science relevant is often interpreted as relating it to children's everyday lives in terms of their external environment, but this has often focused on explaining the science behind everyday items, or activities. This, of course, is valid and important and can form the basis of innovative, interesting and engaging learning activities. However, how often do we as teachers see a role for science as part of anti-bullying strategies, or assuaging children's fears about school and the wider world? If we really want children to engage with science we need to at least consider using science to help reduce their fears and concerns, after all, ecology is the science of relationships.

SCIENCE AND GENDER EQUALITY

When it comes to gender differences in academic performance at primary level, research has usually concentrated on the lower achievement levels attained by boys and the efficacy of strategies that may be adopted to improve them (Harlen and Qualter, 2009). Of course in science we have far greater concerns, namely the internationally recognized under-representation of women in the majority of science subjects.

> It is universally accepted that learning science is important for the future lives of all citizens and because of this it is a required part of primary and secondary education in practically all countries. Science is a major area of human mental and practical activity and the knowledge it generates plays a vital part in our lives and in the lives of future generations. (Harlen and Quilter, 2009, p. 35)

So important and so vital is the perception of students that when it is no longer compulsory, students particularly girls, drop it with alarming readiness. Despite females outperforming males in UK schools (Sheppard, 2011) there is still a significant under-representation of females studying science beyond the age of 16 and the disparity in some areas of science has become progressively worse (OECD, 2008).

Research into the reasons for this disparity has shown that there is little variation in the academic performance of females (Hyde and Linn, 2006) and that at degree level, female graduates in science gain slightly better degree classifications than their male counterparts (OECD, 2008). We can therefore reject any difference in cognitive performance.

Given a lack of identifiable differences in cognition and academic performance, relative interest has formed the next focus for research. Research studies have indeed identified, in the UK at least, that interest in science topics varies with gender. Jenkins and Pell (2006) as part of the Relevance of Science Education project found that in UK schools the interests were markedly different. The most popular areas of interest listed by girls were nearly exclusively health and well-being related. For boys it was topics concerned with atomic weapons, space and dangerous animals (Jenkins and Pell, 2006).

The image of science, its history and apparently the content of the modern science curriculum seem to be male dominated. Is it any wonder that women are put off? Of course a valid question to ask here is 'does it matter'? If the advances in medical science or physical sciences are made, does the gender of those making such discoveries and contributing to such advancement particularly matter?

Well, to those with an interest in science and who care about it, it does. In fact such gender disparities are of real concern. Ben Barres (2006) has reviewed the gender imbalance in science and finds no evidence of any difference in innate academic or intellectual ability. In fact, so lacking is evidence for differences in performance, interest and ability that he concludes that the gender disparity in science must be the result of discrimination. Barres goes on to point out that this is hard to accept for many and that much of this discrimination is subtle rather than overt. However, it conspires to put girls off continuing with science by undermining their self-confidence. No matter how unintentional, no matter how 'low-level', this is discrimination and we as scientists and more importantly as teachers cannot tolerate this. In fact we need to take an active role in combating it. One of the simplest ways, as Virginia Valian suggested as long ago as 1998, is simply to raise our expectations of girls in science. We can also check our resources, think about our examples and change our histories.

 Activity 14.3

It is good practice generally to remember role models and challenging stereotyped images? However, it is even more important in science. Ways in which this could be achieved could be the study of the work of women scientists, past and present. The latter point may be emphasized by inviting local women scientists to visit the school.

Think of the apparent differences in interest, perhaps individual or group project work may be useful. Can these projects be based around a unifying theme, such as health?

CONCLUSION

Hopefully this chapter has given you a few things to think about. You may not agree with some of the points discussed here, or you may think that strategies to promote diversity and inclusion are best done in other ways. However, the point here is that we can be imaginative in our science teaching. We can integrate it into all areas of the curriculum, but we can also use science in creative ways to promote many of the wider commitments of tolerance and understanding that we share as professional teachers. As Barres (2006) points out;

We can teach young scientists how to survive in a prejudiced world. Self-confidence is crucial in advancing and enjoying a research career. From an early age, girls receive messages that they are not good enough to do science subjects or will be less liked if they are good at them. The messages come from many sources, including parents, friends, fellow students and, alas, teachers. When teachers have lower expectations of them, students do less well. But we are all at fault for sending these messages and for remaining silent when we encounter them. (Barres, 2006)

If you also see yourself as a teacher of science, well, science is a subject limited only by imagination. We therefore need people with imaginative, creative and perceptive minds and to exclude anyone with those criteria is to undermine the future of our subject. Therefore a science based on equality isn't just a laudable aim. It should be the very basis of our philosophy and of our practice.

FURTHER READING

Peirce. E. (2008) *Activity Assemblies to Promote Peace: 40+ Ideas for Multi-Faith Assemblies for 5–11 Years: 50 Ideas for Multi-faith Assemblies for 5–11 Years.* London: David Fulton Publishers
A useful resource book of ideas dealing with issues of peace from a multi-faith perspective.

Hill, D. and Helavaara-Robertson (2011) (eds) *Equality in the Primary School: Promoting good practice across the curriculum.* London: Continuum
Excellent 'in-depth' discussions on a variety of topics relating to equality issues.

Online resources may be found at http://peace-education.org.uk/

For general peace education resources and ideas

Some 'debunking' of ideas relating to boys and girls may be found at:
http://www.theguardian.com/science/blog/2013/feb/08/pseudoscience-stereotyping-gender-inequality-science

For ideas specifically relating to equality and science the ASE has the following resource:
http://www.ase.org.uk/resources/scitutors/professional-issues/ethnicity-and-gender-issues-in-science/#3.2Primary

REFERENCES

Baress, B. (2006) Does Gender Matter? *Nature*, 442, pp. 133–6
Bernstein, G. (2002) 'Advances in child and adolescent anxiety disorder research', *American Academy of Child and Adolescent Psychiatry*. [Online] Available at: http://www.aacap.org/training/DevelopMentor/Content/2002Fall/f2002_a2.cfm (accessed 13.11.13)
Briffault, R. (1919) *The Making of Humanity*. New York: Macmillan
Chow-White, P. (2009) Genomic databases and an emerging digital divide in biotechnology. [Online] Available at: https://www.hastac.org/blogs/mhstorment/2012/03/15/race-after-internet-chapter-13-review (accessed 12.11.13)

Department for Education (1999) National Curriculum Science Key Stage 1. [Online] Available at: http://webarchive.nationalarchives.gov.uk/20100413151441/http://curriculum.qca.org.uk/key-stages-1-and-2/subjects/science/keystage1/sc2-life-processes-and-living-things/index.aspx

Department for Education (2011) Teachers' standards: statutory guidance for school leaders, school staff and governing bodies July 2011, (introduction updated June 2013). [Online] Available at: https://www.gov.uk/government/uploads/system/uploads/attachment_data/file/283198/Teachers__Standards.pdf (accessed 13.11.13)

Department for Education (2012) National Curriculum for science. Key stages 1 and 2 – draft. National Curriculum Review. [Online] Available at: http://webarchive.nationalarchives.gov.uk/20130904095348/http://media.education.gov.uk/assets/files/pdf/d/draft%20national%20curriculum%20for%20science%20key%20stages%201%202.pdf

Department for Education (2013) Science programmes of study: Key stages 1 and 2 National Curriculum in England. DFE-00182–2013

Dillon, J. and Manning, A. (2010) (eds) *Good Practice in Science Teaching*. London: Open University Press

Eastwood, J.L., Sadler, T.D., Zeidler, D.L., Lewis, A., Amiri, L. and Applebaum, S. (2012). Contextualizing nature of science instruction in socioscientific issues. *International Journal of Science Education*, 34(15), 2289–315

Harlan, W. and Quilter, A. (2009) *The Teaching of Science in Primary Schools*. 5th edn, London: Routledge

Harris, S. (2012) *The Moral Landscape: How Science Can Determine Human Values*. London: Bantam Press

Hyde, J.S. and Linn, M.C. (2006) Gender similalrities in mathematics and science. *Science*, 314(5799), pp. 599–600

Jenkins, E.W. and Pell, R.G. (2006) The Relevance of Science Education Project (ROSE) in England: a summary of findings. [Online] Available at: http://roseproject.no/network/countries/uk-england/rose-report-eng.pdf

Njoroge, W., Benton, T., Lewis, M.L. and Njoroge, N.M. (2009), What are infants learning about race? A look at a sample of infants from multiple racial groups. *Journal of Infant Mental Health*, 30, pp. 549–67

OECD (2008) Education at a glance. [Online] Available at: http://www.oecd.org/education/skills-beyond-school/41284038.pdf

Ofsted (2008) TellUs3 Report. [Online] Available at: http://www.ofsted.gov.uk/resources/tellus3-national-report

Peacock, A. (1991) (ed.) *Science in Primary Schools: The Multicultural Dimension*. New York: MacMillan Education

Quillen, E.E and Shriver, M.D. (2011) Unpacking human evolution to find the genetic determinants of human skin pigmentation. *Journal of Investigative Dermatology*, 131 (November). [Online] Available at: http://www.nature.com/milestones/skinbio4/pdf/skinbio20113a.pdf

Sargeant, J. (2010) The altruism of pre-adolescent children's perspectives on 'worry' and 'happiness' in Australia and England. *Childhood*, 17(3), pp. 411–25

Sheppard, J. (2011) Girls surge ahead at GCSE to open up record gender gap at 16. *Guardian*. [Online] Available at: http://www.theguardian.com/education/2011/aug/25/girls-gcse-gender-gap-16

Silverman, W.K., La Greca, A.M. and Wasserstein, S. (1995) What do children worry about? Worries and their relation to anxiety. *Child Development*, 66(3), pp. 671–86

Talwar, D. (2012) More than 87,000 racist incidents recorded in schools. [Online] Available at: http://www.bbc.co.uk/news/education-18155255

INDEX

The 21st Century Teacher, 80

Abbot, Luke, 105–106
Abrahams, I., 60
accuracy, 73
Adey, P.S., 22
ADHD (Attention Deficit Hyperactivity Disorder), 140–141
adventure, 130
affective engagement, 134
Allen, M., 20
altruism, 165–166
analytical thinking, 5–6
animals, 37, 46, 116, 121, 141
animation software, 84
annotated drawings, 59
apple meditation, 117
Arabic science, 167
art
  and communication, 95–96
  and curiosity, 91
  and enquiry, 90
  and investigation, 93–95
  materials, 92
  and observation, 91–93
  resources, 97
artists, 89–90
Ashbridge, J., 35
Asoko, H., 46
Assessing Pupils' Progress, 60–61
assessment
  benefits of, 58
  and creativity, 63
  current state of, 57–58

assessment *cont.*
  elicitation of children's ideas, 58–59
  enquiry work, 39
  involvement of children, 61–62
  observation in, 60
  of practical skills, 59–61
  resources, 63–64
  types of, 56–57
  validity and reliability, 57, 58
astronomy, 81
Attention Deficit Hyperactivity Disorder (ADHD), 140–141
Atwood, Margaret, 166
audio recording, 82
Ausubel, David, 18

Bad Science, 11
Bake Your Lawn, 142
Barres, Ben, 168–169
Bartholomew, H., 31, 32
basic needs, sustainability, 116–117
BBC website, 82
Beare, Headley, 115
Becta, 79, 80, 85
behaviour, 140–141, 165–166
Bew, P., 57
big-C creativity, 23
biological altruism, 165–166
biology, 17, 42, 46, 47, 82
biophilia, 122, 134–135
Bird, W., 141
Black, P., 61–62
Briffault, R., 167
Brock, A., 104

Brundtland Report, 116, 117
Brunellesci, Filippo, 15
Bruner, Jerome, 18–19, 22
bullying, 164, 168

Çalyk, M., 20–21
Cambridge Primary Review, 15
cameras, 82, 85
Carson, Rachael, 115, 120, 129
CASE (cognitive acceleration through science
    education), 22
CCEA (Council for the Curriculum, Examinations
    and Assessment in Northern Ireland), 29,
    38–39, 89
Centre for Eco-literacy, 117
charts, 74, 83, 84
chemistry, 17, 33, 42, 46, 47, 48–49, 130
Chi, M.T.H., 21, 22
children
    child protection, 145
    conceptions of, 20–25
    concerns and priorities, 145
    health, 138–140
    wellbeing, 138–139, 146–147
Children's Society, 138, 145
Chiu, M-H., 42
Cinderella, 102
classrooms, healthy, 143
clay modelling, 92, 93
closed investigation, 31–32
cognitive acceleration through science education
    (CASE), 22
collaboration, 79
combinatorial creativity, 55
Commoner's Four Laws of Ecology, 118
communication, 95–96
compassion, 147
composting, 119–120
computer science, 81
concept cartoons, 22
concept maps, 22, 47–48, 59
conceptual change
    children's conceptions, 21–22
    creative approaches to, 22–25
    theories of, 18–21
conscience or decision alley, 106, 108
constructivism, 19, 20–22, 25, 35
controversial issues
    learning outcomes, 153–154
    promoting values, 158
    resources, 159
    role of discussion, 155–157
    in science education, 150–151, 152
    teaching approaches, 154–155
core concepts, science, 48–49
Cornell, Joseph, 67, 121, 122, 130, 134
correlative subsumption, 18

Council for the Curriculum, Examinations and
    Assessment in Northern Ireland (CCEA), 29,
    38–39, 89
Cox, Brian, 15
Craft, A., 57
craft projects, 97
Creative Partnerships Programme, 15
creativity
    art and design, 15–16, 90
    and assessment, 63
    combinatorial, 55
    definitions, 5, 6, 75
    exploratory, 55
    facilitating, 5–7
    importance in science education, 7–9
    key characteristics, 62
    little-c, 23
    Ofsted, 28–29, 75
    and science, 14–15, 68–69, 91
    teacher skills, 55–56
Cremin, H., 105
culture, 165
Cunliffe, L., 55
curiosity, 91
curriculum
    England *see The National Curriculum in
        England (2014)*
    integrated, 80
    Northern Ireland *see The Northern Ireland
        Curriculum Primary*
    science and technology *see* digital technology
    Scotland *see Curriculum for Excellence*
    spiral, 22
    Wales *see Developing the Curriculum
        Cymreig*
Curriculum for Excellence, 7, 29, 43, 100

Daniel, A.K., 100
Darwin, Charles, 69, 130, 153
data
    analysis, 84, 85
    data loggers, 82
    harvesting, 81–83
    presentation, 73–74, 83, 84
Davies, D., 6
Davies, T., 56
deductive reasoning, 92, *93fig*
democratic creativity, 5
Denning, S., 100
dependent variable, 72
derivative subsumption, 18
Desailly, Juliet, 15, 55–56
design *see* art
Developing the Curriculum Cymreig, 29, 43
Dickens, Charles, 113
diet, 140, 143
difference *see* equality

digital technology
  data analysis, 84
  data harvesting, 81–83
  data presentation, 83
  expenditure in schools, 77–78
  impact on learning outcomes, 78–79, 85
  promoting dialogue and collaboration, 79, 84
  recreation, 128, 129
  in science education, 79–81, 85
Dillon, J., 167
discussion, 20, 29, 39, 155–157
Dolan, A.M., 103, 110
drama, 104–110, 153, 157
drawing, 59, 97, 132, 153
Dyer, A., 146–147

earthwalk activities, 122, 134
ecology, 118, 120, 141–142, 165
  see also environment
Education Act (2011), 138
Education for Sustainability, 113, 124
Education Scotland, 7, 30, 33, 81
Einstein, Albert, 15
elite creativity, 5
Embercombe, 131
emergent environmentalism, 121
emotion, 165–166
emotional engagement, 121, 131–132
empathy, 121, 132, 147, 166
enquiry *see* science, scientific enquiry
enthusiasm, 66–67, 75
environment
  crises, 113 *see also* sustainability
  emergent environmentalism, 121
  healthy, 141–142
  impact of humans, 117–118
  see also ecology
epistemology, 19
equality
  emotion and behaviour, 165–166
  ethnicity and culture, 165
  Eurocentrism in science education, 166–167
  gender equality, 168–169
  human differences, 162–163
  resources, 170
  and science, 163–164, 168–169, 170
  in science education, 161–162, 167–168
  Teachers' Standards (2011), 160–161
error, in experimental design, 72–73
ethnicity, 165
eudiamonic wellbeing, 145, 147
Eurocentrism, 166–167
European Commission, 33
Evagorou, M., 96
evaluative thinking, 5–6
Every Child Matters, 145

Every Child Outdoors, 129
evidence, 91
evolution, 69, *103tab*, 150–151, 152, 153, 157
Excel, 83, 84
Excellence and Enjoyment Framework, 15
exercise, 140, 141, 143, 144
experimentation, 71–73
exploration, 130, 133–134
exploratory creativity, 55

fairy tales, 102
fictional-world-making play, 105–106
field observation, 82
Finding Nemo drama activities, 107–109
flashbacks and flash forwards, 106
Flow Learning, 67, 130, 134
flowers, 89–90
food chains/webs, 107, 108, 119, 120, 121, 142
food miles, 82
foods, 37, 117, 120, 139, 143–144, 165
formative assessment, 56
forum theatre, 106
Foster, C., 22
freeze-frame, 106, 107–108

Gauss, Carl Friedrich, 161
gender
  equality, 168–169
  stereotyping, 162
generative thinking, 5–6
genetics, 163
Gilbert, J.K., 44–45
Goethe, Johann Wolfgang von, 161
Gompertz, B., 93, 122
Good Childhood Report, 145
Goodall, Jane, 120, 130, 166
Google Earth, 81–82
Gottschall, Jonathan, 100
Gove, Michael, 126, 129
graphs, 74, 76, 83, 84, 85
Great Acceleration, *114tab*
Gresnigt, R., 45, 80
Gripshover, S.J., 144
group moderation, 58
group work, 101, 154

Hahn, C.L., 151
happiness *see* wellbeing, hedonic
Harlen, W., 44, 57, 58, 63
Harwood, A.M., 151
Harwood, D., 155–157
health
  children and, 138–140
  healthy classrooms, 143
  healthy environments, 141–142
  healthy menus, 144

health *cont.*
   healthy schools, 142–143
   human health, 143–145
   and wellbeing *see* wellbeing
hedonic wellbeing, 145, 146–147
Heywood, D., 45–46
Hodgson, J., 146–147
hot-seating, 106
Howard-Jones, Paul, 6
Human Genome Project, 163
hypotheses, 70–71, 75

IBSE (inquiry-based science education), 31–33,
   39, 90
ICT (information and communication technology)
   see digital technology
illustrative approach, 31–32
The Importance of Teaching White Paper, 138–139
improvisation, 106
Independent Review of the Primary Curriculum, 15
independent variable, 72
inductive reasoning, 92, *93fig*
infographics, 84
information technology *see* digital technology
inquiry *see* scientific enquiry
inquiry-based science education (IBSE), 31–33,
   39, 90
integrated curricula, 80
interconnectivity, 117, 120
International Union for Conservation of Nature, 127
internet, 36, 81–82, 83–84
   see also digital technology
investigation, 93–94
in-vitro fertilizaton (IVF), 150
İpek, 20–21
Irish Primary School Curriculum for English, 100
Islamic science, 167
IVF (in-vitro fertilizaton), 150

Joesphidou, J., 35

Kaku, Michio, 69
Kaplan, H., 104
Key Stage 2 testing, 57, 64
Kind, P.M., 90, 96
Kind, V., 44–45, 90, 96
KWL grids, 58–59

language, 20, 96
Lanier, Jaron, 15
Large Hadron Collider, 158
*Learning: creative approaches that raise
   standards*, 28–29
Leonardo da Vinci, 15
Lewin, Roger, 161
Lin, H-S, 89

*Linking Thinking: New Perspectives on Thinking
   and Learning for Sustainability*, 119, 124
little-c creativity, 23
Liu, S-C, 89
Louv, R., 136
Lunn, M., 91, 95

macro photography, 92–93
Manning, A., 167
Mantle of the Expert, 105–106, 109
Markman, E.M., 144
materials, 48–49
meaningful learning, 18
measurement, 73–74
menus, healthy, 144
Mesure, S., 96
microscopes, 82
Microsoft Excel, 83, 84
misconceptions, childen's, 20–25
mitochondrial transfer, 150
mixtures, 144
Monet, Claude, 90
Monteiro, A., 22
Morton, T., 20
Moss, S., 127
Murphy, C., 6, 19, 81, 84, 101

NASA, 81
National Advisory Committee on Creative and
   Cultural Education (NACCCE), 5, 34–37
National Association for Environmental
   Education, 127
National Children's Bureau, 138
The National Choice: A White Paper, 127
*The National Curriculum. Handbook for primary
   teachers in England (1999)*, 17, 112, 162
The National Curriculum in England (2014)
   animals, 37
   assessment, 57
   computer science, 81
   contents areas, 37, 46, *47fig*, 50
   creativity, 15–16
   evolution, 152
   Finding Nemo drama activities, 109
   health and wellbeing, 138–139
   observation, 75
   opportunity offered by, 3–4
   outdoor learning, 126–127
   overview of, 46–49
   Science Programmes of Study, 74–75, 116, 133,
      141–142, 162
   scientific enquiry, 17, 30–32, 39, 43, 66, 67, 68,
      *93fig see also The National Curriculum in
      England (2014)*, working scientifically
   slimmed down, 46–47
   spoken language, 20

The National Curriculum in England (2014) cont.
  storytelling, 100
  sustainability, 112–113, 116, 117–118, 120–121
  teaching approaches, 29
  working scientifically, 17, 43, 50, 66, 67, 68–69,
    74–75
The National Curriculum Review for Science, 162
National Healthy Schools Standard, 138
Natural Environment, 127
natural selection *see* evolution
nature, 89–90, 131–132, 136
NESTA, 78, 85, 150–151
New Generation Science Standards, 51–52
Noble, A., 91, 95
The Northern Ireland Curriculum Primary, 29, 43
Nuffield Science Teaching Project, 10–11
nutrition, 140, 143–144
  see also foods

obesity, 140
observation
  in assessment, 60
  of human differences, 162–163
  The National Curriculum in England
    (2014), 75
  in outdoor learning, 130, 132, 134
  in science, 69–70, 75
  in science education, 91–93, 122
  see also data, harvesting
Ødegaard, M., 105
Odena, O., 55
Ofsted
  arts materials, 92
  Assessing Pupils' Progress, 60
  creative approaches to learning, 28–29, 75
  effective science education, 30
  ICT in schools, 80
  Key Stage 2 testing, 57
  outdoor learning, 129, 135
  pupil involvement, 135
  sharing ideas by children, 59
  subject knowledge, 44–45
Olympics, 140
ontology, 19–20
Open Air Laboratories Project, 79
open-ended problem-solving, 90
Orr, David, 113, 123
Osborne, J., 17–18, 21, 30, 96
outdoor learning
  behavioural disorders, 141
  child play patterns, 128–129
  contemporary approaches, 134–135
  educational advantages, 129–131
  engagement with nature, 131–132
  The National Curriculum in England (2014),
    126–127
  observation, 130, 132, 134
  Ofsted, 129, 135

outdoor learning *cont.*
  promoting ethical science, 132–133
  resources, 135–136
  school trips, 128
  and science, 131–134
  sustainability, 120–122
  and wellbeing, 146–147
outdoor play, 128–129

Parker, J., 45–46
Parkinson, R., 100
PBL (problem-based learning), 34–37
peace, 170
Peacock, A., 33, 165
pedagogical content knowledge, 45–46, 51
physical activity, 140, 141
  see also exercise
physics, 17, 42, 46, 47
Piaget, Jean, 19
picture books, 103–104, 110
planets, 81, 82
plants, 46–47, 89–90, 116, 119, 141, 142, 146
play, outdoor, 128–129
poetry, 105
POGIL (process-oriented guided inquiry learning),
  33–34
Pollard, A., 45, 46
Posner, G.J., 19
practical skills, 59–61
practical work, 31, 60
precision, 73
Primary National Curriculum (2008), 112
Primary School Curriculum: English Language, 100
problem-based learning (PBL), 34–37
process-oriented guided inquiry learning (POGIL),
  33–34
programming, 81
progression
  in understanding materials, 48–49
  in working scientifically, 50
pseudo-science, 11
Public Health England, 140
puppets, 104–105

Qualified Teacher Status, 46
quantification, 73–74
questions, 31–34, 38, 50, 61, 70–71, 73, 91, 116,
  122, 134
  see also hypotheses

racism, 161, 164
Raspberry Pi, 81, 82
reasoning skills, 21
recycling, 119–120
relaxation, 144
reliability and validity, 57
replication, 72–73, 131
research documentaries, 154–155

risk, 129
Robinson, Sir Ken, 6–7
Rocard, M., 33
role play, 95, 101, 104, 105, 106, 153, 157
Root-Bernstein, R.S., 15
Roscoe, R.D., 21, 22
routines, 54–55
Royal Horticultural Society, 142
rubrics, 60

schemas, 19
schools
    healthy schools, 142–143
    school gardens, 120, 142
    school trips, 128
Schools Council Integrated Science
        Project, 10
Schwarz, R.S., 31
science
    communication, 95–96
    conceptions of, 16–17
    controversial issues, 150, 151–152
    creativity in, 14–15, 29, 68–69, 91
    data generation, 73–74
    digital technology *see* digital technology
    drawing conclusions, 74
    and equality, 163–164, 168–169, 170
    ethical approaches, 132–133
    Eurocentrism in, 166–167
    experimental design, 71–73
    hypotheses, 70–71, 75
    nature of, 30–31, 42–43, 48–49, 68–69
    observation, 69–70, 75
    and outdoor learning, 131–134
    pseudo-science, 11
    resources, 75–76
    scientific attitudes, 91
    scientific enquiry, 17, 30–32, 39, 43, 66–68,
        90, 92–93 *see also* science, working
        scientifically
    scientists, 15, 120
    scope of, 157–158
    and technology curricula, 80
    working scientifically, 17, 43, 47, 50, 60, 66–69,
        74–75, 131, 133, 135
Science and Engineering Education Advisory
        Group, 78
*Science programmes of study (National Curriculum
    2014)*, 74–75, 116, 133, 141–142, 162
*Science: Social, Environmental and Scientific
    Education Teacher Guidelines*, 29, 43
scientists, 15, 120
second life technologies, 133
sex education, 153
Sharing Nature with Children, 121, 130
Shayer, M., 22
Shtulman, A., 21–22
Shulman, L., 45–46

Sigman, A., 128, 129
Silent Spring, 129
Simon, S., 105
sleep, 144–145
social awareness, 4
spiral curriculum, 22
stereotyping, gender, 162
Sterling, S., 122
storytelling
    resources, 110
    role in science education, 100, 101–104
    traditions, 99–100
structured controversy, 105
subject matter knowledge, 44–45
substantive knowledge, 46
summative assessment, 56–57
sustainability
    basic needs, 116–117
    definition, 115
    Education for Sustainability, 113, 124
    educational approaches, 113–115, 119–120
    environmental impact of humans, 113,
        117–118
    The National Curriculum in England (2014),
        112–113, 116, 117–118, 120–121
    outdoor learning, 120–122
    resources, 124–125
    whole school approach, 122–123
sustantive knowledge, 44, 45
syntactic knowledge, 44, 45, 46

TagCrowd, 84
A Tale of Two Cities, 113
teacher identity, 55–56
Teachers' Standards (2011), 160–161
tests, 57, 64, 66
textbooks, 24–25, 42–43
The Teachers' Standards, 46
thought tapping, 106, 107–108
Torrance, E.P., 6
transparent technology, 78–79
trees, 90, 94, 100, 119, 122, 131, 133, 146

UN Decade for Education for Sustainability, 113
UNICEF, 138, 146, 147

Valcarcel, J., 21–22
validity and reliability, 57
Valkanova, Y., 104
values, 158
Van de Broek, P., 24–25
variables, in experiments, 72
visual media, 154–155
visualisation, 97
Vygotsky, Lev, 19

Ward, H., 32
Watts, M., 104, 105

wellbeing
   children, 138–139, 146–147
   eudiamonic, 145, 147
   hedonic, 145, 146–147
   importance of, 145–146
   outdoor learning and, 146–147
   resources, 147–148
Wildlife Trust, 131
William, D., 61
Wilson, E.O., 134
Wolk, S., 33
wonder, 91

Woodland Trust, 131
Wordle, 84
worksheets, 24–25
writing, 95, 96
WWF (World Wildlife Fund), 119, 123, 124, 125
Wynder, M., 56

Young Internet surveys, 145
Young Minds, 147

Zone of Proximal Development, 19